Typing: College Edition

ITT Educational Services, Inc.
Business Education Series
Series Editor, Verleigh Ernest

Basic Accounting, Calvin Engler
Business Correspondence, Waldo C. Wright
Business English: College Level, Donald Sheff
Business Spelling and Word Power, A. H. Lass
Dictation and Transcription
Medical Dictation Course, College Edition, Goodwin W. Gilson
Speedwriting Shorthand Dictionary, College Edition
Typing: College Edition, Verleigh Ernest

Typing: College Edition

Verleigh Ernest

ITT Educational Services, Inc.
New York, New York

ITT Educational Services, Inc.
55 West 42 Street
New York, New York 10036

Library of Congress Catalog Card Number: 72-142516

International Standard Book Number: 0-8455-1600-0   (cloth)

International Standard Book Number: 0-8455-1601-9   (paper)

Printed in the United States of America

9 8 7 6 5 4 3 2

Contents

Section 1 ALPHABETIC KEYBOARD AND PUNCTUATION MARKS

Section 2 ALPHABETIC KEYBOARD MASTERY

Section 6 JOB TYPING

Section 7 A RECAP

Typing: College Edition

Index

Section 1
ALPHABETIC KEYBOARD AND PUNCTUATION MARKS

HOME KEYS

Each finger controls a zone of keys as indicated in the illustration above. The keys *a, s, d, f, j, k, l,* and *semicolon* represent the "home keys" and the fingers are named for these home keys; for example, the left little finger is the *a* finger and the right little finger is the *sem* finger. The home keys are the base of operation.

HAND POSITION

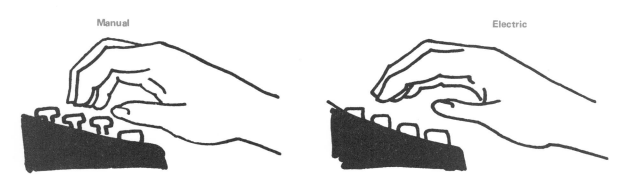

Manual

Curve your fingers tightly.

Electric

Curve your fingers slightly and hold them close to the home keys.

Look at the keyboard and locate the home keys. Place the correct fingers on these keys with fingers curved. Remove your hands from the keys to your lap. Practice lifting your hands to home position two or three times.

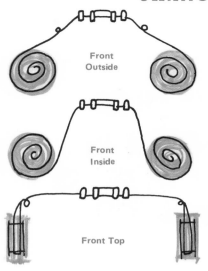

Front
Outside

Front
Inside

Front Top

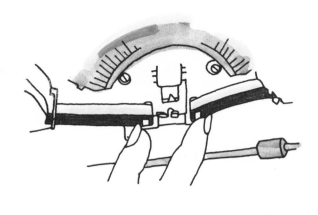

Ribbon Threaded Through the Ribbon-Carrier Mechanism

The techniques for changing ribbons vary from machine to machine. The following steps are basic to all machines:

1. Before removing the old ribbon, note how it is threaded and the direction in which it winds.
2. Wind the ribbon to one spool.
3. Remove this spool and discard the ribbon, noting the way in which the ribbon is hooked to the spool.
4. Depress the shift lock and set the ribbon control for typing on the lower part of the ribbon. Depress and lock any two central keys.
5. Fasten the end of the new ribbon to the empty spool and wind a few inches of the ribbon to the spool in the correct direction.
6. Place both spools in their holders and thread the new ribbon into place.
7. Release the shift lock, return the ribbon control to type on the upper portion, and unlock the two keys.

For more specific directions, refer to the operations manual that was prepared for your particular brand of typewriter.

SPACE BAR

To space after typing a letter or between groups of letters, use the space bar. Use the right-hand thumb to strike the bar. Tap the center of the space bar with a sharp stroke, releasing the bar immediately. Keep your other fingers in position, as motionless as possible.

STRIKING KEYS

Strike each key with a firm, sharp stroke. Release quickly by snapping the finger slightly toward the palm of the hand. Keep the fingers poised directly over the keys so that each key is hit in the center.

Watching your fingers, type this drill:

ffff ffff jjjj jjjj fjfj fjfj ffff jjjj fjfj fjfj

Check your paper. Did you type four letters in each group with a space following each group?

&	One space before and after the ampersand. `Mark & Sons`
#	Do not space between the number sign and the number it identifies. `Style #34, Bill #45`
$	Do not space between the dollar sign and the number it identifies. `We have a bill for $35.`
%	Do not space between the percent sign and the number it identifies. `A discount of 18%.`
*	Often used to refer to a footnote. Do not space between the asterisk and the word that precedes it. `This article* appeared two months ago.`
@	One space before and after the "at" sign. `4 @ $3.50`
¢	Do not space between the cent sign and the number it identifies. `15 lbs @ 18¢`
/	In fractions, do not space between the numbers of the fraction and the diagonal. `A total of 4 3/8 inches.`

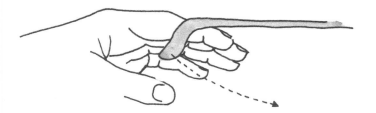
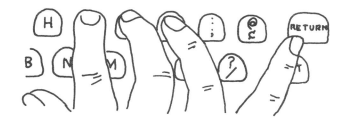

The carriage return spaces the paper forward and returns the carriage to the beginning of the line.

To return the carriage on a manual machine, raise the left hand in a continuous sweep, placing the hand against the lever as shown in the preceding illustration.

Flip the lever with a toss of the wrist, continuing this sweep down to the home-key position. Do not allow the hand to follow the carriage across the machine. By the time the carriage hits the left margin, your left hand should be back on the keyboard, ready to continue typing.

If you are using an electric typewriter, the carriage return key is touched with the little finger of the right hand. Extend the *sem* finger to the right, press the return key, and return the finger to home-key position.

The return key on the Selectric returns the typing element to the left margin.

TYPING POSTURE

The semicolon, colon, and dash are always typed outside the quotation marks.

`The following are considered "standard equipment":`

—	Use two hyphens to indicate a dash and do not space before, between, or after the hyphens. `He came today--didn't you meet him?`

-	No space before or after the hyphen.
	
	`A first-class job`
	`Second-hand car`

'	No space before or after an apostrophe.
	
	`I can't find Mary's record.`
	`I'll check it at two o'clock.`

( )	Space once before typing the opening parenthesis and once after typing the closing parenthesis, but do not space between the parentheses and the words they enclose.
	
	`In the illustration given (see below) the purpose`
	`is made clear.`
	
	Type the comma, semicolon, colon, and dash after the closing parenthesis.
	
	`Although we are not satisfied with our order (there are`
	`too many broken pieces), we are paying the bill.`
	
	A period, question mark, or exclamation point is typed outside the parentheses when it punctuates the entire sentence. These marks of punctuation are placed inside the parentheses when they punctuate the enclosed material.
	
	`They met at the Waldorf (Hotel).`
	`We have waited 30 days (doesn't it seem longer?)`
	`for the package.`

Sit well back in the chair, head erect, back straight, shoulders level, and elbows hanging loosely at your sides.

Center your body opposite the *J* key approximately 8 to 10 inches from the base of the machine. You should reach ever so slightly for the keyboard. The forearms should be parallel to the keyboard.

Check yourself for the correct position at the machine:

1. Are you sitting erect in your chair with your feet resting flat on the floor?

2. Do your arms hang naturally from your shoulders, and are your elbows held comfortably close to your body?

3. Are your fingers curved, and do your hands slope parallel to the keyboard?

If you can answer "Yes" to these questions, you are ready to type!

Home Row Drill

1   ffff dddd fdfd fdfd jjjj kkkk jkjk jkjk fdfd jkjk

2   fdss ssss fdss ssss jkll llll jkll llll fdss jkll

3   fdsa aaaa fdsa aaaa jkl; ;;;; jkl; ;;;; fdsa jkl;

4   as ask asks all fall falls add adds lad lads fads

5   flask flasks salad salads a flask; a salad; a lad

6   all lads; ask all lads; a lad falls; all lads add

I AND T KEYS

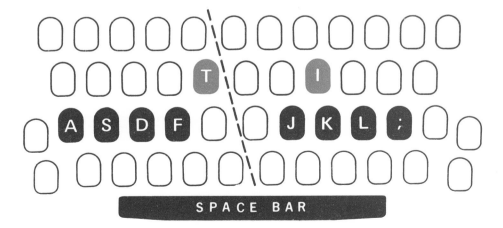

Note the location of the *i* key on the chart. The *i* is struck with the *k* finger.

In reaching for a third-row key, unbend the finger slightly, raise it far enough to strike the desired key, and then return the finger quickly to its home-row position. Note the curved fingers in the following illustration.

?	Space twice after a question mark. `Did you go?  No.`
!	Space twice after an exclamation point. `No!  Yes!  Not really!`
:	Space twice after a colon. `as follows:  bills, clips, and pencils.`
,	Space once after a comma. `Invoices, bills, and statements.`
;	Space once after a semicolon. `All orders must be entered; all bills must be paid.`

"	No space between opening quotation marks and the first word of the quoted material. Space once after the closing marks if they are not at the end of the sentence.
	
	`She marked "paid" on the bill.`
	
	A period or a comma is typed before the quotation marks.
	
	`"The book," she said, "is very interesting."`
	
	If the quoted material is a question or an exclamation, but the rest of the sentence is not, type the question mark or exclamation point inside the quotation marks.
	
	`I heard her ask, "Where are you going?"`
	
	`The man said, "What a beautiful sight!"`
	
	If the entire sentence is a question or an exclamation, type the question mark or exclamation point outside the quotation marks.
	
	`Who purchased "Typing Techniques"?`

Place your hands in the home-key position and find *i* on the typewriter. Make the reach to *i* with the *k* finger a few times.

I Drill

1   `kik kik kid kids skid skids aid laid said lid did`

2   `ill fill fills dill sills skill skills ails jails`

3   `fail sail sails silk silks is kiss disk dial dais`

4   `a lad said a lass is ill; silk sails; fill a jail`

To strike *t* raise the *f* finger slightly to the right.

Locate *t* on the typewriter and practice making this reach; then type the drill.

T Drill

1   `ftf ftf sat fat kit kits lit sit sits fit fits it`

2   `lift sift flit flat fast talk tiff tall tail task`

3   `till jilt jilts still fast fists tilts slits skit`

4   `list it; it still is; at last; it did fit; it is;`

5   `lift it; it tilts; it is flat; it lasts; is still`

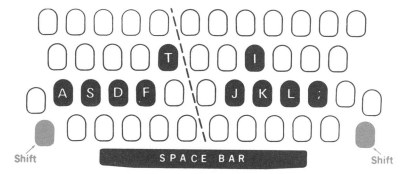

Notice that there is a shift key on each side of the keyboard. The *right* shift key is used to capitalize a letter that is struck with the *left* hand, and the *left* shift key is used to capitalize a letter that is struck with the *right* hand.

Common nouns, such as model or chapter, should be capitalized when used before reference numbers.

```
Chapter 7

Lesson III

Room 2
```

Time

Use figures with o'clock for emphasis; use words for formality.

```
four o'clock

4 o'clock
```

Use figures with a.m. and p.m. Do not space after a. or p.

```
4 a.m.
```

Use a colon to separate hours from minutes and minutes from seconds.

```
4:03 p.m.

4:03:26
```

When time appears without a.m. or p.m. or o'clock, spell out the hour.

```
I shall expect you at three.
```

SPACING FOR MARKS OF PUNCTUATION AND SPECIAL CHARACTERS

Space twice after a period at the end of a sentence. Space once after a period at the end of an abbreviation. Do not space after a period within an abbreviation consisting of single initials typed in small letters. Abbreviations consisting of capital letters are sometimes written without periods. When periods are used, there is usually no space after the internal period.

```
Order now.  It's not too late.

Mr. C. L. Bradley

p.m.  f.o.b.  sq. ft.  op. cit.  M.D.  U.S.A.

CPA ITT CDT
```

To capitalize a letter that is struck with the right hand:

1. Reach for the left shift key with the *a* finger. Keep your other fingers in their correct position over the home keys.

2. Fully depress the left-hand shift key.

3. While the shift key is depressed, strike the letter to be capitalized.

4. Release the shift key and return the *a* finger to its home key.

To capitalize a letter that is struck with the left hand, follow the same procedure outlined above, using the *sem* finger to depress the right shift key.

Practice depressing the left shift key and returning to home-key position; then practice the reach to the right shift key.

Shift Key Drill

1   aAa sSs dDd fFf tTt All Ask Did Fall Flask Salads

2   A lad asks; Add a salad; A flask falls; All lads;

3   lLl kKk jJj iIi I It Lad Jail Kits Lass Kid Lists

4   It is I; List it last; It still fits; It is flat;

Check your paper. Are any of your capital letters above or below the line of writing? If so, remember to strike the letter to be capitalized while the shift key is fully depressed.

Money	Use figures, except in extremely formal legal documents. Do not space after the dollar sign.

```
$12.73
```

```
$8.05
```

Omit the decimal point and ciphers for even amounts (except in checks).

```
$12
```

```
$3.45 list, $3 net
```

For amounts under $1, use the cent sign (¢) only in invoices and other business forms.

```
4 @ 8¢            We paid 8 cents.
```

For extremely large round numbers, the ciphers may be replaced by the word million or billion.

```
The deficit was $7 billion.
```

Spell out indefinite amounts of money.

```
Many thousands of dollars.
```

Percentages	Use figures to express percentages. Percent may be written as one word or as two.

```
12 percent
```

```
12 per cent
```

Use the percentage sign (%) in business forms and statistical work only. Do not space before the percentage sign.

```
12%
```

Reference Numbers	Use figures for reference numbers that identify a model, style, policy, invoice, purchase order, page, volume, etc. Generally omit all commas in such numbers.

```
Model #23456
```

```
Policy No. S98467
```

```
Invoice 20741
```

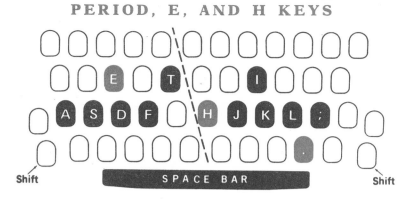

The period is struck with the *l* finger. Move the *l* finger downward and slightly to the right to strike the period. Note that the period is the same whether typed in the lower case or with the shift key.

Strike the space bar twice after a period at the end of a sentence.

Locate the period on the typewriter and practice making this reach.

Period Drill

1   l.l l.l l.l l.l It is I. It fits. Al sat still.

2   Ada is ill. Ask Sal. List it. Kati did a skit.

Use the *d* finger to type the letter *e*. Locate *e* on the typewriter and practice the reach.

E Drill

1   ded ded ded deed desk east takes likes tell tests

2   let less left leads sled fled settle little tales

3   ate fate estates feels feed feet likes jade jaded

4   Let Jed take less. Ask if it is at East Estates.

5   Stella likes a little desk. I settled all deals.

Use the *j* finger to type the letter *h*. Locate *h* on the typewriter and practice the reach by moving the *j* finger to the left while the *k, l,* and *sem* fingers remain in home-key position.

H Drill

1   jhj jhj jhj hit hits hid hide hill hiked his this

2   hat hail hale has hall halts half that he she the

3   dash dish lash fish sash Edith Faith Hattie Hilda

4   She left the hall. Take this desk. He has that.

5   She likes Edith. Hilda is late. Dale has a jet.

Age	In general, spell out numbers designating ages and anniversaries. Use figures for an age stated in years, months, and days. Omit commas between the years, months, and days.
	`I am eighteen.`
	`I am 18 years 4 months and 27 days old.`
Dates	Use figures except in extremely formal documents. Use -st, -nd, -rd, -th in a date only when the day is written before the month.
	`August 6, 19--`
	`the 6th of August`
	In U.S. military correspondence and in letters from foreign countries, the date is expressed in date-month-year sequence.
	`14 October 1971`
	The year may be abbreviated by using an apostrophe for the century in a historical sense.
	`Class of '61`
	`the blizzard of '88`
Dimensions **Feet** **Inches** **Weights** **Distance**	Use figures for dimensions. In technical material, use the apostrophe (') to represent feet, and quotation marks (") to represent inches. Do not space between the number and mark. Note use of number sign (#) for pounds.
	`4 by 6 feet` `4' x 6'`
	`4 feet 6 inches` `4'6"`
	`6 lbs.` `6#`
	`3 miles`
Legal Documents	Numbers are often spelled out, followed by the figure in parentheses, in legal documents. `We agreed to sell thirty-three (33) acres.`

MEASURING TYPING SPEED

Five strokes are counted as one standard word. The scale below the sentences shows the number of 5-stroke words in a line.

```
Fred left five gifts for the staff in our office.
....1....2....3....4....5....6....7....8....9....10
Fred left fi
....1....2..
```

To determine the number of words typed in the preceding example, add the figure for the portion of a line typed to the figure for the complete line or lines typed (10 + 2 = 12 gross words). If this copy was typed for one minute, the score would be 12 gross words a minute (GWAM).

REMOVING, INSERTING, AND STRAIGHTENING THE PAPER

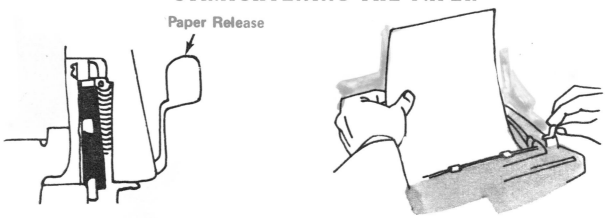

Move the paper bail away, depress the paper-release lever, draw out the paper with your left hand, release the lever with your right hand, and replace the paper bail.

Inserting the Paper

Left Edge at Zero

Plural Numbers	Form the plural of a figure by adding the letter *s*. If a number is spelled out, just add the letter *s*. Some authorities still recommend the apostrophe and *s* but this is unnecessary.
	
	`8s and 9s`
	
	`8's and 9's`
	
	`eights and nines`
	
	`1900's`

Decimals	A period is used to express a decimal point. Do not skip a space before or after the period.
	
	`1.06         12.412         128.627`
	
	Do not use commas in the decimal part of a number. Always write decimals in figures.
	
	`1.08`
	
	`47.62432`
	
	`2,974.4216`

Fractions	There are two kinds of typewritten fractions—those that are on the keyboard (½) and those that are made by using the diagonal (1/19). Note that there is no space before or after the diagonal.
	Use figures for all mixed numbers. With a "keyboard" fraction, no space is left between the whole number and the fraction. With a "made" fraction, one space is left.
	
	2½ `2 5/16`
	
	4¼ `18 4/100`
	
	Do not use a "keyboard" fraction (½) in the same sentence with a "made" fraction (1/8).
	
	`    The lot measures 84 1/2 by 26 1/8 feet.`
	
	`NOT:  The lot measures 84½ by 26 1/8 feet.`
	
	Spell out all isolated fractions. Hyphenate such a fraction.
	
	`The job is two-thirds completed.`

If your machine is equipped with a "0" mark on the paper guide scale:

1. Set paper guide at "0."

2. Raise paper bail away from the cylinder.

3. Hold the sheet of paper loosely with the left hand and place it on the paper table with the left edge of the paper resting against the paper guide.

4. Twirl the right cylinder knob with the thumb and first two fingers of the right hand.

5. When paper is in the correct position, the left edge will be at "0" on the cylinder scale (see illustration). Then place the paper bail over the paper to hold it firmly against the cylinder.

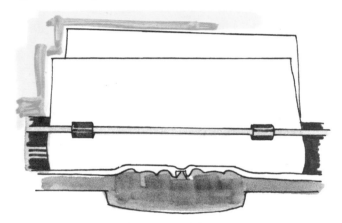

Paper not straight

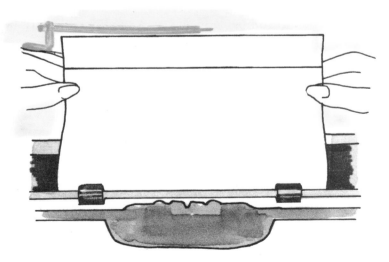

Straightening the paper

Now check your paper to see if it is straight. To do this, roll the paper forward several inches to see if the top left edge of the paper lines up with the bottom left edge. If it does, your paper is straight—if it does not:

When a series of numbers includes numbers both above and below ten, use figures for all the related numbers.

We ordered 8 boxes of paper, 12 boxes of envelopes, and 20 cartons of index cards.

Tabulation and Statistical Typing	Use figures in all statistical typing, tabulation, and business forms.

4 cartons	No. 10 envelopes
3 boxes	8" x 10" letterheads
12 cartons	3" x 5" index cards

Hyphens with Numbers

Hyphenate spelled-out numbers from twenty-one through ninety-nine.

Twenty-one	Forty-six	Ninety-nine

Do not hyphenate before the words hundred, thousand, etc. (**NOTE:** The *and* may be omitted.)

One hundred and twenty-one

One thousand three hundred forty-six

Seventy-six thousand four hundred and ninety-nine

When a number appears as a modifier directly before a noun, the entire modifier should be hyphenated.

It will be a 12-page booklet.

They ordered a 6,000-letter mailing.

It will be a four-story building.

Commas in Numbers

Figures of 1,000 or more are generally written with commas to separate every three digits except when writing years, page numbers, house or room numbers, serial numbers, and decimals. This permits ease of reading. Leave no space before or after the comma.

1,000	1,426
1,932	7,320

A RECAP

1. Lift the paper bail.

2. Use the paper release lever to loosen the paper.

3. Line up the left edges of the paper.

4. Reset the paper release lever and return the paper bail to typing position.

PICA AND ELITE SPACING

Most typewriters have either elite or pica type. Elite type, which is the smaller of the two, permits the typing of 12 strokes to an inch. Pica has 10 strokes to an inch. Since most typing is done on paper that is 8½ inches wide, it is possible to type 12 × 8½, or 102 strokes across the line with an elite machine. A machine equipped with pica type, however, allows for only 10 × 8½, or 85 strokes across the line.

Notice the difference in the size of the type on the following lines:

ELITE: This is a sample of elite type.   Notice the size.

PICA: This is a sample of pica type.   Notice the size.

To determine whether your machine is equipped with elite or pica type, insert a standard-sized sheet of typing paper into the machine so that the left edge of the paper is at "0" on the cylinder scale. Notice the position of the right edge of the paper on the scale. The number indicated represents the number of strokes that can be typed across your paper. Therefore, if the right edge of the paper is at 102, you are using a machine that is equipped with elite type; if your paper ends at 85, your machine is equipped with pica type.

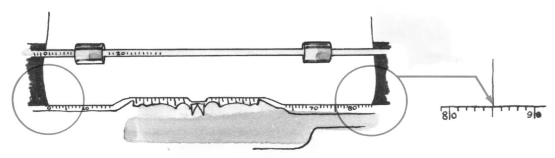

Pica — 10 strokes per inch — 85 strokes across the page.

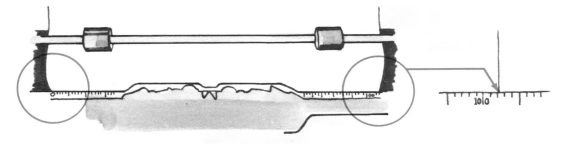

Elite — 12 strokes per inch — 102 strokes across the page.

Whole Numbers	Spell out whole numbers from one through ten, whether exact or approximate. Use figures above ten.
	
	`We sent four packages.`
	`He received ten letters.`
	`They ordered 11 sets of books.`
	`This mailing consisted of 10,500 letters.`
	
	When writing is of a formal or literary nature, spell out all numbers from 1 through 100 and all round numbers above 100 that require no more than two words.
	
	`More than eleven million people heard the`
	`program.`
	`Over three hundred people participated.`
	`But:  Over 375 people participated.`

Numbers at Beginning of Sentence	Spell out numbers that begin a sentence, no matter how large. (When a long number begins a sentence, it is often better to rearrange the sentence.)
	
	`Two hundred twenty-eight men applied for`
	`the job.`
	`The job was applied for by 228 men.`

Ordinal Numbers	Ordinal numbers are "first," "second," "third," etc.
	Spell out ordinal numbers that can be expressed in one or two words, except for dates.
	
	`This is my fourth visit to your city.`
	`He succeeded on the eleventh attempt.`
	`This is my twenty-fifth crossing.`

Numbers in Series	When two numbers appear one after the other, spell out the smaller number and express the larger number in figures.
	
	`The purchasing department ordered eleven`
	`55-gallon drums.`
	`We need 11 three-cent stamps.`
	
	If spelling out the smaller number requires more than two words, express both numbers in figures and separate by a comma.
	
	`Of 1700, 123 were rejected.`

CENTERING THE CARRIAGE

To center the carriage, depress either the right or the left carriage release key and hold it down as you move the carriage to the center of the typewriter.

SETTING THE MARGINS

"Spring Set"

To set the left margin with the "spring-set" margin key, depress the left margin-set key, move the carriage to the desired point on the scale, and release the set key. To set the right stop, depress the right margin-set key, move the carriage to the desired point on the scale, and release the set key.

"Hand Set"

To set the margins with the "hand-set" margin key, center your machine and slide each margin stop to the desired point on the scale.

"Hook On"

MAR SET

Do you have only one margin-set key that must be used to set both margins? Then you have the "hook-on" type of margin key.

To set the left margin stop, move the carriage to the left as far as possible. Hold down firmly on the margin-set key, move the carriage to the desired point, and release the set key. To set the right margin, move the carriage to the right as far as possible. Hold down firmly on the margin-set key, move the carriage to the desired point, and release the set key.

Set the margins at 15 and 70 for pica type and at 25 and 75 for elite type for all drill work in Section 1.

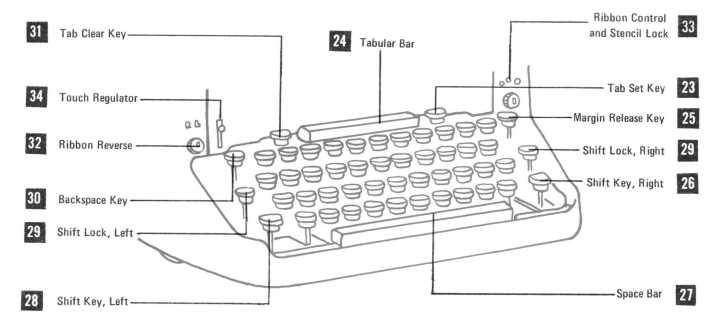

31 Tab Clear Key

34 Touch Regulator

32 Ribbon Reverse

30 Backspace Key

29 Shift Lock, Left

28 Shift Key, Left

24 Tabular Bar

33 Ribbon Control and Stencil Lock

23 Tab Set Key

25 Margin Release Key

29 Shift Lock, Right

26 Shift Key, Right

27 Space Bar

Lower Segment of a Manual Typewriter

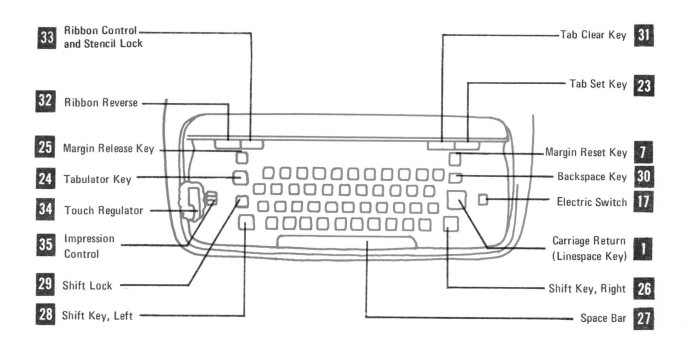

33 Ribbon Control and Stencil Lock

32 Ribbon Reverse

25 Margin Release Key

24 Tabulator Key

34 Touch Regulator

35 Impression Control

29 Shift Lock

28 Shift Key, Left

31 Tab Clear Key

23 Tab Set Key

7 Margin Reset Key

30 Backspace Key

17 Electric Switch

1 Carriage Return (Linespace Key)

26 Shift Key, Right

27 Space Bar

Lower Segment of an Electric Typewriter (check for different positions of ¢ @ * and ___ . Note that some keys have repeat action. Extra keys that are used are ⌐ = ! 1.

A RECAP

1   she likes feel life he fate his see it is fast as

2   hits jet at lake left had staff ask the shall let

3   She likes this life. He left his hat. It is he.

4   He likes fast hits. Set it at the left. Hit it.
     ....1....2....3....4....5....6....7....8....9....10

V AND O KEYS

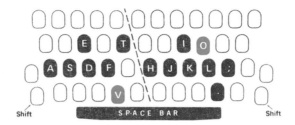

Locate *v* on the typewriter and practice the reach by dropping the *f* finger and moving it slightly to the right. Keep the *a* finger in the home-key position. Avoid twisting the hand or elbow out of position.

V Drill

1   fvf fvf fvf vie five veils have saves vistas visa

2   velvet dive live vital valid vest hive vivid vale

3   I have five vests. Ask Eve if the test is valid.

4   Jessie likes velvets. David lives at Vista Lake.

5   Save that vase. I shall visit Jill at Eastville.
     ....1....2....3....4....5....6....7....8....9....10

Locate *o* on the typewriter and practice the reach with the *l* finger. Extend the *l* finger to make this reach without changing the hand alignment with the keyboard. The *j* finger remains in the home-key position.

O Drill

1   -lol lol lol told fold so sold hold lot slot total

2   to too do took look hook of off odd oil toil soil

3   Fold at the slot so that it fits. Oil the tools.

4   He sold the odd lots of tools. Total the losses.

5   Joe looked at the jade. She took it to the sale.
     ....1....2....3....4....5....6....7....8....9....10

OPERATIVE PARTS OF A TYPEWRITER

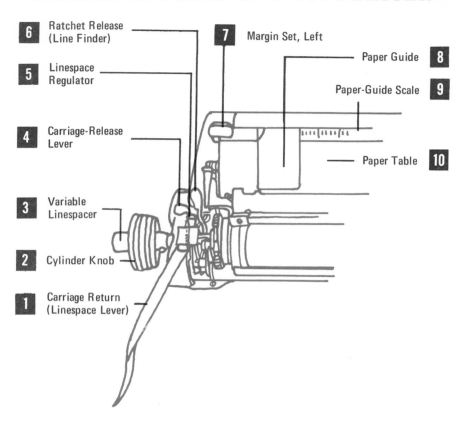

6 Ratchet Release (Line Finder)

5 Linespace Regulator

4 Carriage-Release Lever

3 Variable Linespacer

2 Cylinder Knob

1 Carriage Return (Linespace Lever)

7 Margin Set, Left

8 Paper Guide

9 Paper-Guide Scale

10 Paper Table

Top Left Segment of a Typewriter

NOTE: The Underwood margin sets are located at the front of the machine.

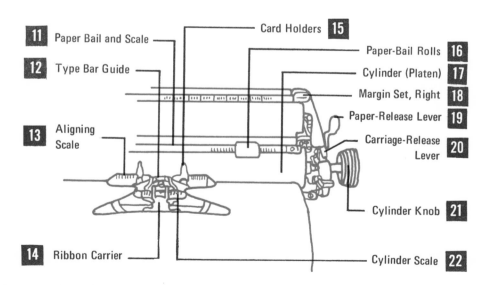

11 Paper Bail and Scale

12 Type Bar Guide

13 Aligning Scale

14 Ribbon Carrier

15 Card Holders

16 Paper-Bail Rolls

17 Cylinder (Platen)

18 Margin Set, Right

19 Paper-Release Lever

20 Carriage-Release Lever

21 Cylinder Knob

22 Cylinder Scale

Top Right Segment of a Typewriter

G AND M KEYS

Locate *g* on the typewriter and practice the reach by moving the *f* finger to the right. Keep the *a*, *s*, and *d* fingers in home-key position. Practice the drill.

G Drill

1   fgf fgf fgf go ago good glad glass get gives gave

2   high sight fight light age Giles Gail dog log gas

3   .Give the glasses as a gift. Giles is glad to go.

4   This light is too high. He gave his age to Gail.

5   The edge is jagged. She leads the fight to vote.
....1....2....3....4....5....6....7....8....9....10

Locate the *m* on the typewriter and practice the reach by moving the *j* finger down and slightly to the right. Avoid twisting the hand or elbow out of position.

M Drill

1   jmj jmj jmj am made mailed makes most almost them

2   small Jim Amelia time fame miss me some them game

3   Mail them to Jim at home. She made a small gash.

4   Let Miss Small take the mail. Amelia made a hat.

5   Avoid jams at games. I am home most of the time.
....1....2....3....4....5....6....7....8....9....10

Review

1   _if it is ill its feels fat fits fates fatal fakes

2   falls fills fail faith feet fast fifth filth flat

Section 7
A RECAP

```
 3   take tie task tells tale tall tests this that the
 4   see settle stale staff sits sat set sake sift she
 5   shall shifts shale shall shakes salt skills still
 6   as all asked ash at aft kills kale kid khaki keel
 7   lifts left liked lakes lets lash less lest little
 8   he his hats half hated hill hit hall ham had home
 9   eat east elated estate edge eve eagle ease eddies
10   valet valid velvet veto vivid vigils viola violet
11   go good gold gait gall game gas gasket gate gavel
12   mad maid mailed makes malt medal media meet Midas
13   jets jot jailed jam James jellies jig joke jovial
14   I shall go to Easthill Lake to settle his estate.
15   The fifth is the date of the game.  Go to see it.
16   She asked Mike to go to the Village Hall to vote.
17   Jim took all of the tests; Joe took half of them.
18   Omit it.  All he asks is that the lease is legal.
     ....1....2....3....4....5....6....7....8....9....10
```

R AND Y KEYS

Locate *r* on the typewriter. Practice the reach to *r* using the *f* finger. Move the *f* finger up to *r* without moving the hand forward and without moving the other fingers out of home-key position.

Remember: two spaces follow a period at the end of a sentence; one space follows a period after an abbreviation within a sentence.

```
STATE OF NEW YORK    )
                     )  s.s.
COUNTY OF NEW YORK   )
```

John Doe being duly sworn deposes and says:

That he resides at 17½ Broadway, Borough of Manhattan, City of New York and is over twenty-one (21) years of age.

That he executed the foregoing bill of sale and that he is the sole and absolute owner of the property described in said bill of sale and has the full right to transfer the same; that he is not indebted to anyone and has no creditors; that there are no judgments existing or entered against him; that there are no replevins, attachments or executions issued against him now in force; that no petition in bankruptcy or arrangement proceedings has been filed by or against him; and that he has not taken advantage of any law relating to insolvency.

That this affidavit is made for the purpose of inducing Richard Roe the buyer of said property to purchase the same, knowing full well that he will rely thereon and pay the sum of ONE THOUSAND ($1,000) DOLLARS therefor.

Sworn to before me this

1st day of October, 19--

_____

_____ (L.S.)

Notary Public State of New York

No. 100 qualified New York County

Term expires March 30, 19--.

R Drill

1 frf frf frf girl first tires fair large dear here

2 red read order short folder letter Mrs. Dr. dress

3 Dr. Short read the folders. The address is here.

4 Mrs. Read ordered a red dress. Rate the letters.

5 Fill the jars. Look over the order for mistakes.
....1....2....3....4....5....6....7....8....9....10

Locate *y* on the typewriter and practice the reach using the *j* finger. Straighten the *j* finger and move it to *y* without arching the wrist or moving the other fingers out of home-key position.

Y Drill

1 jyj jyj jyj ray jay may day say Friday they loyal

2 very my try every system yes yell year ready yolk

3 Mrs. Jay may arrive Friday. They are very loyal.

4 Mr. Ray mailed my letter today. Try this system.

5 I talked to Dr. Daley early Friday. He is ready.
....1....2....3....4....5....6....7....8....9....10

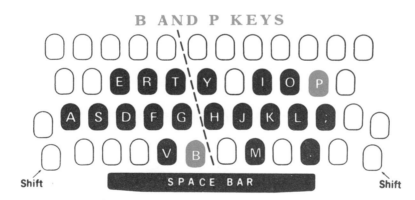

B AND P KEYS

Locate *b* on the typewriter and practice the reach, moving the *f* finger down and to the right without moving the hand out of home-key position.

B Drill

1 fbf fbf fbf be better believes Barbara bills book

2 Bob both broke boys bottles by bare balls batters

3 Bob broke the bottles. Bill them for both books.

4 Barbara believes these boys to be better batters.

5 Mr. Bar is based at Brits. He is able to travel.
....1....2....3....4....5....6....7....8....9....10

ASSUMPTION OF CHATTEL MORTGAGE

KNOW ALL MEN BY THESE PRESENTS, that SUPREME MOUNTING
AND FINISHING COMPANY, INC., of 10 West 103 Street, New York
City, does hereby assume and guarantee to Daniel Martin, of
2115 West 191 Street, New York City, the satisfaction of a
certain Chattel Mortgage given by Ernest Carlson and Lawrence
Lambert on the sixth day of June, 19--, to the said Daniel
Martin, to secure the payment of the sum of $5,000.00 and does
further absolutely guarantee the payment of all the promissory
notes recited in the said Chattel Mortgage, and the absolute
payment of the said sum of $5,000.00, according to the terms,
conditions, and tenor of the said Chattel Mortgage.

IN WITNESS WHEREOF, the said SUPREME MOUNTING AND
FINISHING COMPANY, INC., has subscribed its name and caused
the seal thereof to be affixed hereunto this 20th day of
November, 19--.

SUPREME MOUNTING AND FINISHING COMPANY, INC.

By_____
President

_____
Treasurer

Locate *p* on the typewriter and practice the reach, moving the *sem* finger up to *p* without twisting the hand or elbow out of position and without raising the wrist.

P Drill

1   `;p; ;p; ;p; pad pay paid page prove ports reports`

2   `post possible paper happy people please keep type`

3   `Please post the letter.  Keep these people happy.`

4   `Proof all pages of the report before Joel leaves.`

5   `It is possible that Peg may visit late this year.`
    `....1....2....3....4....5....6....7....8....9....10`

U AND X KEYS

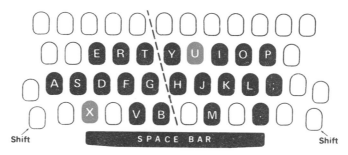

Locate *u* on the typewriter. Using the *j* finger, try the reach up to *u* keeping the other fingers in home-key position to guide the finger back to *j*.

U Drill

1   `-juj juj juj us use used our four out about pupils`

2   `full dull group built value push you jumps Judith`

3   `Four pupils of our group built this stage for us.`

4   `It is a pleasure to see future leaders take part.`
    `....1....2....3....4....5....6....7....8....9....10`

Locate *x* on the typewriter. Move the *s* finger down to the right, keeping the *f* finger in home-key position. Keep fingers curved. Practice the reach.

X Drill

1   `sxs sxs sxs box fox fix mix six sixty tax axe lax`

2   `examples expert extra expose expressed Ajax oxide`

3   `Box the extra items; express them to Mr. Joe Fox.`

4   `Experts prepared tax reports for their employees.`

5   `The sixty boxes expressed to Max Poster are lost.`
    `....1....2....3....4....5....6....7....8....9....10`

POWER OF ATTORNEY

KNOW ALL MEN BY THESE PRESENTS:

THAT I, THE UNDERSIGNED, John B. Adams, of New Orleans, Louisiana, do hereby make, constitute, and appoint William DeGroaf, of Baton Rouge, Louisiana, my true and lawful attorney, for me, and my name, place, and stead.

THAT I DO THESE PRESENTS grant and give unto my said attorney full authority and power to do and perform all and every act and thing whatsoever necessary and requisite to be done in and about the premises, as full to all intents and purposes as I might or could do if personally present, with full power of substitution and revocation, hereby ratifying and confirming all that my said attorney shall lawfully do or cause to be done by virtue hereof.

IN TESTIMONY WHEREOF, I hereunto set my hand and seal this 30th day of July, 19--.

_____

Executed and delivered in the presence of

_____
                Notary Public

Q AND N KEYS

Locate *q* on the keyboard. Watch your *a* finger as it moves up to type *q*. Hold the elbow and wrist in position and keep the other fingers in home-key position. Practice the reach.

Q Drill

1 aqa aqa aqa quit quite quiet quotes quota require

2 required requests qualify quality equaled quorums

3 Employees are required to meet quotas to qualify.

4 Quarterly reports are requested from all dealers.

5 Good quality paper is required for the extra job.
   ....1....2....3....4....5....6....7....8....9....10

Move the *j* finger down and to the left to type *n*. Practice this reach and then type the drill.

N Drill

1 jnj jnj jnj an and any plan thank than then noted

2 on only money bonds additional personal equipment

3 Any plan for additional equipment requires money.

4 Thank you for your personal note about the bonds.

5 Join Don in studying the trends in money markets.
   ....1....2....3....4....5....6....7....8....9....10

Z AND COMMA KEYS

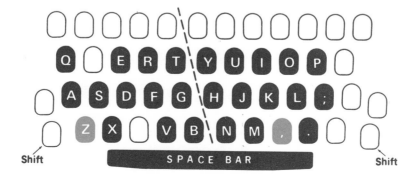

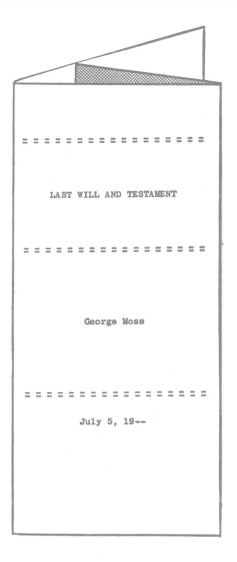

After studying the information given in Job 2 on legal typing, type the next three jobs on legal cap paper. Either use the paper provided in the workbook or prepare your own. The double line on the left is drawn 1⅜ inches from the edge of the paper and the line on the right is ⅜ of an inch from the edge.

Locate *z* on the keyboard and practice the reach from *a* to *z*. Curve the *a* finger and avoid moving the hand or elbow.

Z Drill

1   aza aza aza zip zeal zest zero zoo zone haze size

2   quiz quizzes jazz amaze prize hazard organization

3   Amazing prizes are given for passing all quizzes.

4   Zoning rules apply to organizations of all sizes.

5   Size five does not fit Mr. Zans; order size nine.
     ....1....2....3....4....5....6....7....8....9....10

The comma is typed with the *k* finger. Note that comma is the same whether typed in the lower case or with the shift key.

Practice the reach from *k* to comma.

Space **once** following a comma.

Comma Drill

1   k,k k,k k,k I am sure, if he is, too, so, if not,

2   If Roberta types the report, you should proof it.

3   Harry, Tom, and James attended the same meetings.

4   Karl talked to Joe, and they realized the danger.

5   In his opinion, Inez has an extraordinary talent.
     ....1....2....3....4....5....6....7....8....9....10

C, DIAGONAL, AND QUESTION MARK KEYS

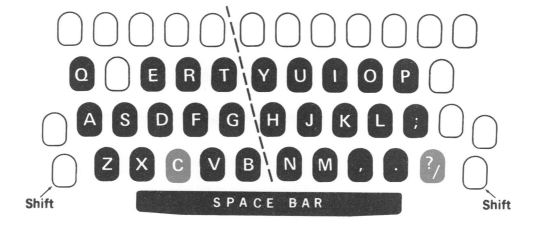

Locate *c* on the keyboard. Using the *d* finger, practice the reach a few times.

To prepare a legal back, fold the top down one inch. The papers will be stapled in this fold. Bring the bottom edge of the sheet even with the creased top edge and crease this fold. Bring the last fold to the top and crease again. The legal back will then be folded into four equal parts, not counting the one-inch binding fold. The endorsement is then typed on the back of the sheet in the second fold from the top.

Common legal forms include: acknowledgments, deeds, guardianships, summonses, subpoenas, petitions, powers of attorney, orders to show cause, writs, garnishments, injunctions, proxies, miscellaneous types of contracts, and patents and copyrights.[4]

---

[4] Ibid.

LEGAL PAPERS

Folding and Endorsing

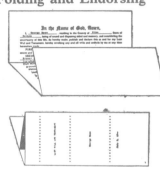

Legal documents must be specially folded and titled to facilitate filing. If the document is on 8½-by-11-inch paper, it should be folded horizontally into three parts. On the outside of the middle panel certain information required for identification should be filled in, as indicated. This panel is called the endorsement (or indorsement).

If the document is typed on legal-size 8½-by-13-inch paper, the sheet should be folded in half, then in half again. The endorsement is typed on the back of the document, on the second panel from the top.

To protect certain documents, these documents are enclosed in a separate cover. This cover, usually consisting of a heavy blue paper, is slightly larger than the document sheet. It should be folded with a 1-inch flap at the top, then folded in half twice.

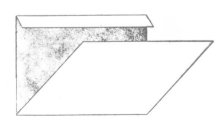

The endorsement is typed in the second panel. The cover should be opened, the document inserted under the 1-inch flap and stapled firmly in place. The two should then be folded for filing.

C Drill

1   dcd dcd dcd can call cases cost could Charles cap

2   each office include services receive acquired cut

3   I call the office each day to check on the cases.

4   Mr. Charles did not include the cost of services.

5   A secretary must be an accurate and rapid typist.
    ....1....2....3....4....5....6....7....8....9....10

Locate the diagonal (/) on the keyboard. Using the *sem* finger, practice this reach. The question mark (?) is the shift of the diagonal. Practice this reach.

Do not space before or after the diagonal.
Space twice after the question mark at the end of a sentence.

Diagonal and Question Mark Drill

1   ;/; ?; ;/; ?; ;/; ;?; ;?; ;?; a/c n/c B/L Jack? Marie?

2   May I go? Has he gone? Did you go? Is he here?

3   Mark this bill n/c. Indicate a/c or d/c current.

4   Is she a registrant and/or a member of the group?

5   The letter is addressed c/o Mr. Leonard M. Johns.
    ....1....2....3....4....5....6....7....8....9....10

W, COLON, AND HYPHEN KEYS

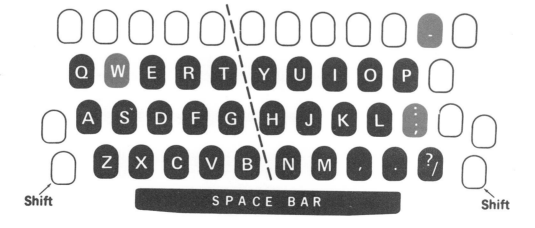

Locate *w* on the keyboard. Watch your *s* finger as it moves from *s* to *w* and back to *s*. Practice the reach a few times.

The most common types of legal documents which must be typed are: acknowledgments, affidavits, pleadings, wills, answers, deeds, petitions, leases, guardianships, mortgages, verifications, powers of attorney, summonses, contracts, garnishments, proxies, abstracts, miscellaneous documents, depositions, and patents and copyrights.[3]

[3] National Association of Legal Secretaries, *Manual for the Legal Secretarial Profession*, West Publishing Co., St. Paul, Minn., 1965, p. 19.

Every secretary should have a loose-leaf binder to hold copies of each kind of legal instrument used frequently in her office. This copy will show not only the style in which the instrument should be typed but also the wording used by the lawyer.

There are general directions that apply to most legal papers. All require a high degree of accuracy. Erasures are even prohibited in some instances. Great care must be taken in punctuating so that the meaning is absolutely clear.

An original, a file copy, and varying numbers of carbon copies of all legal documents are necessary. There may be as many as five to ten carbons required so care must be taken in inserting the carbon pack so that all paper is aligned in the typewriter. Place the sheets beneath the flap of an envelope before inserting. Make sure that each sheet is straight.

Legal papers are typed on legal cap paper, which is 8 or 8½ by 13 or 14 inches, or brief paper, which is 8 by 10½ inches. Both kinds of paper have ruled vertical lines on the left and right.

All typing must be within the marginal lines without touching the lines. Begin typing two spaces to the right of the left ruling and end two spaces to the left of the right ruling.

Legal papers typed on legal cap are bound at the top. Begin typing two inches from the top of the paper on each page and leave a one-inch bottom margin.

Double space the copy except for land descriptions and quoted matter, which are single spaced. Indent paragraphs ten spaces and indent descriptions and quoted matter ten spaces from both margins.

The first page is usually not numbered except on a will. Subsequent pages are numbered one half inch from the bottom of the page, centered between the vertical rulings. Type a hyphen before and after the page number.

The title of a legal paper is typed in all caps and is centered between the vertical rulings for margins.

The makers of a legal instrument sign at the right of the page and the witnesses, if any, sign at the left. Type signature lines approximately three inches long and leave two or three blank lines between them.

Legal documents may be bound in a cover known as a legal back. This is made from heavy paper slightly larger than legal cap. Information that is typed on the outside of a legal back is called an endorsement, and it gives the name of the document and the names of the parties concerned.

W Drill

1   sws sws sws who whom what when where while how we

2   were week will with wait way women would work two

3   We saw James while we were waiting in the subway.

4   What will the women do during the next two weeks?

5   He wants to work with Win, but there are no jobs.
    ....1....2....3....4....5....6....7....8....9....10

The colon is the shift of the *sem* key. Practice sem, colon, sem.

The colon is followed by two spaces except to separate hours and minutes (6:45); the semicolon, by one space.

Colon Drill

1   ;:; ;:; ;:; ;:; Dear Frank: Dear Mary: Dear Al:

2   Dear Sir: Dear Madam: as follows: these items:

3   Order the following: pens, pencils, and folders.

4   Dear Bill: Meet me on Wednesday morning at nine.

5   Dear Willis: What can we do to entertain Walter?
    ....1....2....3....4....5....6....7....8....9....10

Locate the hyphen on the keyboard. Watch the *sem* finger as it moves up and slightly to the right to type the hyphen. Practice the reach. Straighten the finger slightly without arching the wrist, keeping the elbow in position.

Hyphen Drill

1   ;-; ;-; ;-; first-class; past-due; self-conscious

2   up-to-date; five-cent; part-time; brother-in-law;

3   We can do a first-class job of promoting our mer-

4   chandise if we adopt these up-to-date procedures.

5   An air-conditioning expert gives reliable advice.
    ....1....2....3....4....5....6....7....8....9....10

The dash is typed with two hyphens (--) without spacing between the dash and the words before and after it.

6   John talked to the group--all well-known writers.
    ....1....2....3....4....5....6....7....8....9....10

---

bargain price, or when it offers additional sweetening, that it becomes an attractive investment.[1]

[1] David S. Salisbury, *So You Want to Invest,* Globe Publishers, Atlanta, 1957, p. 18.

JOB 2

Type the following manuscript to be bound on the left side.

TYPING IN A LEGAL OFFICE

The secretary, stenographer, or typist in a legal office has tremendous responsibilities. The typing is extensive and varied, often requiring work on both the manual and electric typewriters.

The typewriting duties include: copying letters, memorandums, and reports; typing letters, memorandums, and reports from employer's long-hand notes; typing duplicating machine stencils; typing legal documents using previously prepared documents as guides; and typing legal documents using fill-ins as a basis.[1]

[1] Mary Jane Howell, "An Investigation and Analysis of the Duties of Legal Secretaries," Business Administration paper, Texas Christian University, p. 33.

The same survey indicated that the competent legal secretary should be capable of typing at the rate of 80 words a minute with a high degree of accuracy.

The same procedures are used in legal correspondence as those used in business correspondence. Letterheads are usually more conservative, thus adding to the prestige of the attorney and his law firm.

The titles of *Messrs., Honorable,* and *Esquire* are used more frequently in legal letters than in business letters. For example, a firm of attorneys is addressed: *Messrs. Rogers, Dean, and Judson. Hon. Arthur M. Edwards* is the correct way to address anyone who holds or has held an important government position. The title *Esquire* is sometimes used after the name of a lawyer. When it is used, no title is necessary before the name. The correct way to use this title is: *George L. Burke, Esq.* finish.

Legal correspondence will probably contain a subject line more often than will business correspondence. This line may be introduced by *SUBJECT:, Re:,* or *In re:,* or the subject may be stated without any introductory word or phrase.

When any material is to be copied, write the word *COPY* at the top of the first page unless special printed copy paper is used. Copy the material exactly as it is typed on the original even if there are errors.[2]

[2] Lois Hutchinson, *Standard Handbook for Secretaries*, 8th ed., McGraw-Hill Book Company, New York, 1969, p. 431.

Section 2
ALPHABETIC KEYBOARD MASTERY

Investors buy common stocks for one or both of two purposes—the dividend income they may receive from their investments, either currently or in the future, and the anticipation of gain from a rise in the market value of a stock.

Common stock represents the basic share in the ownership of a corporation. Exactly what percentage of ownership a particular stock represents depends upon the number of shares that the corporation has issued. Thus, if you own 100 shares of the ABC corporation, and that corporation has issued one thousand shares, you own 10 percent of the total equity of that corporation.[4] On the face of each share of stock is mentioned what is called

---

[4] Charles Rapport, *Economics of the Corporation*, Dell Publishers, Los Angeles, 1955, p. 18.

---

the "par value" of the stock. This par value, however, has little or no relevance to the actual market value of the stock. Market value is determined wholly by the laws of supply and demand. As a corporation prospers, more and more investors will try to buy its stock and, as a result, the price of the stock will rise. On the other hand, when a corporation suffers a setback, many of its investors will want to sell their shares and as they pour stock on the market, the price of that stock will fall.[5] Actually, the

---

[5] Robert C. Ryan, *Financing the Corporation*, Square Publishers, New York, 1954, p. 36.

---

factors that enter into the creation of supply and demand for stocks depend upon the anticipated dividend income from the stock, the anticipated market value of the stock, and the general attitude of the public toward investing in general.

Preferred stock represents a form of ownership of a company with special privileges—notably, the receiving of a specific amount of dividends before any dividends may be paid to common stockholders. While, on its face, this would seem to be an advantage, preferred stocks are inherently a poor form of investment.[6] The holder of preferred stock enjoys none of

---

[6] Richard R. Howe, *Preferred Stocks*, Triangle Press, Chicago, 1957, p. 271.

---

the assurances of repayment of his investment that come to the bondholder and none of the possibilities for sharing in the profits with common stockholders. The directors need only fail to declare his dividend, whether profits have been earned or not, and his return is delayed or lost. He is safeguarded only by the desire of the directors to declare a dividend on the common stock. In periods of depression, the preferred stockholder is in a particularly weak position, and in periods of inflation and business boom his return is strictly limited. It is only when preferred stock is selling at a

1 a;sldkfjghfjdksla;sldkfjghfjdksla;sldkfjghfjdksla;

2 ab ac ad ae **af** ag ah ai al am an ao ap aq ar as at

3 ba be bi bl bo br bu by ca ce ch ci cl co cr cu cy

4 da de di do dr du dy ea eb ec ed ef eg ei ej el em

5 en ep eq er es et eu ev ex ey fa fe fi fl fo fr fu

6 ga ge gi **gl** gn go gr gu **gy** ha he hi ho hu hy ia ib

7 ic id ig il im in io ir is it iv ja je ji jo ju ka

8 ke hk ki kn ko ku la le li lo lu **ly** ma me mi mn mc

9 mo mu **my** na ne ni no nu ny oa ob oc od of oh oi ol

10 om on oo op or os ot ou ov ox oy oz pa pe ph pi pl

11 pn po pr ps pu **py** qu ra re rh ri ro ru sa sc se sh

12 si sk sl sm sn so sp sq st su sw sy ta te th ti to

13 tw tu ty ub ud ug uh uk ul um un up ur us ut ux va

14 ve **vi** vo **vu** wa **we** wh **wi** wo wr **wy** xa xe xr xy ya ye

15 yi yo yt yu za ze zi zo zu zw zy am ame awn aze an

16 on-no ton not now nose noun pond north gone onion front

17 cr-rc cry crave arched crime crack critics march scrubs

18 yo-oy you yours youth yodel foyer ahoy employ youngster

19 be-eb bet beds deb ebb best bent debts beer ember debut

20 better ebony barbers pebble rebels beaten trebled

21 ly-yl ply lye ally styles amply silly only nylons fully

22 ct-tc facts tract deducted evict doctors stitched catch

23 mu-um mud mug dumps slum mules mumps tumor music mumble

24 mural must umpires stumped immune muffle grumbled

25 rv carved nerve curved fervently services deservedly

26 ni-in nights lining niece finely spineless alpine union

27 ce-ec cede accepted centers echoes pieces sectors place

STOCK OWNERSHIP

One does not have to be a millionaire to own stock. Stocks come in all prices, from a few pennies to over $6,000 a share. Who owns stock? Over 6,500,000 different people own stock in their own name or through beneficial interests and trusts, mutual funds, etc.[1] One corporation, American Telephone and Telegraph Company, has 1,100,000 shareholders, of whom one-third own five shares or less. In the larger corporations, it is not uncommon to find that 90 percent of all stockholders hold less than 100 shares.[2]

However, there is another angle to this analysis of stockholders. The five largest corporations in America, American Telephone and Telegraph, General Motors, General Electric, Standard Oil of New Jersey, and U. S. Steel, account for more than 2,000,000 shareholders. All in all, these five companies have more than 23 percent of all stockholders.[3]

---

[1] George C. Hunt, The American Investor, Circle Publishing Co., New York, 1956, p. 17.

[2] Peter Mizner, "The Five Great Corporations" in Dow Institute Reports, Washington, D. C., 1955, p. 204.

[3] Ibid., p. 307.

28 ab-ba	able babbled stab grabs bathes above banner about
29 ve-ev	very never every cleverly wives have grave divers
30 bt-tb	debts obtrude outboard debtors subtlety subtracts
31 mp	lamp stamp sample swamp tempt pamper example camp
32 rb-br	verbs herbs urban curbing barb brag carbon abroad
33	orb brands brave urban orbit brides harbor verbal
34 x	tax lax flax exit laxity examined oxen waxes taxi
35 py-yp	jumpy poppy pygmy happy hypnotics copy snappy spy
36 ny-yn	many thorny syntax rainy tiny cynical pony dynamo

SUBSTITUTION DRILLS

1 r-t	Try to retain the right posture.
2 m-n	The amount of income he demands is enormous.
3 o-i	In my opinion we should obtain action tonight.
4 a-s	I saw a sample of the latest safety regulations.
5 e-i	I received a beautiful linen handkerchief.
6 s-d	We should like to send a deposit.
7 r-e	—Read the brochure to learn about our free service.
8 v-b	I believe he described the best value available.
9 w-e	Where were the jewels when we needed them Wednesday?
10 o-l	We are obliged to make allowances when policies are lost.
11 f-g	Miss Ferguson forgot to do the filing again on Friday.
12 i-u	Inquire about the quality of equipment issued to Mr. Austin.
13 a-e	Establish a permanent site near the beach.
14 k-l	We are looking for a person with remarkable skills.
15 c-d	Direct mail service could include cards in December.
16 u-y	He inquired about a quantity of sturdy boxes.
17 d-e	Let us develop your ideas for the advertising media you need.

[4]Doris and Miller, loc. cit.

[5]Doris and Miller, op. cit., p. 420.

[6]Style Manual, Rev. ed., United States Government Printing Office, Washington, 1967, p. 249.

1. This footnote shows a book with two authors.

2. This footnote shows a magazine article.

3. *Ibid.* refers to everything in the preceding footnote except the page number.

4. If a footnote reference is precisely the same as one that is not immediately preceding, use the author's name and *loc. cit.*

5. When a footnote refers to a different page in a source previously cited and other footnotes separate the two, use the author's surname and *op. cit.* with the page number.

6. This reference is to a book that carries no author's name.
   Instead of using *loc. cit.* and *op. cit.* in footnotes 4 and 5, a more informal style could have been used:
   [4] Doris and Miller, *Complete Secretary's Handbook*, p. 505.
   [5] Doris and Miller, *Complete Secretary's Handbook*, p. 420.

JOB 1

Type the following manuscript for top binding. Type the illustration and then continue with the copy to complete the job. If you are using elite type, your copy will not agree line for line with the illustration.

18 f-d	Did you find the fare more than you could afford?	
19 c-v	His clever conversation convinced them of his objective.	
20 g-h	The huge desk Mr. Wright bought is just right.	
21 y-t	Try to stay an extra twenty minutes on Tuesday.	
22 s-w	He will bestow awards at the showing Wednesday.	
23 d-k	They liked the kind of damask used in the curtains.	
24 f-r	Four officers retired from the board on Friday.	
25 p-o	I reported their opposition to the popular proposal.	
26 j-h	June and July are too hot to hold meetings.	
27 r-u	We urge you to return the manuscript.	
28 s-e	The teachers have expressed interest with this series.	
29 g-t	Work together in your struggle against the rise in taxes.	
30 e-t	Take time to have the experts test the equipment.	
31 z-a	They were dazzled by the size of the bazaar.	
32 s-c	It is customary to draw conclusions from statistics.	
33 x	The experts were expected to examine the texts.	
34 b-n	Bulletin boards may benefit a number of bank employees.	
35 g-b	Baggage can be bought at a bargain at Bridges.	
36 i-k	Pick up the kitchen knives which I bought.	
37 q-a	They quarreled over the quality and quantity of music.	

CARRIAGE-THROW DRILLS

		WPM		
		20"	30"	60"
1	You have heard..	9		
2	We hope to sell...	10		
3	The time is good..	10		
4	I will always try.......................................	11		
5	This list is small......................................	12		

Direct quotations having three typewritten lines or fewer are typed in full line length and enclosed in quotation marks. Those quotations of more than three typed lines should be typed in a separate paragraph, single spaced, and indented at least five spaces from each margin. When a quotation is set off in this indented style, quotation marks are not needed.

If there are omissions in the quoted material, they are indicated by using the ellipsis (three alternating periods and spaces or four if the end of a sentence is included in the omission):

Titles of books, booklets, magazines, and newspapers may be typed in solid caps or they may be underscored.... Titles of essays and magazine articles ... are enclosed in quotation marks.

FOOTNOTES

Footnotes are used to indicate the source of a quotation or an opinion mentioned in the body of a manuscript. Authorities do not agree on style in typing footnotes, but the guides recommended here are based on common practices.

References are usually numbered consecutively with superior figures. The footnote is given the same number and must appear at the bottom of the same page as the reference. Estimate three or four lines for each footnote. This will allow for the blank lines above and below each footnote reference.

After typing the last manuscript line, single space and type a 2-inch line with the underscore beginning at the left margin. Double-space and type the first footnote. Indent the first line and begin the second and succeeding lines at the left margin. Single-space each footnote and leave a blank line between footnotes.

The general arrangement of the elements of footnotes is: footnote number, authors, article, book, publisher, place of publication, date of publication, and page numbers, This pattern can be modified to fit the circumstances; for example, if the author's name is not known, omit this portion of the footnote.

Examine these footnotes with the keyed explanations following them.

[1]Lillian Doris and Besse May Miller, Complete Secretary's Handbook, Rev. ed., Prentice-Hall, Inc., Englewood Cliffs, N.J., 1960, p. 505.

[3]Ibid., p. 106.

6	Bill cannot qualify.	12
7	Would you like to go?	13
8	Meet me at the square.	13
9	You need zeal to excel.	14
10	Do all the good you can.	15
11	I shall send these cards.		10
12	To see it is to admire it.		10
13	A man is known by his talk.		11
14	Will the men call to see us?		11
15	Let us try to go to the lake.		12
16	I cannot give the information.		12
17	The jet zoomed through the sky.		13
18	We will do our best to help you.		13
19	Let us hope that things are good.		13
20	Zephyr yarn is exceptionally soft.		14
21	You have a good chance for success.		14
22	We shall send a free list and rates.		14
23	Yes, it is a joyful, exciting moment.		15
24	The space bar is used after each word.		15
25	She may lend them a hand with the work.		16
26	Higher speeds result from good stroking.		16
27	This is a rule known to all the men here.		16
28	We must try to do it the best that we can.		17
29	Sit back in the chair; do not lean forward.		17
30	This has happened in just a few short years.		18

MINUTES OF A MEETING

The official record of a meeting is known as the "minutes." Often a secretary is expected to attend meetings and assume the responsibility of recording the minutes and of preparing a typewritten transcript of them.

Minutes usually follow the outline of the order of business that is recommended by organization bylaws. They usually include:

1. The name of the organization; the time, date, and place of the meeting; and the type of meeting held.

2. The names of the presiding officer and the secretary, and the result of the roll call.

3. A statement regarding the reading of the minutes of the previous meeting and the approval.

4. Reports of officers and chairmen of various committees.

5. A summary of action taken on unfinished business from previous meetings.

6. A summary of action taken on new business brought up for consideration.

7. The announcement of the date of the next meeting.

8. The time of adjournment.

9. The signature of the secretary who prepared and typed the minutes.

		20"	30"	60"

31 The largest nugget of gold came from
Australia. 19

32 In the future, send their money to them
by wire. 20

33 He will write to them when the manager
gets here. 20

34 Strike each of the keys with quick, sharp
strokes. 20

35 Many earthquakes have been recorded over
the world. 10

36 The discovery of gold has excited men
through the ages. 11

37 You sometimes hear someone boast that he
is a self-made man. 12

38 Bananas grow well only in intense sunlight
and abundant rainfall. 13

39 Most of us must find for ourselves that
haste quite often makes waste. 14

40 Volumes have been written about the various
volcanoes throughout the world. 15

41 You have often heard men and women say that
there are too few hours in each day. 16

42 The paper used in our paper money is the
most exacting product in the paper industry. 17

43 Air travel has rapidly reached the leading
position as the chief method of transportation. 18

44 Dear Bill: Do you plan to attend the meeting
next week? If not, let me know when we can meet. 19

PACING DRILLS

16 WORDS

You will learn how to type in a short time if you will do
all you are told to do.

18 WORDS

You must keep in mind that your speed will not go up with
each test you take in your class.

20 WORDS

If you wish to build high speed, you must be sure to learn
how to strike each key in the right way.

II. Magazines

    A. Name of author, inverted, period

    B. Title of article in quotation marks, comma inside quotation marks

    C. Name of periodical, underlined, period

    D. Numerals indicating volume, comma, and number if necessary for identification

    E. Date of publication, comma

    F. Page reference abbreviated, period

Body

Review pages 233 and 234 for the procedures to follow in margins, spacing, and pagination of manuscripts.

XXXXXXXX XXXXXX	← Title
XXXXXXXXXXXXXXXXXXXXXXXXXXXXXXXXXXXXXXXXXXXXXXXXXXXXXXXXXXXXXXXXXXXXX XXXXXXXXXXXXXXXXXXXXXXXXXXXXXXXXXXXXXXXXXXXXXXXXXXXXXXXXXXXXXXXXXXXXX XXXXXXX	← Body
XXXXXX	← Subtitle
XXXXXXXXXXXXXXXXXXXXXXXXXXXXXXXXXXXXXXXXXXXXXXXXXXXXXXXXXXXXXXXXX XXXXXXXXXXXXXXXXXXXXXXXXXXXXXXXXXXXXXXXXXXXXXXXXXXXXXXXXXXXXXXXXX	
<u>XXXXXXXX</u>	← Side Heading
XXXXXXXXXXXXXXXXXXXXXXXXXXXXXXXXXXXXXXXXXXXXXXXXXXXXXX XXXXXXXX XXXXXXXXXXXXXXXXXXXXXXXXXXXXXXXXXXXXXXXXXXXXXXXXXXXXXXXXXXXXXXXXXXXXX	

Type the following job in manuscript style using one-inch margins. Note that the body is double spaced but each enumeration is single spaced.

Jan 29.

As you go through life, you learn that a man must be judged by what he does and not by what he talks of doing.

Feb 5

If its purpose was to put out of power those who did not answer when first called upon, we shall not support the motion.

Feb 6

To most of us who use a typewriter day in and day out, the ribbon is just an inkpot that comes by the yard instead of by the bottle.

Feb 6

One of the urgent things we trust that each member of our staff will remember is that, in the eyes of the people he meets, he is our firm.

Feb 8

Air expands as it rises. Vapor is chilled and becomes visible in the form of clouds. When chilled, it comes down in the form of rain, hail, or snow.

Feb 9

The typing student who is able to type forty or fifty net words in a minute should not expect to see her speed increase with each test she takes.

Feb 14

When trying to gain the higher speeds, the student sometimes appears to be traveling across a plateau. Failure to notice gain in speed is discouraging.

ALPHABETIC PARAGRAPHS

Set margins at 15 and 75 for pica and at 20 and 80 for elite.

		Words
→ 1	This is to let you know that our shop is not able	10
	to fix the topaz and jade pin you sent to us. In	20
	view of this, it is being sent back to you; and I	30
	am quite sure it will reach you in a week or two.	40

....1....2....3....4....5....6....7....8....9....10

Type 3 times — 1 mistake per paragraph

The title "Bibliography" is centered 2 inches from the top of the page and is followed by a triple space. Margins should agree with those in the body of the manuscript.

Start the first line of each entry at the left margin and indent each subsequent line of a given reference five spaces. Single space the lines of a single entry, and double space between entries.

BIBLIOGRAPHY

Bendixen, Ethel T., and Juanita E. Carter. Production Typing, 3d ed. Cincinnati: The South-Western Publishing Co., 1967.

How to Invest in Stocks and Bonds. New York. Merrill Lynch, Pierce, Fenner and Smith, Inc., 1966.

Lessenberry, D.D., S.J. Wanous, and C.H. Duncan. College Typewriting, 8th ed. Cincinnati: The South-Western Publishing Co., 1969.

Lloyd, Alan C., John L. Rowe, and Fred E. Winger. Gregg Typewriting for Colleges, 2d ed. New York: McGraw-Hill Book Company, 1964.

Montoya, Sarah. "Word Wise," The Secretary. August-September, 1970, p. 30.

Style Manual. Washington: United States Government Printing Office, 1967.

The order of the elements in a bibliography is as follows:

I. Books

   A. Name of author, inverted, period (if an editor is cited in place of an author, his name is used)

   B. Title of book, underlined, period (if an edition number is cited, follow the title with a comma, abbreviate edition number and follow by a period)

   C. Place of publication, colon

   D. Name of publisher, comma

   E. Date of publication, period

2 The sky was hazy, and the cold wind brought tears   10
to our eyes as we stood to watch the pilots climb   20
quickly aboard their jet and taxi down the field.   30.
We did not move until the plane was out of sight.   40

3 I was very glad to hear from you and to know that   10
you will be able to meet me one day next week for   20
lunch. I know a quiet little place near the lake   30
that you are sure to enjoy. It is not very large   40
in size, but the food is the best you have eaten.   50

4 If you wish to build your typing speed easily and   10
quickly, you must first of all learn how to relax   20
as you type; and you must learn how to focus your   30
mind on the job that is at hand. As you type, be   40
aware that a lazy typist is also a very slow one.   50

5 There is no sight so amazing as that of an expert   10
typist at work. If you will study his habits for   20
just a moment, you will see that in his quest for   30
high speeds he makes every typing motion swiftly.   40
You will see as you watch that he wastes no time.   50

6 You may wish to know how a boy or girl becomes an   10
expert typist. The answer is quite simple; it is   20
just a question of deep desire and hard work. If   30
you also want to be a fine typist, then recognize   40
the fact that it can come only through hard work.   50

7 There is no doubt of the fact that you will learn   10
how to type if you will just make up your mind to   20
work hard at it every day. As you type, be aware   30
that your goal is to form the habit of striking a   40
key with a quick, sharp motion; and that you will   50
never be an expert typist by using a lazy stroke.   60
....1....2....3....4....5....6....7....8....9....10

INDENTING WITH THE TABULATOR

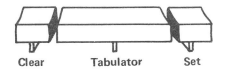

Clear   Tabulator   Set

(Refer to the reference section on page 253 to determine where these operative parts are located on the different makes of machines.)

To indent a paragraph five spaces by striking the space bar five times is time consuming. Each machine has a tabulator mechanism that enables you to indent much more quickly; all you do is strike the tabulator key or bar once and the carriage moves directly to the assigned point.

The tabulator mechanism has three controls:

In the illustration, the title begins 2½ inches from the top of the page; the name begins 2½ inches below the title; and the date begins 2½ inches below the name. If the manuscript is to be bound at the left, center the lines between the margins rather than using the center of the sheet. To determine the center of any given line, add the numbers where the margins are set and divide by 2. For example, the margins for a given line are 15 and 92. The sum of these two numbers is 107. Divide 107 by 2 to get the center, which is 53 in this illustration.

The title is typed in all caps. If it is very short, spread the letters. If it is very long, make two lines. All other lines are typed with initial caps for the important words.

Table of Contents

The table of contents is a list of the major divisions and subdivisions, with corresponding page numbers, to show how the manuscript is organized. The table of contents is not necessary for a short report but is desirable for a long manuscript. It follows the title page.

Because it is necessary to include the page numbers, this page cannot be prepared until the manuscript typing is completed.

TABLE OF CONTENTS

Chapter		Page
I	Appointment Letters	2
II	Acceptance Letters	5
III	Acknowledgment Letters	7
IV	Letters of Congratulations	10
V	Letters of Introduction	13
VI	Letters of Recommendation	18
VII	Thank-You Letters	25

Bibliography

A bibliography is an alphabetic list of publications or sources used as references in the preparing of the manuscript. This list follows the body of the manuscript and contains all sources cited in the footnotes as well as additional references that are not specifically cited.

Tab-Clear Key: This key is used to clear an individual tab stop that was previously set.

Tab-Set Key: This key is used to set a pin at the back of the machine that is called a tab stop. The carriage will stop at the point where the tab stop is set when the tab key is pressed.

Tab Key (or *Bar*): This key is used to make the carriage spring to the desired point with one operation.

Only one tab stop is set to indent paragraphs.

Procedure:

1. Set the margins.

2. Clear any tab stops already set by moving the carriage to the right margin and then returning the carriage *while pressing the clear key.* (Some machines have an all-clear key that eliminates simultaneously all stops that have been set previously.)

3. Space five spaces from the left margin with the space bar and press the tab-set key.

4. Test the setting by returning the carriage to the left margin and then firmly pressing the tab key or tab bar.

Indention Drill

Set margins at 20 and 70 for pica and at 25 and 75 for elite. Set one tab stop for a 5-space paragraph indention.

		Words
1	Dear Mr. Black:	3
	This is just a brief letter to thank you for	14
	the help you gave in our drive to raise the money	24
	required to increase the size of our gym. We now	34
	expect the gym to be ready in about three months.	44
2	Dear Bill:	2
	Mr. Chance told us today that our final math	13
	quiz will be given on the fifth or sixth of June.	23
	Most of his tests in the past have been easy, but	33
	we think we should take the time to study for it.	44
3	Dear Students:	3
	If you wish to know the joy of being a truly	13
	expert typist, it is vital for you to seize every	24
	chance to develop proper techniques and good work	34
	habits. Believing this will insure your success.	44

BUSINESS CORRESPONDENCE SYLLABUS

Carl C. Matthews

July 17, 19--

LINESPACING

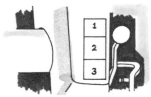

The amount of blank space between lines of typing is controlled by the linespace regulator, which adjusts the machine for single, double, or triple spacing. When the machine is set at "1," there are *no* blank spaces between lines of typing. When the machine is set at "2," there is *one* blank space between lines of typing. When the machine is set at "3," there are *two* blank spaces between lines of typing.

SINGLE SPACING

```
This is an example of
copy being typed with
single spacing.  The
linespace regulator
has been set in the
"1" position.  As you
can see, there are no
blank lines being left
as the cylinder turns
from one line to the
next.
```

DOUBLE SPACING

```
In this example, the

copy is being typed with

the regulator in the "2"

position.  There is now

one blank space between

lines of copy.
```

TRIPLE SPACING

```
With the linespace


regulator in the "3"


position, there will


be two blank lines


between lines of copy.
```

To leave extra space between some lines of typing such as between two drills, advance the paper two lines by returning the carriage twice instead of once.

Remember always to advance the paper one more line than the number of lines to be left blank.

WORDS, SENTENCES, AND PARAGRAPHS
STRESSING INDIVIDUAL LETTERS

Set margins at 17 and 67 for pica and at 25 and 75 for elite.

Use single spacing with double spacing between drills. Indent paragraphs 5 spaces.

```
1a    as ask all add ago are any ace art able also away
1b    areas again stanza arena ahead banana drama tiara

1c    An aged man sat all day beneath an ancient maple.
1d    Ann called to say that the ball game was delayed.
1e    Are you aware that many local dealers have sales?
      ....1....2....3....4....5....6....7....8....9....10
```

III. HEADINGS

A. Main Headings
1. Centered over the line of writing in solid caps
2. Followed by a triple space

B. Secondary Heading (subheading)
1. Begins at left margin, or is centered over the line of writing on a separate line and is underlined
2. Initial caps for main words
3. Preceded by triple space and followed by double space

C. Tertiary Heading (paragraph headings)
1. Indented as first line of paragraph and underlined
2. First word capitalized
3. Preceded by double space

IV. PAGINATION

A. Unbound and Leftbound
1. Omit the page number on the first page
2. Page number centered ½ inch from bottom of paper or ½ inch from top of page at right margin
3. Page number separated from text or footnote by a triple space

B. Topbound
1. Omit the page number on the first page
2. Page number centered ½ inch from bottom edge of paper
3. Page number separated from text or footnote by a triple space

C. Introductory pages are numbered with small roman numerals

Title Page

The title page introduces a manuscript to the reader. This page contains the title, the name of the author, and the date. Short, informal reports usually do not require the preparation of a title page.

There is no single format or arrangement that must be followed in typing a title page. The important point to remember is that all necessary information is included in an easy-to-read, attractive format.

1 f   We are glad to hear that you and your family   10
are planning to stay at our camp again this year.   20
As in the past, we will save an extra large cabin   31
for you and will arrange for the lease of a sail-   41
boat at the usual rate. As you will see, we have   51
made a great many changes since last year that we   61
are certain will increase your vacation pleasure.   71
....1....2....3....4....5....6....7....8....9....10

2 a   both bend bale herb able webs tube numb swab cube
2 b   barb bribe babes abbot object babble bible barber

2 c   He will probably publish both books by September.
2 d   A number of boys climbed nimbly aboard the boats.
2 e   Betty was able to buy a rubber ball for the baby.
....1....2....3....4....5....6....7....8....9....10

2 f   We will probably be able to obtain the black   10
and brown fabrics about which you ask, but we are   20
obliged to say that there will possibly be delays   31
before the fabric is brought to our shop. We buy   41
this fabric from a company that is beset by labor   51
problems, and orders are often subject to delays.   61
....1....2....3....4....5....6....7....8....9....10

3 a   case cram core race sect such acts back tact come
3 b   critic action checked scarce church accept circle

3 c   He expects to check and copy each piece of music.
3 d   The doctors carried the sick child to the office.
3 e   Carol came back to discuss the call she received.
....1....2....3....4....5....6....7....8....9....10

3 f   Once each month, our club conducts a contest   10
to choose a citizen in our city whose actions are   20
such as to indicate a sense of civic duty. Since   31
this contest attracts so much public notice, your   41
council must screen each prospect very carefully.   51
....1....2....3....4....5....6....7....8....9....10

4 a   deal desk does dash edge buds herd wood code void
4 b   dodge dread dandy giddy dowdy drudge admit divide

4 c   Dad demanded a refund when the order was delayed.
4 d   Bridges and roads were damaged by a sudden flood.
4 e   Ida decided to spend the holiday at a dude ranch.
....1....2....3....4....5....6....7....8....9....10

4 f   After reading the detailed study made by our   10
staff, I find that I am ready to defend those who   20
have demanded that we provide additional roads to   31
serve this district. I also understand why these   41
men had decided we need to rebuild the old bridge   51
badly damaged by a dreadful tornado during April.   61
....1....2....3....4....5....6....7....8....9....10

TOPIC OUTLINE

I. Headings

   A. Title centered in all caps
   B. Major headings in all caps
   C. Subheadings with initial caps

II. Vertical Spacing

   A. Title followed by a triple space
   B. Main headings preceded by triple space and followed
      by a double space
   C. Subheadings may be single- or double-spaced

MANUSCRIPTS AND REPORTS

I. MARGINS

   A. Unbound manuscripts and reports
      1. Top: first page, 2 inches; other pages, 1 inch
      2. Sides: 1 inch
      3. Bottom: 1 inch

   B. Leftbound manuscripts and reports
      1. Top: first page, 2 inches; other pages, 1 inch
      2. Sides: 1½ inches at the left; 1 inch at the right
      3. Bottom: 1 inch

   C. Topbound manuscripts and reports
      1. Top: first page, 2½ inches; other pages, 1½ inches
      2. Sides: 1 inch
      3. Bottom: 1 inch

II. SPACING

   A. Body
      1. Double space and use 5- or 10-space paragraph
         indentions
      2. Single space quoted material of four or more lines
         and indent five space from each margin
      3. Single space tabulated material
      4. Single space enumerations.
   B. Footnotes
      1. Separate from last line of manuscript by a 1½-inch
         divider line; precede divider line with a single
         space and follow with a double space
      2. Indent and single space; double space between footnotes

5a ends ease echo real tend vest week bend haze axes
5b erect elder every beset expel clever agree severe

5c Every member felt that the meeting was excellent.
5d They expected each of them to type these letters.
5e We are eager to help her whenever she needs help.
....1....2....3....4....5....6....7....8....9....10

5f   Have you been to see the new steel desks our   10
dealers now sell? These models are the very best   20
we have ever made, and we feel sure that everyone   31
who sees them agrees. We are eager to show you a   41
number of them and would welcome a chance to have   51
you judge for yourself the value of these models.   61
....1....2....3....4....5....6....7....8....9....10

6a fish fair flag surf raft left doff fame roof tuft
6b fifty fluffy graft fresh offer staff gifts relief

6c With effort, Flora finished the file before five.
6d No firm can afford to forfeit such fine benefits.
6e Four of our office staff found the fifty folders.
....1....2....3....4....5....6....7....8....9....10

6f   On the first of February, we informed you of   10
a defect in the fans we had bought from your firm   20
four or five months ago. A few days later, a man   31
from your office came to fix the fans but did not   41
seem able to find the reason for this difficulty.   51
We feel that you should furnish us with new fans.   61
....1....2....3....4....5....6....7....8....9....10

7a glad gone gift eggs urge figs stag bugs gasp dogs
7b gangs gadget gorge degree gurgle baggage staggers

7c George could not judge the weight of the package.
7d The big barge struggled against the evening tide.
7e The eight hungry girls managed to find the lodge.
....1....2....3....4....5....6....7....8....9....10

7f   Our great luggage sale is going to get under   10
way this week. Each single piece of baggage will   20
go for bargain prices, and we suggest you arrange   31
to take advantage of the huge savings we are mak-   41
ing possible. One glance at our bags will assure   51
you that good bags can be bought for a low price.   61
....1....2....3....4....5....6....7....8....9....10

8a hole hike hurt wish push math such wish sign harm
8b health phones church laughs hurrah through phases

8c He brought a hundred healthy bushes to the ranch.
8d I watched the hero march with his head held high.
8e He thought the truth was worth whatever happened.
....1....2....3....4....5....6....7....8....9....10

MANUSCRIPTS

Any typist will probably be required to type manuscripts of such materials as reports, handbooks, manuals, and minutes. Some of these may contain footnotes. The materials are often either copy that has been roughed out by hand or corrected typewritten rough drafts.

Use a good quality bond paper, usually 8½ x 11 inches. Type on one side only and make at least one carbon copy.

The rules for margins, spacing, headings, and pagination are given on page 233.

A ruled backing sheet will help keep margins uniform on all pages. Draw a rectangle with heavy lines to indicate typing area. Place this visual guide between the original copy and the first carbon sheet so that the rulings will show through the original copy.

Another kind of visual guide is a line-by-line page gauge. On onionskin paper number the lines down the right side of the page beginning with 1 in the first linespace and numbering through 33. Continue the numbering in reverse order so that the last line on the page is 1. Insert this sheet behind the carbon pack with the numbered edge extending beyond the copy at the right. A glance at the gauge will indicate where to type the page number, where to begin the first line of typing, and where to end the typing on the page.

Regardless of the length or formality of a manuscript, it may contain these structural parts: title page, table of contents, body, appendix, and bibliography.

Outlines

Since clear organization is essential for effective writing, the writer should prepare an outline before any writing is attempted. This outline may accompany the finished work in place of a table of contents. A good outline seldom carries its subdivisions of main topics further than two or three subtopics.

```
I.   Roman numerals for primary subjects

     A.   Capital letters for secondary topics
          1.   Arabic numerals for tertiary items
               a.
                    (1)
                         (a)
```

The Arabic and Roman numerals are aligned at the right and each is followed by a period and a double space. Each step is indented five spaces.

Do not punctuate the ends of lines in a topic outline. Use the appropriate punctuation for ends of lines in a sentence outline.

8 f   On the fourth of March, I sent you the rough   10
draft of a pamphlet we wish to publish. Have you   20
had a chance to check it? As we wish to go ahead   31
with its printing shortly, we shall appreciate it   41
very much if you would go through it and give any   51
ideas you happen to have about its general worth.   61
....1....2....3....4....5....6....7....8....9....10

9 a   item fill tick suit silk pint milk jilt sign king
9 b   victim origin inhibit finish idiom italics vision

9 c   Our firm wants girls with good skill and ability.
9 d   If you insist, I will visit the sick girls again.
9 e   I think I will wait until you finish your typing.
....1....2....3....4....5....6....7....8....9....10

9 f   If your firm is willing to wait until April,   10
I think I will find thirty girls in this city who   20
will fit into your training program. If you find   31
it too difficult to work with such a small staff,   41
I will again solicit aid from local high schools.   51
....1....2....3....4....5....6....7....8....9....10

10 a   jail jamb jury jump jilt jinx join just joke jack
10 b   ajar banjo jerky jaunt adjust jersey major object

10 c   This jolly major was injured in the jeep in July.
10 d   Judge Jones held the objects for the jury to see.
10 e   Jan joined the junior squad for the July journey.
....1....2....3....4....5....6....7....8....9....10

10 f   You joined our Junior Book Club in June, and   10
this is just to inform you that the selection for   20
July will be a jumbo edition of jungle stories by   31
John J. Jewel. If you object to this subject, be   41
sure you jot us a note giving us your objections.   51
....1....2....3....4....5....6....7....8....9....10

11 a   kind keep kill rock junk took bulk hack mark know
11 b   kicks khaki kayak knack kinky smirk market skills

11 c   I think Karl kept the broken knife in his pocket.
11 d   Speak to Frank about the lock on the black trunk.
11 e   We thank you for picking up the sticks and rocks.
....1....2....3....4....5....6....7....8....9....10

11 f   Thank you for the check and the kind remarks   10
you made. I spoke to Mr. King about the book for   20
which you asked, and he thinks it will be back in   31
stock next week. I will keep it for you and have   41
our clerk call you so you can quickly pick it up.   51
....1....2....3....4....5....6....7....8....9....10

Name	Address	City	State	ZIP Code
Charles W. Allen ①	182 W. Seventh St.	Casper	WY	82601
Edwin T. Barton ⑤	4610 Bay Road	Goshen	UT	84633
John Mc Pherson ⑪	14 Euclid Ave. NE.	Scranton	PA	18532
Albert Farnum ⑥	Box 197	Spartanburg	SC	29301
Matthew Hollis ⑦	37 Park Place	Salem	OR	97301
Robert T. Martin (Dr.) ⑩	162 / 11 Davis Street	Rosewell	NM	88201
Thomas M. Kelly ④	General Delivery	Enid	OK	73701
Harry F. Carr ③	617 Ames Avenue	Omaha	NB	68116
Joseph Whitley ⑨	Highland Hotel	Zanesville	OH	43701
Terrence White (Mrs.) ⑤	5012 27th Ave.	Bismarck	ND	58501
Ronald J. Carson ④	2814 Front Street	Hannibal	MO	63403
Ronald W. Short ⑫	Box 89	Heron Lake	MN	56137
Alan W. Corwin ⑥	455 Carlyle Street	Winston-Salem	NC	27102
Oliver Woods (Mrs.) ⑮	14 University Road	Pontiac	MI	48053
Harold B. Hopkins ⑧	Rural Route 3	Hazard	KY	41701

12a   lame lute lyre halt land silk told sulk yell plot
12b   ally local loyal lowly legal liable lapels letter

12c   This client is fully liable for all legal claims.
12d   Ella lost a flannel muffler rolling in the field.
12e   None are able to excel the skill of my employees.
    ....1....2....3....4....5....6....7....8....9....10

12f   As is our usual policy, we will mail you one   10
of our booklets that tells the details of why our   20
plant is able to supply bottles of such excellent   30
quality. You will learn from this little booklet   40
why our label on a bottle is a sign of excellence   50
and reliability. We will gladly fill all orders.   60
    ....1....2....3....4....5....6....7....8....9....10

13a   maps more myth milk must jump calm time jamb mute
13b   omit dumb lime lame moth miss plum make game meet

13c   Tommy must come home from camp for the Army game.
13d   Mary made some attempt to meet him at the museum.
13e   Many men in the mine managed to move the machine.
    ....1....2....3....4....5....6....7....8....9....10

13f   Millions of dollars were spent on the scenic   10
highway in the movement to save the majestic red-   20
wood trees. You may motor for miles through sub-   31
lime beauty. There among the mammoth trees time   41
seems to stand still; sounds seem muffled and far   51
distant. You speak in a somber, awe-filled tone.   61
    ....1....2....3....4....5....6....7....8....9....10

14a   nook nuts nose unit hand lynx pony hunt join pint
14b   nation onion nouns annoy inner penny nylon ninety

14c   I know Nancy left at the end of the ninth inning.
14d   We know you can obtain a frank and honest answer.
14e   A definite change in this situation is necessary.
    ....1....2....3....4....5....6....7....8....9....10

14f   I think it is necessary to arrange for every   10
agent in the field to attend the conference being   20
held in June. Since we intend to outline several   31
new plans of national interest, I am certain they   41
will benefit from being on hand for the meetings.   51
    ....1....2....3....4....5....6....7....8....9....10

15a   oven only owls pony look mold lion yoke hold nose
15b   spool cookie piano opinion motion common location

15c   I told your son he could borrow some of our wood.
15d   Do not do the work until I show you how to do it.
15e   It took over a month to locate the proper motors.
    ....1....2....3....4....5....6....7....8....9....10

Many firms store information on 3″ by 5″ index cards. Generally the card is filed according to the first line. Therefore, the first line is typed so that it stands out from the rest of the information. The line may be typed all in capital letters, or it may be separated from the rest of the card by a double space.

To insert an index card into the typewriter, follow the procedure for inserting a label outlined on page 228.

Allow a left-hand margin of ½ inch and two blank spaces at the top.

```
        ✓ 3  ≠
                #
  ⌐sp⌐Stewart, Martin

       376 Beaumont Street
       Topeka, Kansas    66612

       Account No. 3756
```

The sample shown is for a card that is filed alphabetically according to the person's name. If the card is to be filed numerically by account number, this number is typed on the first typewritten line, and the three-line address is typed two lines below it.

If the card is to be filed geographically, the state, city, and ZIP code are typed on the first line and the name and address is typed two lines below it.

Omit *Mr.* and *Miss* but indicate all other personal titles by typing them in parentheses at the end of the name, for example, Stewart, Martin (Dr.)

JOB 1

Type the following names and addresses on index cards to be filed alphabetically, according to the person's name:

15 f   I am sorry to inform you that our company is   10
not in a position to forward the report for which   20
you ask. However, I have enclosed a copy of some   31
of the opinion polls conducted by our offices and   41
hope this will prove of some worth to you in your   51
work. I am truly sorry I cannot do more for you.   61
....1....2....3....4....5....6....7....8....9....10

16 a   pans pole plan pint pack pawn pool pulp pomp prop
16 b   open polo spot drop lamp hump pipes papal propels

16 c   Stop to help Pam put up paper lamps on the porch.
16 d   Peter was prompt to pay me for typing his report.
16 e   Pat appreciated the opportunity to improve speed.
....1....2....3....4....5....6....7....8....9....10

16 f   We are happy to report that the paper plates   10
and cups ordered by your shop will be shipped the   20
latter part of April. These popular products can   31
be supplied at prices that appeal to most people.   41
May we hope for prompt payment for this shipment.   51
....1....2....3....4....5....6....7....8....9....10

17 a   quad quay quiz aqua equal quaff quail quart quake
17 b   squad quartz quince equals quicken quiver qualify

17 c   We require a large quantity of high-quality sets.
17 d   Quincy acquired the quartz at their antique shop.
17 e   Quite a few boys qualify to handle the equipment.
....1....2....3....4....5....6....7....8....9....10

17 f   Your inquiry concerning the prices we quoted   10
for our antiques came in quite some time ago. We   20
quickly wrote a reply to your query and requested   31
that you come in person to put your question to a   41
qualified person who could acquaint you with this   51
unique system used to equate quality with prices.   61
....1....2....3....4....5....6....7....8....9....10

18 a   roof raft rove grub trap errs brag crab writ drag
18 b   virus barber rivers refer cracker reserve tractor

18 c   The river rose four feet during the summer storm.
18 d   Our firm is sorry to report a very serious error.
18 e   The editors wrote an article for our trade paper.
....1....2....3....4....5....6....7....8....9....10

18 f   I regret to report that your radio cannot be   10
repaired because the parts required are no longer   20
on the market. I made every effort to obtain the   31
parts through various dealers, but no one appears   41
able to furnish them. I am sorry I cannot repair   51
the radio, but I am certain that you understand.   61
....1....2....3....4....5....6....7....8....9....10

Plain labels in performed sheets are also used, especially for mass mailings, because they are faster to address than envelopes.

```
Miss Charlotte Dudley
c/o Mrs. Robert Clarke
Pine and Elm Streets
Madison, WI   53711
..........................................

Mr. Henry Perry
871 Race Street
Cincinnati, OH    52549

..........................................

Mr. Malcolm T. O'Day
Melody Appliance Center
Pinecrest Avenue and Sixth St.
Endicott, NY    13764
```

Insert the entire sheet into the typewriter and type all of the labels in the first column, then type those in the second column, and then type those in the third column.

Begin typing on the second line below the perforation and two or three spaces from the edge, blocked and single spaced.

JOB 2

Address plain labels to the following:

1. Miss Charlotte Dudley, c/o Mrs. Robert Clarke, Pine and Elm Streets, Madison, WI 53711

2. Mr. Henry Perry, 871 Race Street, Cincinnati, OH 52549

3. Mr. Malcolm T. O'Day, Melody Appliance Center, Pinecrest Avenue and Sixth Street, Endicott, NY 13764

4. Mr. Joseph Maybury, Winterhaven Ski Lodge, Route 3, Rutland, VT 05703

5. Mr. James Gross, 1516 South Street, Bristol, CT 06011

6. Mr. Joseph Miles, Jr., Box 67, Rutland, VT 05703

7. Mrs. Frank J. Willis, 182 Eighth Avenue, Altoona, PA 16601

8. Mr. James K. Weir, 197 Elm Street, San Angelo, TX 76901

19 a says sips suns easy robs cost dish fish eggs zoos
19 b basis spring sense system passed satisfy distress

19 c I saw the scissors his sister used for the dress.
19 d She says you should send a small deposit shortly.
19 e Susy discussed the mistakes in these last essays.
......1....2....3....4....5....6....7....8....9....10

19 f   We publish a series of six short essays that   10
      should be of special interest to the students who   20
      are in your various science classes. These works   31
      have been used with the utmost success in schools   41
      all over this state, and teachers have assured us   51
      they stimulate a great desire for advanced study.   61
......1....2....3....4....5....6....7....8....9....10

20 a take than task left part debt past bath pets next
20 b exit battle started patent static tenant thoughts

20 c Thank them for testing the quality of my product.
20 d I trust the time is right to institute this plan.
20 e The tractor must be sent by fast freight tonight.
......1....2....3....4....5....6....7....8....9....10

20 f   For the first time in thirty years, we shall   10
      grant drastic discounts on certain items we carry   20
      in stock. We trust that this method will attract   30
      steady streams of customers and result in greater   40
      profits to our store. Most of the stores in this   50
      city have tested and proved this method recently.   60
......1....2....3....4....5....6....7....8....9....10

21 a upon ugly unto jump push yule soul hulk junk numb
21 b lucky skull pumps murmur unique juncture stadiums

21 c Our music club is buying a number of instruments.
21 d You must urge your pupils to study the situation.
21 e This opportunity will insure a successful future.
......1....2....3....4....5....6....7....8....9....10

21 f   During the past four years, we have built up   10
      a successful business because each customer knows   20
      of the unusual quality that goes into the product   30
      we produce. We are very proud of our reputation,   40
      and we will continue to supply superior products.   50
......1....2....3....4....5....6....7....8....9....10

22 a vast very vows five view ever give oven wove even
22 b verve velvet valve starve given valor novel waved

22 c He advised covering every heavy vase with velvet.
22 d Several moving vans avoid driving on this avenue.
22 e I have proved the value of giving prompt service.
......1....2....3....4....5....6....7....8....9....10

From:

SPEEDWRITING/NANCY TAYLOR DIVISION
ITT EDUCATIONAL SERVICES, INC.
55 West 42nd Street, New York, New York 10036

A SERVICE OF INTERNATIONAL TELEPHONE AND TELEGRAPH CORPORATION

To:

```
Mr. Ronald Shipman
842 Main Street
Columbus, GA    31908
```

Return Postage Guaranteed

When typing from a roll of labels, insert the labels as a continuous strip rather than tearing them off and inserting individually.

When typing individual labels, follow these steps to prevent slippage:

1. Insert a full-size sheet of paper until about ½ inch of the sheet is visible above the ribbon.
2. Place the blank label behind this ½-inch edge of the sheet and roll the cylinder back until the label is in position for typing the first line.
3. After typing the address, roll the cylinder forward until ½ inch of the edge of the paper is once again visible.
4. Remove the typed label and insert the next one. Continue until all the labels are typed.

JOB 1

Address shipping labels to the following:

1. Mr. James Gross, 1516 South French Street, Bristol, CT 06011

2. Brantley Lumber Supply Company, 90-96 Brookfield Avenue, Baltimore, MD 21209

3. Mrs. Eleanor Corinth, One Marlene Place, Albany, NY 12204

4. Emerald Gift Shop, 64 West Seventh Street, Akron, OH 44319

5. John Channing & Sons, 14 67th Road, Columbus, GA 31908

6. North Shore Motor Sales, 197 Calden Street SW, Topeka, KS 67203

22 f   I was very happy to receive your invitation.   10
I know that a visit with you would prove valuable   20
and would provide me with a chance to observe the   30
methods you have used to solve your various prob-   40
lems.   However, we are having our office moved in   50
five weeks, and it is obvious I should not leave.   60
....1....2....3....4....5....6....7....8....9....10

23 a   wash walk wise sway flew cows twin brow away gown
23 b   widow swallow twelve watchword withdraw woodwinds

23 c   We wondered whether we would be allowed to leave.
23 d   They saw crowds waiting to view the crown jewels.
23 e   The widow went with her when she borrowed a gown.
....1....2....3....4....5....6....7....8....9....10

23 f   How would you like to get away from the cold   10
winds and snows of winter?   Would you welcome the   20
chance to walk down a white beach with a warm sun   30
overhead?   Well, Hawaii is the answer.   Would you   40
allow us to show you how you can afford the trip?   50
....1....2....3....4....5....6....7....8....9....10

24 a   flex text exit coax oxen flax hoax next flux axis
24 b   sixth taxed extra exalt relax oxygen tuxedo excel

24 c   Extra boxes of index tabs are on the sixth shelf.
24 d   Six experts examined the texts with extreme care.
24 e   They expected the sixty fixtures to be exchanged.
....1....2....3....4....5....6....7....8....9....10

24 f   The sixteen jars we expected for our Mexican   10
exhibit next week came today.   An expert examined   20
each and found the texture of the clay exactly as   30
you explained in your exciting note.   These extra   40
jars are now being boxed and sent out by express.   50
....1....2....3....4....5....6....7....8....9....10

25 a   yoke yule yarn hymn jays play many pays lynx tiny
25 b   zeal zest zone daze czar zero buzz hazy quiz zinc

25 c   They say a luxury yacht was completely destroyed.
25 d   Twenty loyal army men may stay to defy the enemy.
25 e   Hazel and the lazy boys were puzzled by the quiz.
....1....2....3....4....5....6....7....8....9....10

25 f   We are puzzled and amazed to learn that your   10
bill has not been paid.   We realize that you have   20
problems, and we recognize that your organization   30
could not utilize its equipment during the freez-   40
ing weather.   However, if you do not pay, we will   50
authorize our attorney to bring suit against you.   60
....1....2....3....4....5....6....7....8....9....10

Pay To: Fuller Outdoor Furniture Co., 276 Jackson Blvd., Baltimore, MD 21200

Amount: $483.06   Check No.: 4322

Date	Description	Charges	Credits	Total
3/25	Invoice No. 3437	127.50		
3/26	Invoice No. 3443	249.95		
3/27	Invoice No. 3462	108.45		
3/28	Credit Memo No. 469		2.84	
				483.06

LABELS

The same style is used in typing shipping labels as in addressing envelopes. The general rule is to begin typing three lines down and five spaces from the left edge of the part of the label designated for the address. The size of the label will determine placement. If the word *To* is printed on the label, align the first line of the address with the printed word and block all other lines with the first one.

Section 3
NUMBERS AND SYMBOLS

CENTRAL OFFICE SUPPLY CO.

201 Central Ave. ● Akron, Ohio 44312

July 15, 19-- No. 20765

PAY Two hundred forty and 27/100--- DOLLARS

To the Order of

Mark Supply Company
1407 Regal Avenue
Topeka, KS 66612

$240.27

CENTRAL OFFICE SUPPLY COMPANY

(For Class Use Only)
Authorized Signature

Bankers National ● AKRON, OHIO

. . . . DETACH BEFORE DEPOSITING . . . .

Date	DESCRIPTION	CHARGES	CREDITS	TOTAL
6/2	Invoice No. 8936	117.20		
6/15	Invoice No. 9623	25.00		
6/22	Credit Memo No. 422		55.53	
6/28	Invoice No. 9987	153.60		
				240.27

Type the following voucher checks using the forms in the workbook.

JOB 1

Pay To:　Mark Supply Company, 1407 Regal Avenue, Topeka, KS 66612
Date:　　August 15, 19-- 　　　Check No.: 21493
Amount: $372.95

Date	Description	Charges	Credits	Total
7/5	Invoice No. 12956	126.42		
7/16	Invoice No. 13642	269.75		
7/28	Credit Memo No. 446		126.42	
7/29	Invoice No. 13879	103.20		372.95

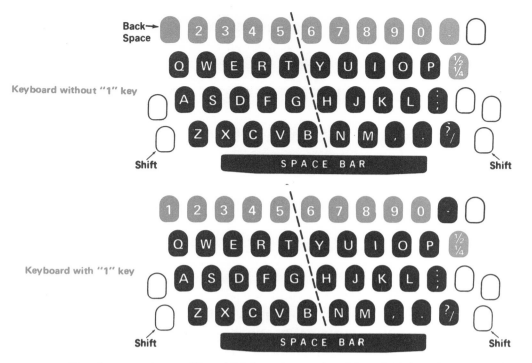

Keyboard without "1" key

Keyboard with "1" key

Set the margins at 15 and 75 for pica and at 20 and 80 for elite. Set tab for a 5-space paragraph indention for paragraph drills.

Use the *f* finger for *4*. Locate *4* on the keyboard and practice reach *f, r, 4, f.*

4 Drill

1   fr4f fr4f f4f f4f 44 fads 44 facts 444 files 4:44

2   We had **44** orders from the **44** stores for **444** sets.
....1....2....3....4....5....6....7....8....9....10

Use the *d* finger for *3*. Locate *3* on the keyboard and practice the reach *d, e, 3, d.*

3 Drill

1   de3d de3d d3d d3d 33 days 33 desks 3 doors 3/4 3.

2   I saw 33 men buy 343 games at 333 East 34 Street.
....1....2....3....4....5....6....7....8....9....10

Use the *s* finger for *2*. Locate *2* on the keyboard and practice the reach *s, w, 2, s.*

2 Drill

1   sw2s sw2s s2s s2s sales 22 seats 22 stars 22 sums

2   We need 22 books, 42 pens, 32 pads, and 234 cards.
....1....2....3....4....5....6....7....8....9....10

Atlantic Builders Co., 4825 Gulf Road, Meridian, MS 39301

Date	Invoice No.	Charges	Credits	Balance
			Balance:	125.00
5/2	593	1,567.00		1,692.00
5/6	C243		24.75	1,667.25
5/9	652	48.50		1,715.75
5/22	687	718.10		2,433.85

Checks

When typing a check, the words and figures are typed slightly above the printed lines. The name of the payee is typed as close to the words "Pay To the Order of" as possible to help prevent alteration. This is also true of the amount—type it as close to the printed dollar sign as possible. The amount is spelled out on the next line beginning at the extreme left end of the printed line. Fill in the space at the right with hyphens. The name of the signer must be written in ink.

not one hundred and thirty five

use hundred thirty five and

CENTRAL OFFICE SUPPLY CO.
201 Central Ave.

No. 235

Akron, Ohio May 11, 19 --

PAY
To the Order of Robert Johnson, Inc.----------------------- $ 35.20

Thirty-five and 20/100------------------------------------DOLLARS

BANKERS TRUST COMPANY
AKRON, OHIO

(For Class Use Only)
Authorized Signature

The purpose of a voucher check is to provide a stub on which is explained the origin of the amount of the check. Voucher checks are usually designed to be mailed in a window envelope so the name and address of the payee must be typed within the area that will be visible through the window.

Some machines have a "1" key on the top row, which is controlled by the *a* finger. If your typewriter has a "1" key, practice the reach *a, q, 1, a*

If there is no "1" key on the typewriter, use the small letter *l* for this number.

1 ll aims ll aides ll acres ll Arabs 1/2 11:34 1.21

2 Dan was ll on March 4; Bill was ll on January 23.
....1....2....3....4....5....6....7....8....9....10

1 These 23 boys and 14 girls had visited 43 states.

2 Out of 243 attempts, the 23 boys missed 34 shots.

3   I know it will take at least 22 days to move
our shop from 432 Main Street to 324 River Drive.
I hope our new shop can open on January 23 or 24.
....1....2....3....4....5....6....7....8....9....10

Use the *j* finger for 7. Locate 7 on the keyboard and practice the reach *j, u, 7, j.*

1 ju7j ju7j j7j j7j 77 jets 77 jobs 77 jugs 2/7 747

2 —I sold 37 pens and 47 kits to 12 firms on May 17.
....1....2....3....4....5....6....7....8....9....10

Use the *k* finger for 8. Locate 8 on the keyboard and practice the reach *k, i, 8, k.*

1 ki8k ki8k k8k k8k 88 key.s 88 kinds 888 kilos 8:14

2 The 88 women left on May 8 for an 18-day journey.
....1....2....3....4....5....6....7....8....9....10

Use the *l* finger for 9. Locate 9 on the keyboard and practice the reach *l, o, 9, l.*

1 lo9l lo9l l9l l9l laps 99 laws 99 loads 9.48 9:12

2 Passengers for Flight 199 will leave from Gate 9.
....1....2....3....4....5....6....7....8....9....10

Use the *sem* finger for *0*. Locate *0* on the keyboard and practice the reach *;p 0;.* Keep the *j* finger in home-key position.

Statement

Mark Supply Company

1407 REGAL AVENUE
TOPEKA, KANSAS 66612

Date_____ June 30, 19--

Central Office Supply Co.
201 Central Avenue
Akron, OH   44302

always end of month for date

Terms: 2% cash discount if paid on or before the 10th of the month following date of invoice. Net thereafter.

DATE	INVOICE	CHARGES	CREDITS	BALANCE
			Old Balance:	250.72
6/2	8936	117.20		367.92
6/6	9352	60.33		428.25
6/9	9583	65.50		493.75
6/15	9623	25.00		518.75
6/22	C892		55.53	463.22
6/28	9987	153.60		616.82

Type the following statements using the forms in the workbook (or plain paper).

JOB 1

Robinson Patterson & Co., 462 Wayne Street, Dallas, TX 75210

Date	Invoice No.	Charges	Credits	Balance
			Balance:	142.65
6/3	8957	126.50		269.15
6/8	9495	37.84		306.99
6/10			142.65	164.34
6/18	11427	195.96		360.30
6/22	11863	237.55		597.85

0 Drill

1   ;p0; ;p0; ;0; ;0; 100 pads 10 pegs 100 packs 1/10

2   In 1920, the 40 men marched 300 miles in 10 days.
    ....1....2....3....4....5....6....7....8....9....10

Review

1   This company hired 147 men and 380 women in 1920.

2   You may call me at Main 4-1980 any day this week.

3   I am very sorry to say that I will be unable
to see you when you visit our city on July 28. I
had hoped I could spend at least 7 or 8 days with
you, but our firm is sending 19 men from our shop
to an out-of-town meeting. We will be leaving on
July 20 and will not be returning until August 1.
....1....2....3....4....5....6....7....8....9....10

Use the *f* finger for *5*. Locate the *5* on the keyboard and practice the reach
f, 5, f. Keep the *a* finger in home-key position.

5 Drill

1   f5f f5f f5f f5f 55 fires 55 feet 5 robes 1/5 5:15

2   The 5 girls bought 25 pens and 75 pads on May 15.
    ....1....2....3....4....5....6....7....8....9....10

Use the *j* finger for *6*. Locate *6* on the keyboard and practice the reach
j, y, 6, j without moving the arm.

6 Drill

1   jy6j jy6j j6j j6j 66 jars 66 have 666 more 16 166

2   These 46 coins were minted between 1816 and 1826.
    ....1....2....3....4....5....6....7....8....9....10

Number Drill

1   we 23 rut 475 low 192 tie 583 tory 5946 wiry 2846

2   up 70 put 075 two 529 yet 635 your 6974 pile 0813

3   or 94 pit 085 you 697 owl 921 pity 0856 pier 0834

4   it 85 wet 235 rip 480 eye 363 fuel 4731 tore 5943

5   oy 96 toe 593 toy 596 top 590 pour 0974 wipe 2803

6   er 34 tip 580 wit 285 try 546 rout 4975 pole 0913

7   to 59 wry 246 Tom 597 lie 183 rope 4903 wipe 2803

Type the following credit memorandums using the forms in the work-book (or plain paper).

JOB 1

Credit To: R. C. Cobbs and Sons, 1172 Main Street, San Francisco, CA 94135

Date: January 22, 19 - -   Credit Memo No.:   5162

Invoice No.:   2094   Salesman: B. Burton

Invoice Date: January 15, 19 - -

Quantity	Cat. No.	Description	Unit Price	Total
6 doz	F-81	Transparent Folder	2.40	14.40
8	75-782	Canvas Binder	1.90	15.20
				29.60
			Less 10% Discount	2.96
			Total Credit	26.64

JOB 2

Credit To: Atlantic Builders Co., 4825 Gulf Road, Meridian, MS 39301

Date: June 15, 19 - -   Credit Memo No.:   243

Invoice No.:   593   Salesman: J. Adams

Invoice Date: June 1, 19 - -

Quantity	Cat. No.	Description	Unit Price	Total
2 ctn	109	Asbestos Tile	11.25	22.50
1 gal	65	Wood Preservative	2.25	2.25
				24.75
			Less 10% Discount	2.48
			Total Credit	22.27

Statements

A statement lists all the charges, payments, and credits recorded during the previous month and shows the balance due at the beginning and end of that month.

8	pi 08	pot 095	lye 163	row 492	pure 0743	pore 0943
9	re 43	rye 463	rue 473	rot 495	sock 2938	pert 0345
10	ow 92	roe 493	vie 483	hum 677	port 0945	wire 2843
11	oe 93	lop 190	out 975	yew 632	tore 5943	tire 5843
12	oi 98	ere 343	rep 430	opt 105	hymn 6676	wept 2305

....1....2....3....4....5....6....7....8....9....10

FRACTIONS

The ¼ is the shift of ½ and this key is controlled by the *sem* finger. Locate this key on the keyboard and practice the reach ; ½ ¼ ;.

½ and ¼ Drill

1 ;½¼; ;½¼; ;½½; ;¼¼; ½ hour ¼ mile 10½ 47¼ 38½ 29¼

2 —The stock sold for 75½ on June 30; it is now 79¼.
....1....2....3....4....5....6....7....8....9....10

1. When typing fractions that do not appear on the typewriter, use the diagonal with no spaces before or after it (7/8; 3/4; 1/8).

2. When typing mixed numbers (a whole number with a fraction), there is no space between the whole number and the ½ or ¼, but there is one space between the whole number and the "made" fraction (10½ and 23¼, BUT 37 1/8 and 42 3/4).

3. If one fraction must be made with a diagonal, use a diagonal with all fractions that are in the same sentence. (The rate is 4 7/8 instead of 4 1/2.)

Fraction Drill

1 Divide 144½ by 12¼; then add 20¼ and subtract 8½.

2 Does George know how to divide 144 3/4 by 12 1/4?
....1....2....3....4....5....6....7....8....9....10

Hyphenate spelled-out compound numerals below 100 (thirty-three). Always spell out numbers that begin a sentence.

Paragraphs Containing Numbers   Words

1	Twenty-five copies of your latest 12-page	9
	catalog are to be sent to Mrs. Jane Roth, 267	18
	Fourth Avenue, Boston, Massachusetts 02143, and	28
	Mr. R. Dunn, 4348 East 41 Street, Los Angeles,	37
	California 90152.	41

2	The dealer sold 3/4 of a bushel for 56 cents,	10
	37 2/3 cases for 18 cents per case, and the bal-	20
	ance of the order at a flat rate of 40 cents per	30
	pound, even though it cost him 9 cents per	40
	pound for shipment.	43

....1....2....3....4....5....6....7....8....9....10

To: North Shore Supply Company, 197 Elm Street, Madison, WI 53719
Ship To: Harold T. Sussman, 305 West 54th Street, Des Moines, IA 50317
Date: November 17, 19--   Invoice No.:   2026
Via: Midwest Trucking   Salesman: R. Stephens
Terms: 2/10; net 30   Purchase Order: 38890

Quantity	Cat. No.	Description	Unit Price	Total
6	1003	Security Vault Boxes	14.95	89.70
8 pr	J51	Desk Sets (Onyx)	4.80	38.40
10	517G	Five-Piece Desk Sets	9.15	91.50
				219.60
		Shipping Charges		6.84
				226.44

Credit Memorandums

A customer may either return merchandise or ask for credit for damaged merchandise he has received. If credit is granted, the customer receives a credit memorandum on which the credit allowed is itemized.

Note that double spacing is used in the illustration because only two items are involved.

CREDIT MEMORANDUM

MARK SUPPLY COMPANY
1407 REGAL AVENUE
TOPEKA, KANSAS 66612

CREDIT TO
Credit applies to:

Central Office Supply Company
201 Central Avenue
Akron, OH 44302

CREDIT MEMO NO. 422
DATE June 22, 19--

INVOICE NUMBER	INVOICE DATE		SALESMAN
1075	June 15, 19--		P. Kass

QUANTITY	CATALOG NO.	DESCRIPTION	UNIT PRICE	TOTAL
1	5411	Sightsaver Floor Lamp	43.95	43.95
5 gal	105	Liquid Paste	3.55	17.75
				61.70
		Less 10% Discount		6.17
		Total Credit		55.53

→ 3 items or less double space (handwritten note)

3   Thank you for your order of March 10 for 385   10
boxes of yellow chalk. We will send 274 boxes to   20
you on April 6, and the rest of the order will be   30
shipped to you by May 29 or June 4 at the latest.   40

4   I have 29 books. Do I have 37 books? Give   10
me 25 more. Here are 33 of them. Take 88 pens   20
to him. Did you give him the 82 pens? He has 46   30
pencils. I sold 830 pencils. Do you have 238 for   40
her? No, but I have more than 318 for him.   49

5   Here are 77. Lend me 55. There are 45, not   10
65. Did you see 69 or 54 men? There were 51.   19
Find 77 papers. There are only 70 left. All 54   29
of them are here. Wait 25¼ hours. I can wait   38
35 minutes. Are there 238 pages? No, only 237.   48

6   They drove 67 miles. Did 93 or 98 men arrive?   10
There were as many as 95 present. He received 61   20
letters. She bought 90 cards. The box contains   30
664 pennies. They lost the 962 coins.   38

7   Your 38-page pamphlet reached me on June 9,   10
and I am happy to enclose my order for 47 leather   20
wallets and 60 silver key chains. I would also   29
appreciate it if you would quote prices on 72   38
storage units that measure 31 by 59½ inches.   47

8   Out of a fleet of 30 trucks, 28 were damaged   10
by a fire in our plant on May 5. That is why the   20
219 books you asked to have sent by June 16 could   30
not go out on time. However, our firm has rented   40
47 trucks; and we are hoping that all back orders   50
will be shipped from here in about 12 or 14 days.   60

9   Her next birthday will be April 18; she will   10
be 32 years old. It took 16 men 52 days to paint   20
40 fire escapes and 37 houses. The report showed   30
that 357 hats, 689 shoes, and 124 bags were ruined.   40
We moved from 7520 Main Street to a new house at   50
6740 Booth Avenue yesterday. We drove 948 miles   60
in two days.   63
....1....2....3....4....5....6....7....8....9....10

SYMBOL KEYS

Backspace Key

Locate the backspace key on your typewriter.

To backspace, extend the little finger and depress the backspace key once for every space needed. Release the key quickly on the electric typewriter to avoid a double backspace. Hold it down for repeat backspacing.

Mark Supply Company

1407 REGAL AVENUE, TOPEKA, KANSAS 66612

Invoice No. 1075
Date June 15, 19--

TO Central Office Supply Company 201 Central Avenue Akron, OH 44312		**SHIP TO** Tanner Stationers, Inc. 6740 Lincoln Drive Chicago, IL 60616	

YOUR ORDER NUMBER	SALESMAN	VIA	TERMS
632	P. Kass	Truck	1/15; net 30

QUANTITY	CATALOG NO.	DESCRIPTION	UNIT PRICE	TOTAL
10	8630	Blue Cloth Dated Diaries	1.81	18.10
3 doz	1790	Jumbo Appointment Calendars	12.80	38.40
2	5411	Sightsaver Floor Lamps	43.95	87.90
5 gal	105	Liquid Paste	3.55	17.75
				162.15
		Less 10% Discount		16.21
				145.94
		Shipping Charges		8.25
				154.19

Type the following invoices using the forms in the workbook (or plain paper), using the underscore for the total line and leaving one blank space between the total line and the total amount.

JOB 1

To: Stanton and Sons, 3307 North Calden Street, Topeka, KS 66612
Ship To: T. M. Morley, 1862 Boxwood Road, Boise, ID 83701
Date: February 19, 19--   Invoice No.:   5107
Via: Truck   Salesman: Richard Holmes
Terms: 2/10; net 30   Your Order No.:   A-72

Quantity	Cat. No.	Description	Unit Price	Total
10	62	Champion Pencil Sharpeners	3.59	35.90
3 doz	106T	Rolls of 3" by 5" Shipping Labels	.60	21.60
2 bx	319	Kleaner Erasers	10.95	21.90
6 bx	358R	Light-Touch Pencils #2	10.85	65.10
				144.50
			Less 10%	14.45
				130.05
			Shipping Charges	4.25
				134.30

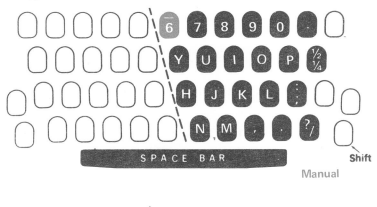

Manual

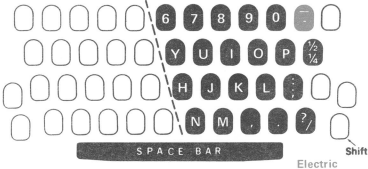

Electric

The underscore is the shift of the *6* key on the manual or shift of the hyphen key on the electric. Locate this key and practice the reach using the left shift key. Type the drill line using (M) for the manual typewriters and (E) for the electric typewriters.

(M)   j6j_6 j6j_j j_j j_j

(E)   ;-;_; ;-;_; ;_; ;_;

To underline one word, depress the backspace key to move the carriage to the first letter of the word or move the carriage by hand. Strike the underscore key once for each letter in the word.

To underline several words, move the carriage to the first letter to be underscored and depress the shift lock key. On the manual typewriter strike the underscore once for each letter and space to be underlined. On the electric typewriter the underscore is an automatic repeat key; depress it and hold down until you have about three letters left to underline. Underline the last few letters individually so that you will be sure to stop exactly at the desired point. (See page 53 for use of the shift lock.)

1   She knew that May, June, and July were very slow.

2   We offer high quality and low prices at our shop.

3   I need all of them no later than Tuesday, May 23.
     ....1....2....3....4....5....6....7....8....9....10

Type the following purchase orders using the forms in the workbook (or plain paper).

JOB 1

To: Mark Supply Company, 1407 Regal Avenue, Topeka, KS 66612
Ship To: High-Grade Supply Company, 67 Millston Avenue, Akron, OH 44302
Date: January 3, 19--   P.O. No.: 852   FOB: Akron
Via: Truck   Terms: 2/10; net 30

Quantity	Cat. No.	Description	Unit Price
4	598	Multiple Posting Binders	12.50
2 doz	62J	A-2 Dividers for 5 x 8 Cards	1.95
10 bx	2937	Carbon Paper—Medium	3.20
2	9529	Desk Drawer Expanding Trays	4.00
2 gal	385	Rubber Cement Solvent	1.25

JOB 2

To: Mark Supply Company, 1407 Regal Avenue, Topeka, KS 66612
Ship To: King and Company, 318 East 24th Street, New York, NY 10026
Via: Railway Express   P.O. No.: 737B   Date: May 7, 19--
Terms: 2/10 eom   FOB: New York

Quantity	Cat. No.	Description	Unit Price
2 doz	4725	Green Desk Calendars	12.60
1 pr	264W	Onyx Book Ends	9.75
3 doz	107	Scrap Books, White	18.00
10 bx	2937	Carbon Paper—Medium	3.20

Invoices

An invoice lists in detail merchandise or services ordered by the customer and how much he owes for it. The information is taken from the purchase order and extensions are calculated.

Note that the underscores in the total column are all the same length as the longest number in the column.

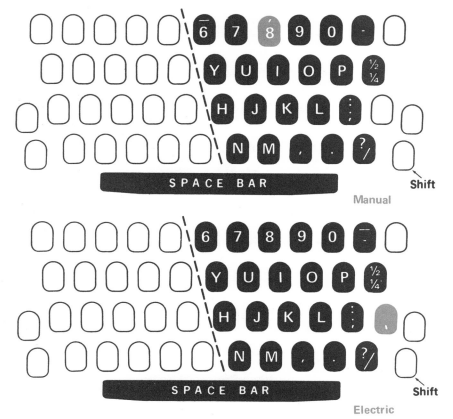

On the manual typewriter the apostrophe is the shift of the *8* key. On the electric it is to the right of the *sem* key and is controlled by the *sem* finger. Locate this key on the machine and practice the reach.

Do not space before or after an apostrophe in the middle of a word.

(M)   k'k k'k k'k k'k We're sure Bill's sister won't go.

(E)   ;'; ;'; ;'; ;'; We're sure Bill's sister won't go.

Exclamation Point

If your machine has a top-row *1* key, the ! is the shift of this key. If there is no exclamation point key on the typewriter, type it in this way:

1. Type a period.
2. Backspace.
3. Type an apostrophe.

Space <u>twice</u> after the exclamation point when it ends a sentence.

        What a day I've had! How happy I'll be when
    it's over! We've all been trying to get ready by
    nine o'clock tomorrow for this year's sale of our
    boys' and men's sneakers. I hope it's a success!
    ....1....2....3....4....5....6....7....8....9....10

3. Make full use of the tabulator mechanism to insure proper alignment of figures and to speed up the work. Center the typing vertically between pairs of lines, beginning at least two spaces to the right of the line and ending at least two spaces to the left of the line. Set the tab stops for the points most often used in the column. Number columns are aligned on the right.

4. When typing amounts in a money column with a vertical line to separate the dollars from the cents, adjust the paper so that the point where the decimal, which is not typed, would fall is exactly on the separation line. Do not use $ on this type of form.

Purchase Orders.

Instead of ordering merchandise or supplies by letter, a standard order form called a Purchase Order may be used.

never use # signs on

Central Office Supply Co.
201 Central Ave. ● Akron, Ohio 44312

PURCHASE ORDER

P. O. NO. 632

DATE June 10, 19--

you are ordering from *sent to*

TO		SHIP TO	
Mark Supply Company 1407 Regal Avenue Topeka, KS 66612			Tanner Stationers, Inc. 6740 Lincoln Drive Chicago, IL 60616

VIA	FOB	TERMS	AUTHORIZED BY
Truck	Chicago	1/15: net 30	

ITEM	QUANTITY	CATALOG NO.	DESCRIPTION	PRICE
1	10	8630	Blue Cloth Dated Diaries	1.81
2	3 doz	1790W	Jumbo Appointment Calendars	12.80
3	2	5411	Sightsaver Floor Lamps	43.95
4	5 gal	105	Liquid Paste	3.55

Flush left, two spaces from line

Flush right, two spaces from line

Flush right to center

Flush right, two spaces from line

Decimal points, one under the other

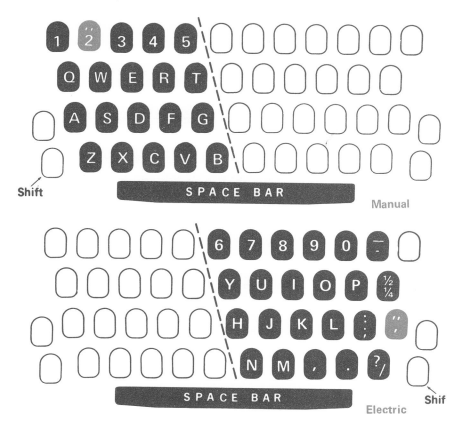

The " is the shift of the *2* key on the manual typewriter and the shift of the apostrophe key on the electric typewriter. Locate this key and practice the reach.

Do not space between quotation marks and the words they enclose.

(M)   s2s"s s2s"s s"s s"s Malcolm said, "Take it easy!"

(E)   ;';"; ;';"; ;"; ;"; Malcolm said, "Take it easy!"

Quotation Marks With Other Marks of Punctuation

1. A quotation mark is always typed after a comma or period.

Our sales staff must be "on the ball."

He said, "Let the chips fall."

Your article, "Southeast Asia," has created a stir.

2. A quotation mark is always typed before a colon or semicolon.

Here are the factors listed in "The Rising Cost of

Living": wages, tariffs, and productivity growth.

Jo is a "go-getter"; Tom is not.

Although business forms vary from company to company, the same general rules apply in typing all of them.

Review the procedures for typing on ruled lines on page 71. In addition to the ruled horizontal lines, business forms also contain ruled vertical lines to separate information.

Business forms are generally typed with one or more duplicate copies. (See page 68 concerning "snap-out" forms.)

Many business forms are mailed in window envelopes, so the name and address must be typed within the area that will be visible through the window when the form is correctly folded. This area is indicated on the printed form by brackets or dots (see page 205). A special space is generally provided for typing the number of the form. Each series of forms is numbered consecutively. The numbers are important for rapid identification.

Here are some general rules to follow when typing business forms:

1. Single space business forms unless a particular form contains three or fewer lines, in which case double space. When more than one line is required for the description column, single space and indent the second line three spaces.

2. Abbreviate measurements of quantity and omit the periods after these abbreviations.

pr pair	lbs pounds	C hundred
ea each	gal gallon	M thousand
bx box	in inch	ft feet
¢ cents	% percent	doz dozen
$ dollars	@ at	# number

A few common abbreviations may be typed in lower case letters with periods when they occur within a sentence but are typed in solid capital letters without periods when they appear on business forms:

c.i.f.	or	CIF	cost, insurance, and freight
c.o.d.	or	COD	cash on delivery
e.o.m.	or	EOM	end of month
f.o.b.	or	FOB	free on board

3. A quotation mark is typed <u>after</u> a question mark or exclamation point <u>if the</u> <u>quotation asks a question or makes an exclamation;</u> when the entire sentence, of which the quotation is a part, is a question or an exclamation, the quotation mark precedes the question mark or exclamation point.

```
"Do you manufacture these?" they asked.

Did you read our article, "The Higher Light"?

"Wow!" was all he could say.

Congratulations on your latest article, "How to
Invest"!
```

Dollar Sign Key

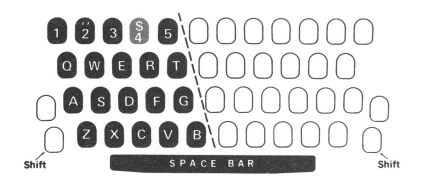

The dollar sign is the shift of the *4* key on both the manual and electric typewriters. Practice the reach.

Do not space between the dollar sign and the amount.

Expressing Amounts of Money

1. In business correspondence, write all amounts of money in figures.
2. When an even amount of money is written in a sentence, the decimal and zeroes are usually omitted.

```
1    f4f$f f4f$f f$f f$f Pay the past-due bill of $41.

2    Your price of $40 is $4 less than the $44 I paid.

3         Thank you for your check for $600 which came

     today.   There now remains a balance of $589.47 on

     your account which may be paid according to these

     terms:   $300 on July 1, $200 on August 1, and the

     remaining $89.47 before the last week in October.
     ....1....2....3....4....5....6....7....8....9....10
```

International Services

The two classes of international services are the full-rate telegram and the letter telegram. Ship radiograms are also available.

The full-rate international telegram (FR) is the fastest but the most expensive service to foreign countries. The minimum charge for the letter telegram (LR) is 22 words.

Abbreviated code names for companies and their cities may be registered at the Central Bureau for Registered Addresses. Each word in the address and signature in international messages is counted in the cost of the message so there is a savings in having a one-word registered address. Each code word is counted at a rate of five, or a fraction of five characters to the word. Each punctuation mark is counted as one word.

Type file copies of the telegrams in Jobs 1 and 2 on plain paper making a carbon to be sent as a confirmation copy. Allow a 2-inch top margin and use a 60-space line.

JOB 1

full-rate telegram/august 18, 19-/11 a.m./william swan/165 english place /crofton maryland/arriving crofton wednesday evening/arrange conference with branch managers on thursday/allen c underwood/sales department/reference initials

JOB 2

overnight telegram/august 20, 19-/3 p.m./george farrell/westward, collins, and reed/209-56 wexford street/detroit michigan/congratulations on your promotion/regret that we will not be working together but am happy that your ability and talent have been recognized/best wishes for success/ ah bonner/reference initials

JOB 3

Type the following Telefax message making one carbon copy.

call letters: KFJ/full-rate/charge to: marathon, inc./denver, colorado, june 15, 19-/robert dowling, president/international supply company/789 east howell street/salem, oregon/duplicate order sent today. should reach you tuesday at latest./paul conners, general manager

JOB 4

Type the following Telefax message making two carbon copies, one for the file and one for the accounting department.

call letters: KFJ/overnight service/charge to: stylewise, inc/detroit, michigan, may 10, 19-/phillip thomas/34 east 39 street/new york, new york/ delighted that lowell accepted our offer. sure he will do a fine job in restoring the branch to former peak of efficiency. arrangements made for him and his family to occupy suite at barkley hotel until he locates a suitable house. you are authorized to issue a check for $500 to cover transportation expenses to new york./harold parks

The left parenthesis is the shift of the *9* key and the right parenthesis is the shift of the *0* key. Practice these reaches with the *l* and *sem* fingers respectively.

There is no space after the left parenthesis nor before the right parenthesis and the material enclosed by them.

1   l9l(l l9l(l l(l l(l This (is the shift of the 9.

2   ;0;);;0;);;);;);This) is the shift of the 0.

3   Send: (1) books, (2) cards, (3) pads, (4) paper.

4   The local paper (Daily Mail) reported five fires.

5   Our agent (John Park) leaves here (Albany) today.
     ....1....2....3....4....5....6....7....8....9....10

Ampersand Key

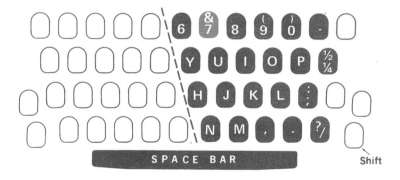

The ampersand (&) is the shift of the 7 key.

The & sign means "and," and it is used in company names, usually when the name consists of the names of persons. Practice the reach.

1   j7j&j j7j&j j&j j&j Smith & Hughes; Jones & James

2   Order 77 boxes from Curtis & Lee or Jordan & Bur.

Special services that are available via telegram are: money orders, hotel reservations, will-call telegrams, gift services and greetings, and messenger service.

Each initial is counted as one word unless the letters are written together, such as **AR MATSON**, which would be counted as two words. Common abbreviations are counted at the rate of one word for each of five letters when they are typed together without periods, such as **COD**. Standard punctuation marks are neither counted nor charged for in the message. Groups of figures and letters and symbols are counted at the rate of one word for each five characters on list. ($500.00 contains six characters and would be counted as two words, but $500 would be counted as one word.)

The name and address and the signature are transmitted free in a domestic message.

When preparing a Telefax message, use a form provided by Western Union and type within the outline border.

The call letters indicate the sending station. Indicate the service desired in the next blank by using FR for full-rate, NL for overnight message, or NL (COL) if the overnight message is to be sent collect. The point of origin and the date are typed on the same line. The address, message, and signature are the same as the file copy of a telephoned message.

ШШШ western union | **Telefax**

CALL LETTERS KDG   FR   CHARGE TO Central Office Supply Co.
Akron, Ohio, January 15, 19--

Raymond Dawson, Manager
Mark Supply Company
1407 Regal Avenue
Topeka, Kansas

Order of January 8 not received by Tanner Stationers.
Check shipment date and notify us.

                        Arnold Matson
                        Manager

SENDING BLANK

Send the above message, subject to the terms on back hereof, which are hereby agreed to

PLEASE TYPE OR WRITE PLAINLY WITHIN BORDER—DO NOT FOLD
WU 1269 (R 5-69)

---

3   We regret to tell you that Lee & Moss cannot

supply the lumber you will need for the units you

are building for Hart & Sons. I have, therefore,

written to Black, Star & Reed to see if they will

contact Gordon & Gray for this special type wood.
....1....2....3....4....5....6....7....8....9....10

Number/Pounds Sign

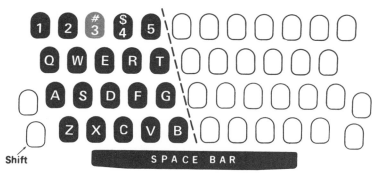

The number/pounds sign is the shift of the 3 key.

Do not space between # and the figure.

When # is typed before a figure, it indicates No.; when it follows a figure,
it indicates pounds. Practice the reach.

1   d3d#d d3d#d d#d d#d Order #33; Order #131; #31245

2   Order #5498 for 2# of nails was sent on truck #7.

3   Our check #3245 in payment of Invoices #9870

and #9936 was sent out today. This means that we

have now paid the full balance due on Order #1985

for 240# of #45-A cement that reached us in July.
....1....2....3....4....5....6....7....8....9....10

Percent Sign

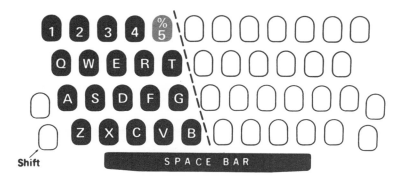

Full-rate Telegram

January 15, 19--, 10 a.m.

Raymond Dawson, Manager
Mark Supply Company
1407 Regal Avenue
Topeka, KS

Order of January 8 not received by Tanner Stationers.

Check shipment date and notify us.

Arnold Matson, Manager
Central Office Supply Company

JW

If a messenger picks up the telegram, it is typed on a form supplied by Western Union. Always type at least one carbon copy.

western union — Telegram

NO. WDS. – CL. OF SVC.	PD. OR COLL.	CASH NO.	CHARGE TO THE ACCOUNT OF	[ ] OVER NIGHT TELEGRAM
			Sender	UNLESS BOX ABOVE IS CHECKED THIS MESSAGE WILL BE SENT AS A TELEGRAM

Send the following message, subject to the terms on back hereof, which are hereby agreed to

January 15, 19 _

TO Raymond Dawson, Manager
Mark Supply Company

CARE OF OR APT. NO.

STREET & NO. 1407 Regal Avenue

TELEPHONE 476-1080

CITY & STATE Topeka, KS

ZIP CODE 66612

Order of January 8 not received by Tanner Stationers.
Check shipment date and notify us.

Arnold Matson, Manager
Central Office Supply Company

SENDER'S TEL. NO. 864-2173

NAME & ADDRESS

Central Office Supply Company
201 Central Avenue
Akron, OH   44312

The percent sign is the shift of the 5 key.

Do not space between % and the number it identifies.

1. Express percentages in figures, preferably with <u>percent</u> spelled out.
2. The symbol % may be used in statistical material, tabulations, invoices, and interoffice memorandums.

```
1   f5f%f f5f%f f%f f%f 15%; 55%; 100%; 15% discount;

2   We sent 35% to Max, 40% to Mary, and 25% to Alex.

3        Your representative offered us a discount of
    15% on our order.  We understand that 5% discount
    is usually granted on such purchases, but we were
    assured that an extra 10% discount would apply in
    our case.
    ....1....2....3....4....5....6....7....8....9....10
```

Asterisk Key

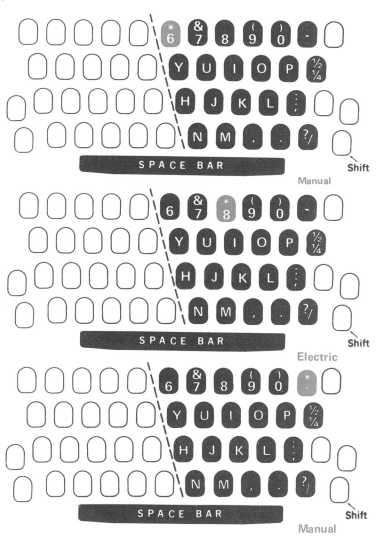

mr robert sacks/1426 maine avenue/topeka ks 66606/date/in looking over our records, we were surprised to find that you have not visited our show-rooms in more than a year. we had always looked upon you as one of our regular customers and would like to count you once more among our many friends. (P) won't you come in during our sensational january sale? you will be astonished at the amazingly low prices./r kane sales manager/reference initials

mr donald t barnes/2714 river drive/topeka ks 66601/date/thank you for your request for our catalog. it is being sent to you today. (P) we are sure you will find that we handle all of your office needs. mark supply company has been pleased to fill your orders in the past. we look forward to many more years of continued service./r kane sales manager/reference initials

miss roberta johnson/426 lane street/topeka ks 66602/date/our annual clearance of office supplies is scheduled for the first week in january. the store will be open from 9 a.m. to 7 p.m. monday through saturday during the sale. (P) come in early to make your selections./mark supply company/reference initials

TELEGRAMS

Domestic Services

Domestic telegrams may be sent to anyone in the continental United States, Canada, or Mexico. A standard charge applies regardless of where the wire originates or where it is to be sent within these three countries.

Almost all telegrams today are transmitted to Western Union by tele-phone, teleprinter, or Telefax. When the telegrams are transmitted by telephone or teleprinter, one or more copies are typed on plain paper for the files. Telegrams are typed on special forms when Desk-fax service is used. There are two classes of services available for domestic messages:

1. The full-rate telegram is the fastest service, and the minimum charge is based on 15 words.
2. The overnight telegram may be sent any time up to 2:00 a.m. for delivery the next morning, and the min-imum charge is based on 100 words.

Time-zone differences must be considered in determining whether to use the full-rate telegram or the overnight telegram. Refer to a map showing the standard time zones to decide which is the most practical service.

When preparing a file copy of a telegram transmitted by telephone or teleprinter, include the following information: class of service desired, account to be charged if other than sender, date and time message was filed, complete address of the recipient, message, sender's name and title, and the reference initials of the typist. The following illustration is a suggested form for file copies.

The asterisk key (*) may be the shift of the 6 key, the 8 key, or the hyphen key depending upon the make of the machine. It is used to refer to a footnote or explanation and is typed adjacent to the word or figure. Locate the * key and practice the reach; then type the drill.

(M)   `j-j*j j-j*j j*j j*j`

(E)   `k8k*k k8k*k k*k k*k`

1. When the asterisk and a mark of punctuation fall at the same point in a sentence, the asterisk <u>follows</u> the punctuation mark with no intervening space.
2. In the footnote, leave <u>one</u> space after the asterisk.

`Use the * and ** for the two footnote references.`

Cents Sign

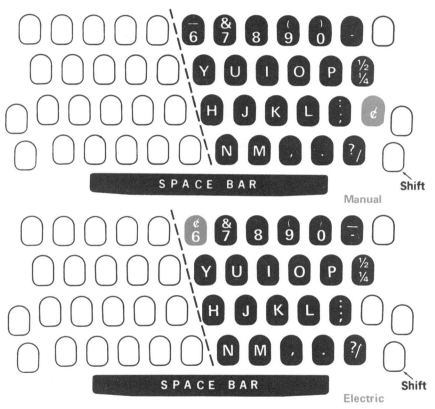

The cents sign is to the right of the *sem* key on the manual and is the shift of the 6 key on the electric. Locate this key and practice the reach.

1 (M)   `;¢; ;¢; ;¢; ;¢; Don't space between ¢ and figure.`

2 (E)   `j6j¢j j6j¢j j¢j Don't space between ¢ and figure.`

3   `We paid John 16¢ for the pen and 25¢ for the pad.`

4   `Prices rose from 18¢ on Tuesday to 21¢ on Friday.`
`....1....2....3....4....5....6....7....8....9....10`

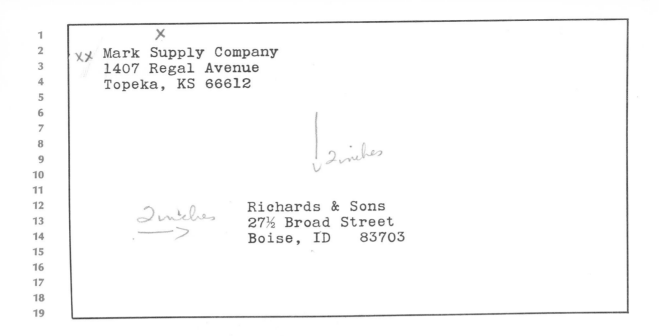

```
1        ✗
2  ✗✗   Mark Supply Company
3        1407 Regal Avenue
4        Topeka, KS 66612
5
6
7
8                                    | 2 inches
9                                    ↓
10
11
12                          Richards & Sons
13        2 inches            27½ Broad Street
14        ──────→             Boise, ID   83703
15
16
17
18
19
```

On the message side allow a three-space margin on each side. Type the date on line three, and begin the message a double space below the date. The inside address and complimentary close are usually omitted, as is penwritten signature. The message may be arranged in block, modified-block, or semiblock style. Type the closing lines a double space below the message. The following illustration is typed in block style.

```
1          ✗
2            ✗
3  ✗✗✗  October 20, 19--                              ✗ ✗ ✗
4          H
5      The file cabinets that you request in your order
6      No. 3764 are no longer available in the F-207
7      model.  This model has been replaced by the F-236.
8      The price of the F-236 file is $52.50.
9          H
10     Please let us know if you want your order filled
11     with the F-236 file.
12         H
13     MARK SUPPLY COMPANY
14         H
15     VJ
16
17
18
19
```

Using the same return address as shown in the illustration and the current date, type the following cards:

1. In the body of a letter, write cents after the figures for amounts under $1.
2. Use ¢ in technical material containing many price quotations.

@ Sign

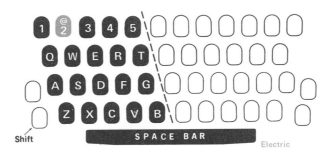

The *per* or *at* sign is the shift of the ¢ key on the manual and the shift of the 2 key on the electric. Locate this symbol and practice the reach.

(M) `;¢;@; ;¢;@; ;@; ;@; Space once before and after @.`

(E) `s2s@s s2s@s s@s s@s Space once before and after @.`

Shift Lock Key

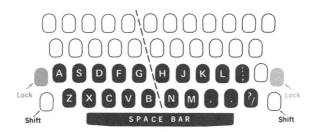

When typing a series of capital letters, use the shift lock. This key locks the machine in a shift position so that only upper case characters are typed (UNICEF).

1. Depress the shift lock key that is above the left shift key.
2. Type the word or words.
3. Release the shift lock by depressing either shift key.

Type Job 1 on a half-sheet memorandum sheet using single spacing and Job 2 on a full-size memorandum sheet using double spacing and 5-space paragraph indentions.

JOB 1

To: Murray L. O'Connor/From: Harriet Minor, Secretary/Date: June 25, 19-/Subject: Plane and hotel reservations/In accordance with Mr. Graham's instructions, I have reserved a room for you at the Crestview hotel in Memphis for the week beginning July 8. (P) Mr. Renalds will send your plane tickets by messenger to your office this morning./reference initials

JOB 2

To: All employees/From: Jason Carter, Director/Date: January 2, 19-/Subject: Elevator service/Effective january 10 the elevator on the north side of the building will be closed for service at 6 p.m. All personnel reporting to work or leaving the building between 6 p.m. and 7:30 a.m. will be required to use the elevators on the south side of the building. In addition, any person entering or leaving the building during these hours will be required to give his name and department to the security officers in the lobby. (P) your cooperation in these new regulations will be appreciated./reference initials

POSTAL CARDS

Postal cards are cards sold by the post office and having the stamp already printed on them. A post card is a commercial printed card, with a picture on one side, to which a stamp must be attached for mailing.

Postal cards are used to handle unimportant, routine correspondence. Postal cards measure 5½ by 3¼ inches.

What is the vertical center of a card 5½ inches wide when using pica? ___ When using elite?___How many horizontal lines are there if a card is 3¼ inches deep? ___

Follow the same rules you learned for addressing an envelope (page 158) when addressing a postal card. Type the return address on line two, beginning three spaces from the left edge.

NOTE: Do not forget to release the shift lock whenever a stroke that cannot be typed in capitals such as a hyphen appears among the capitalized letters (COST-PRICE CONTROLS).

Typing Abbreviations

1. There is no space after the period when the abbreviation is typed with lower case letters (a.m., p.m., i.e.).
2. There is usually no space after the period when the abbreviation is typed with capital letters (A.M., P.M., B.C., but: J. M. Anderson).
3. Some abbreviations have become accepted as words and are written without periods (ad for advertisement).
4. Initials of the names of various government agencies, international organizations, and labor organizations are usually written without spaces and periods (SEC, UN, AFL-CIO).

1   Flight No. 3 departs at 9 a.m.; No. 41, at 7 p.m.

2   The meeting is scheduled for 10 A.M. to 3:30 P.M.

3   Twelve members of UNICEF attended the conference.

4   Pack these circulars. Label them PRINTED MATTER.

5   Mr. Andrews will travel to the West Coast on TWA.
....1....2....3....4....5....6....7....8....9....10

NUMBER AND SYMBOL REVIEW DRILLS

1   Let's see if the boy's able to do John's new job.

2   When did they leave? For how long did they stay?

3   Brown & Clark will send a check to Orin & Peters.

4   If she wishes to go--and she should--I will help.

5   Here are the marks: John, 85; Paul, 92; Ann, 95.

6   Did they receive our check for $3,902 on June 6?

7   Please notice: Flight #39 arrives at 10:45 p.m.

8   Doesn't he know how to divide 144 3/4 by 12 1/8?

9   Please ship 200# of #45 cement to Lowe & Brandin.

10   What traffic! You've gone 24½ miles in 2¼ hours.
....1....2....3....4....5....6....7....8....9....10

The size of stationery most commonly used is 8½ x 11 inches; however, 8½ x 5½ or 8½ x 7¼ may be used. Sometimes colored paper rather than white is preferred.

No salutation, no complimentary close, and usually no signature lines are used on interoffice memorandums. Since the dictator's name is given in the *From* line, it need not be repeated as a signature. Some dictators initial their memorandums. The reference initials, enclosure notations, and carbon copy notations are typed as they are on an outgoing letter.

Set the left margin at a point two or three spaces after the longest guide word in the left half of the printed heading or at the point where the printed guide words begin. Set a tab stop two or three spaces after the longest guide word in the right half of the printed heading. Set the right margin stop at a point equal to the left margin.

Make sure that the typewritten fill-ins are aligned at the bottom with the printed guide words.

Begin typing the message a triple space below the last fill-in line and use single spacing with either blocked or indented paragraphs.

If the dictator wants his name and title typed at the bottom of the message, begin at the tab stop you set for the right side of the heading and type this line a double space below the last line of the message.

MARK SUPPLY COMPANY **Interoffice Memorandum**

TO: Office Managers   DATE: July 10, 19--

SUBJECT: Cancellation of Weekly   FROM: Harold Thompson, Director
Meetings

The regular weekly meetings are canceled until further notice because of the illness of Mr. Clarke.

Until such time as the meetings are resumed, please feel free to contact me in my office to discuss any problems that may arise in your department.

ML

11   Call 279-5570 for an appointment between 2 and 4.

12   Brown & Bolton have reduced the <u>entire</u> stock 20%.

13   Use @ when typing invoices (10 lbs. @ 79¢ a lb.).

14   UA Flight #002 leaves LAX at 9 p.m. each weekday.

15   The correct abbreviation for "In care of" is c/o.

16   The asterisk (*) was used to indicate a decrease.

17   The ballpoint pen is 50¢; a matching pencil, 25¢.

	Words
18 Mr. Arnold's article, "Typing's Fun," included	11
a section describing "Make Your Typing Pay." There	22
were several copies in the school's library, but the	33
librarian said, "We never seem to have enough." The	44
copy I borrowed from Mrs. Brown's shelf was marked	54
"Teacher's Copy."	58

19 Your representatives (Mr. Sims and Mr. Lowey)	10
offered us a discount of 15% on our order. We under-	21
stood (from reading your catalog) that a 5% discount	32
was usually granted on such purchases, but we were	42
assured that this extra 10% discount would apply in	53
our case.	55

20 We paid 10¢ for the pencil, 15¢ for the pen,	10
and 35¢ for the ink. We also bought a blotter that	21
measures 36½ by 24¼ inches, but this was 6½ inches	31
longer than we needed.	36

21 When underscoring a <u>hyphenated</u> word, <u>underscore</u>	11
the <u>hyphen</u> because it is considered a part of the	21
word. <u>For example</u>, underscore the hyphen in the	31
word <u>cross-examined</u>. If you use the asterisk (*)	41
to indicate a footnote, <u>do</u> <u>not</u> <u>space</u> between the	51
word and the asterisk.	56

22 Our check #313 for the air-cooled motor that	10
we purchased in mid-July is enclosed. We are now	20
interested in the slow-burning furnace described	30
in your Booklet #49 to heat our three-story factory	41
building. This Model #843 would replace the old-	51
fashioned equipment we have been using for approxi-	61
mately twenty-three years.	67

23 You may type either 6¼ or 6 1/4. Thus, when	10
typing 18¼ lbs. @ 32¢, the number 18¼ may be typed	20
as 18 1/4. Now, practice typing these items: 7¼	30
yards @ 17¢; 32¼ feet @ 14¢; 8¼ hours @ $2.35.	40

....1....2....3....4....5....6....7....8....9....10

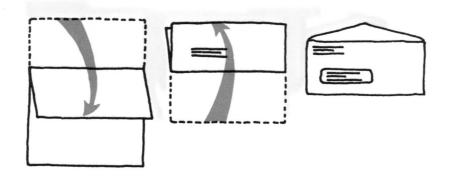

INTEROFFICE MEMORANDUMS

Correspondence within a firm is usually in the form of memorandums. The stationery used for interoffice memorandums is designed to save time in typing and handling. There is usually a special heading that includes: *To, From, Date,* and *Subject.*

BARRETT FURNITURE COMPANY

INTEROFFICE MEMORANDUM

TO: DATE:

SUBJECT: FROM:

SPEEDWRITING/NANCY TAYLOR DIVISION
ITT EDUCATIONAL SERVICES, INC.
55 West 42nd Street, New York, New York 10036
Telephone (212) 565-2262

To: Date:

From: Copies:

Subject:

24   She paid $4.95 for the gloves at Mark & Sons   10
and $4.15 for the scarf at Nelson & Company. I saw   21
those items in the window of Brown & King's for only   32
$4. She had planned to spend between $30 and $40   42
for the table advertised by Jones & Lee, but she   52
saved $5 or $6 by shopping at Handley & Company.   62

25   Your letter of June 26 did not receive my attention   11
until today because I left my office on June 9 and   21
did not return until July 31. However, your order   31
will now have immediate attention and should reach   41
you no later than August 7. As I told you, our Price   52
List No. 591 is complete; and you can order from it   63
at your convenience. An order for 480 books was sent   74
on the morning of May 25 to the following address: 84
H. Hahn, 371 North 28 Street, New York, N. Y. 10031.   95
We were happy to be of assistance.   *no space.*   102

26   We have received your letter of April 18 and   10
have made a change in our records to indicate your   20
change of address from 728 Broadway to 194 South   30
34 Street. The 37 copies of our 29-page catalog   40
will be sent before May 3 and you should have them   50
in time for your sale on May 14. May I remind you   60
that we have not yet received your check for $278   70
to cover our invoice No. G1742. This order for 19   80
Capitol I   cabinets and 32 benches was shipped to you on March 9   91
with the understanding that we would receive payment   102
in thirty days.   105
....1....2....3....4....5....6....7....8....9....10

SPECIAL SYMBOLS

omit

!	Exclamation Point	See page 46.	Alas!
x	Times or By	Use a small letter *x* with space before and after.	a 9 x 12 rug 12 x 12 is 144
—	Minus	Type a hyphen with a space before and after.	10 - 7 is 3
÷	Divided by	Type a hyphen; backspace; type a colon.	10 ÷ 5 is 2
=	Equals	Type a hyphen; backspace; roll the platen forward slightly by hand; hold it in position; type a hyphen; return platen to line position. (Some machines have an equals key on the right side in the top row.)	12 x 11 = 132

Folding and Inserting the Letter

Before folding your letter for insertion into an envelope, make a final check to be sure that the letter is signed, that all corrections have been made, that all enclosures have been included, and that you have the correct envelope.

Follow the steps shown in the illustrations.

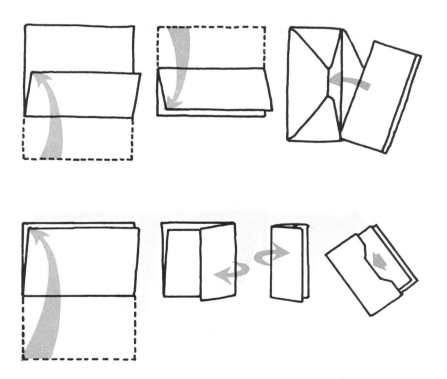

Symbol	Name	Procedure	Example
+	Plus	Type a hyphen; backspace; type a diagonal. (If the machine contains an = key, the shift will have the + sign.)	$18 + 20 = 38$
°	Degrees	Using the ratchet release, turn the platen toward you one-half space; type lower case *o*; return ratchet release to normal position; return the platen to line position.	$32°$ F.
said[2]	Superior Figures	Use the same procedure as that used to type the degree sign.	. . . book^2 had merit.
H_2O	Inferior Figures	Use the same procedure as that used to type the degree sign except that the platen is turned away from you one-half space.	H_2SO_4
III	Roman Numerals	Use capital letters I, V, X, L, C, and M.	Chapter XVIII
Ø	Military Zero	Intersect the zero with a diagonal.	13ØØ hours
[ ]	Brackets	Type diagonals and under-scores facing inside.	/C̄leveland̲/
'	Minutes or Feet	Type the apostrophe.	5' writing 3' square
"	Seconds or Inches	Type the quotation mark.	15" timings 6" line

Special Symbol Drills

1 An algebraic expression is typed: 3ab $(3y^2 - 4x)$.

2 Make brackets to enclose parentheses: /N̄i (CN) 4̲/.

3 It was 10° in Miami and 2° below zero in Chicago.

3 times each

4 This shipping carton measures 4'5" x 3'6" x 3'2".

5 Begin with 15" writings and build to 5' writings.

Expanding or Condensing Letters

If the typist realizes that she has misjudged the length of a letter after it has been started, she need not start the letter over again. The following pointers will compensate for errors in judgment.

To lengthen a very short letter, any one or a combination of these techniques may be used:

1. Lower the date line three to five lines.
2. Allow additional blank lines between the date and the inside address.
3. Use 10- or 15-space paragraph indentions.
4. Double space the body of the letter.
5. Using the variable linespacer, leave one and a half blank lines rather than one blank line between parts of the letter.
6. Allow five or six blank lines for the penwritten signature.
7. Type the dictator's name and official title on separate lines.
8. Lower the reference initials one or two lines.

To shorten a long one-page letter, any one or a combination of the following techniques may be used:

1. Raise the date one or two lines.
2. Allow only two or three blank lines between the date and the inside address.
3. Omit the company name in the closing line.
4. Allow only two blank lines for the penwritten signature.
5. Type the reference initials on the same line as the last line of the closing of the letter.

Submitting the Letter for Signature

Before taking your letter out of the machine, check it carefully for any errors that you may have overlooked. Then assemble your letter and carbon copies in the following order:

1. The envelope, with the original copy inserted under its flap, is placed on top.
2. Under this, place all carbon copies, properly designated for forwarding to other departments or individuals.
3. The file copy, attached to the original correspondence, is at the bottom of the pile.

Section 4
SPECIAL TECHNIQUES

much. (P) during that short time, we did find him to be a conscientious and willing worker, who was always on time and who got along very well with people. incidentally, he left of his own volition. (P) if we learn anything else, we'll certainly let you know./very sincerely yours/maxwell bates/reference initials

JOB 5

Type this letter on standard window stationery using modified-block style with mixed punctuation.

date/mrs thomas walsh/329 jackson street/waukegan illinois 61504/dear mrs walsh/we previously informed you that a branch office of our bank would be opening in your area in the near future. we are happy to announce that the day has arrived, and it will be open for business on monday, june 2, at 9 a.m. (P) according to your wishes, we are transferring your account to this branch. mr watson, the manager, will be happy to give you every possible assistance if you have any questions or need help of any kind./very truly yours/robert madlund/reference initials

Fill-Ins on Form Letters

Form letters are often reproduced to facilitate the answering of written correspondence. The inside address and specific information are filled in where the blanks occur.

The typed-in lines should match the typing of the letter so that it does not appear to be a form letter. Insert the form letter so that the paper is straight and the margins are aligned with the printed copy.

Type the date on the second line below the letterhead. Roll the paper forward until the first line of printed copy is visible and aligned properly in the typewriter. Count the number of lines you need for the inside address and salutation including the blank lines. Roll the paper back the needed number of lines and type the inside address and the salutation.

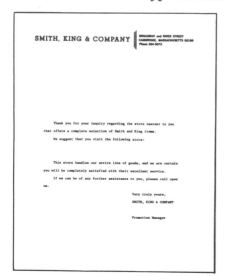

Form Letter

Filled-In Letter

DETERMINING THE MARGINS

1. Decide upon the length of line to be used. The line length may be expressed several different ways, as demonstrated on the chart below. (Review pica and elite spacing, page 11.)

2. Plan where to set the margin stops. To determine the left margin, subtract half the number of spaces in the line from the centering point.

To determine the right margin, add half the number of spaces in the line to the centering point; then ~~add five more spaces~~ and set the right margin. *[omit]* Five spaces are added to the point where you wish to stop typing so that you will hear your bell right at that point and will be able to return your carriage without having to use the margin release key at the end of every line.

Centering Point

```
                                                    Very Imp.
       -20              ∧              +20+5
       ─────────────────────────────────────
               40-space line


         -25            ∧            +25+5
       ─────────────────────────────────────
               50-space line


      -30               ∧               +30+5
    ───────────────────────────────────────────
               60-space line
```

Example: 60-space line on pica typewriter

$$60 \div 2 = 30$$

42	42
−30	+30
12 left margin	72
	+ 5 extra spaces
	77 right margin

Example: 7-inch line on elite typewriter

$$12 \times 7 = 84 \text{ space line}$$

$$84 \div 2 = 42$$

$$50 - 42 = 8 \text{ left margin}$$

50
+42
92
+ 5 extra spaces
97 right margin

JOB 1

Type this letter on Monarch stationery using modified-block form with mixed punctuation.

date/mr richard johnson jr/55 oak avenue/paterson new jersey 07514/dear mr. johnson/thank you for your letter of january 4. i am happy to learn that you are so well pleased with our equipment that you have decided to place an additional order with us. (P) as you requested, we have asked our representative in your area to call on you within the next few days. he will have with him our latest sample catalog from which you may make your selection of style and color./yours truly/john t. barrow/sales manager/reference initials

JOB 2

Type this letter on left-weighted standard stationery in block style.

date/mr and mrs myron wolf/494 parma road/cleveland ohio 92327/dear parents/you have been referred to us by mrs james byrd, the mother of one of your son's classmates. she felt that you would be interested in world encyclopedia for your son. (P) a recent national survey of parents whose children use this encyclopedia disclosed that nine out of ten families feel that their children have benefited greatly from its use. they reported that their children not only get better grades in school but also are developing a much wider range of interests. in addition, they are learning to question things and to look them up. (P) wouldn't you like to give your son these advantages? just return the enclosed postage-paid card to us for full information./sincerely/jason meadows/reference initials

JOB 3

Type this letter on standard stationery with a three-inch letterhead style with indented paragraphs and mixed punctuation.

date/mr burton ives/1540 bedford avenue/wilmington, delaware 19872/dear mr ives/our telephone conversation today made me feel more hopeful about completing our convention arrangements on time. your kind offer to help, plus your vast experience in this area, will surely make it the best one we've ever had. (P) enclosed are the facts you require. as you can see, we are expecting about 350 people to attend this annual affair. (P) may i thank you again for your much-needed and appreciated help./sincerely yours,/charles harper/reference initials/enc.

JOB 4

Type this letter on Baronial stationery using the modified-block style with mixed punctuation.

date/mr william smith/moore, brown & smith/98 north sussex street/jamestown virginia 30031/dear mr smith/we can appreciate your desire to get all the information you can on the background of mr james hastings. since he was with us only one month, however, we cannot tell you very

Determine the left and right margins for each of the following:

Line Length	Pica Left	Pica Right	Elite Left	Elite Right
40-space				
50-space				
60-space	12	77 _72_		
70-space				
4 inches				
5 inches			20 _21_	85 _81_
6 inches			14 _15_	91 _87_
7 inches				
Margin Length				
1 inch				
1½ inch	**15**	**75** _70_		
2 inch				

NOTE: The margins printed in bold face should be memorized and can be used whenever an average length line is required.

MARGIN RELEASE

To type outside the left margin, depress the margin release key and move the carriage to the point at which typing is to begin.

The margin release key is located in several different positions, depending upon the make of typewriter. Locate this key on your machine. It is labeled *Mar. Rel.* or *MR*.

Type the following numbers one under the other at the left margin of your paper. To type "10" in proper alignment, depress and hold the margin release key and backspace once:

```
 7.
 8.
 9.
10.
```

To type outside the right margin, type until the carriage locks, depress the margin release key, and type the remainder of the word.

Set the margins on your typewriter for a 60-space line. Type the following line, using the margin release when the carriage locks.

```
Ignore the bell and use the margin release when the carriage locks.
```

Collins, Bradley & Fox

9 Purchase Street
Boston, Massachusetts 02100

January 7, 19--

Mr. Harold King
7821 Arlington Drive
Boston, MA   02116

3 or 4 sp.

Dear Mr. King:

Last April, at your request, we spoke with our client,
Mr. White, concerning the lowest price we would accept
for his house on Windale Drive. You will recall that
he refused to consider any offer that was below the
original asking price.

Two days ago, I received a call from Mr. White and
learned that he is now willing to accept $30,000 for
the house, provided the sale can be consummated within the next few weeks. If you are still interested
in the house, let me know; and I will set up a meeting so that the details of the sale can be worked out.

Sincerely,

ad

Standard window stationery to use with a window envelope has printed
corners to indicate the proper placement of the inside address. The address
is centered within this area.

Maintaining Right Margin

You cannot always copy material line for line so you must decide where to end each line. To help you make this decision, you listen for the bell warning.

A bell rings six or eight spaces before the right margin stop. These spaces will vary from machine to machine. How many strokes can you make on your typewriter after the bell rings and before the margin locks?

When the bell rings, plan to end the line as close to the desired ending point as you can, preferably *avoiding* the division of words. If typing only two or three strokes beyond the margin will permit you to complete the word, strike the margin release when the carriage locks and type the remaining letters. If the word you are typing is so long that it would make the right margin too uneven, divide the word.

WORD DIVISION

The trend in letter writing today is to avoid dividing words whenever possible. A line may be approximately five strokes longer or shorter than the desired ending. Therefore, the guiding rule for every typist should be to divide words only when it is absolutely necessary to do so in order to maintain a reasonably even right margin.

DO

1. Type the hyphen at the end of the first line, not at the beginning of the second line.

2. Divide words only between syllables.

3. Divide hyphenated words and compounds at hyphen only.

        sister-in-law   self-control   above-mentioned

4. Carry over three or more letters of a word.

    Correct: shortly   Incorrect: short-ly
              lux-ury   luxu-ry

5. Divide after the double letter when a syllable is added to a word ending in a double letter.

        small-est   excel-lence

6. Divide between vowels when they constitute 2 one-letter syllables coming together.

        continu-ation   gradu-ation

7. Divide after a one-letter syllable that occurs within the root of a word.

        edu-cates   simi-lar

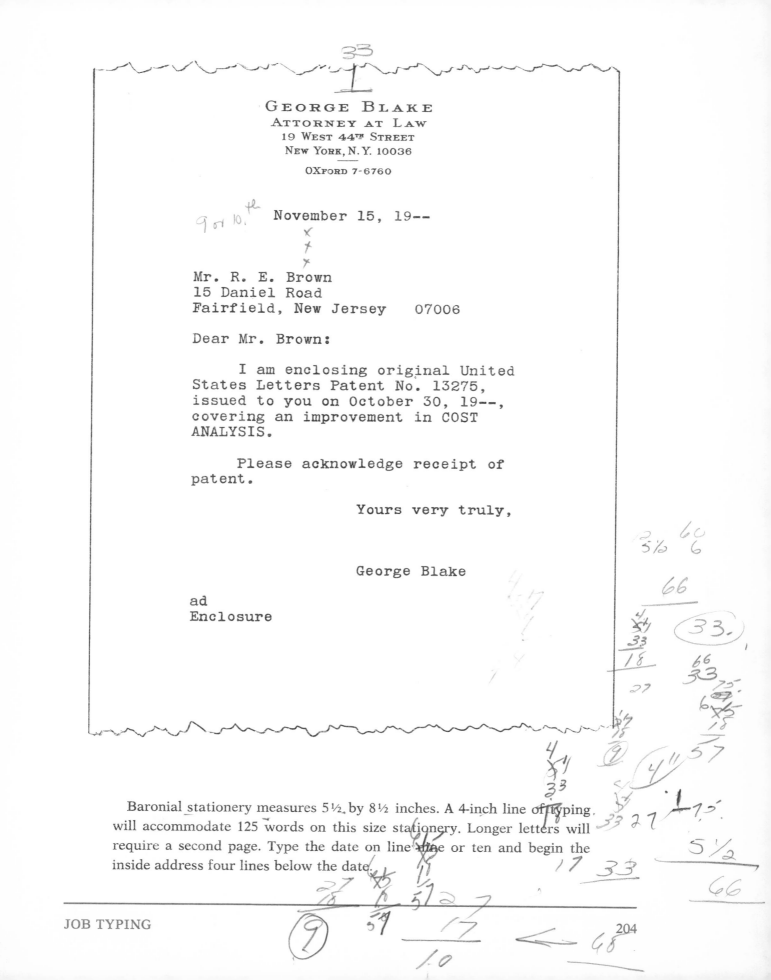

GEORGE BLAKE
ATTORNEY AT LAW
19 WEST 44TH STREET
NEW YORK, N.Y. 10036

OXFORD 7-6760

November 15, 19--

Mr. R. E. Brown
15 Daniel Road
Fairfield, New Jersey   07006

Dear Mr. Brown:

    I am enclosing original United
States Letters Patent No. 13275,
issued to you on October 30, 19--,
covering an improvement in COST
ANALYSIS.

    Please acknowledge receipt of
patent.

                    Yours very truly,

                    George Blake

ad
Enclosure

Baronial stationery measures 5½ by 8½ inches. A 4-inch line of typing
will accommodate 125 words on this size stationery. Longer letters will
require a second page. Type the date on line nine or ten and begin the
inside address four lines below the date.

DO NOT

1. Divide a proper noun, a contraction, an abbreviation, or a number. (Initials or a given name may be separated from a surname when necessary.)

   MR. TOM.   MR. J
   JONES.   JONES

2. Divide a one-syllable word.

   `where`   `think`   `shipped`

3. Divide a word of ~~five~~ 6 or fewer letters.

   `among`   `radio`   `obey`

4. Divide a word in such a way that a single letter is separated from the remainder of the word.

   Correct: `con-tain`   Incorrect: `e-lated`
   `trans-fer`   `a-mong`
   `edu-cates`   `radi-o`
   `con-di-tion`   `o-blige`

imp. ⟶ 5. Divide the last word on a page. *or the last word on the First line of a letter*

AVOID

1. Dividing a two-letter syllable at the beginning ~~of a word.~~

imp. ⟶ 2. Dividing words at the ends of two or more consecutive lines or dividing a word at the end of the last complete line of a paragraph.

   Where would you divide the words in the following list? In those words that can be divided, use a hyphen to indicate all acceptable word divisions in typewritten work. If the word cannot be divided, type it without hyphenating.

Example: `con-tinu-ation`   `edu-cates`   `enough`

in all possible places

shipment	maintained	tallest
develop	modernized	against
unnecessary	first-rate	constitution
departing	percentage	regardless
along	margins	evaluate
running	every	stenography
filling	stopped	secretary
electric	procedure	wouldn't
sentence	performance	salutation
followed	typewriting	upon

GEORGE BLAKE
ATTORNEY AT LAW
19 WEST 44TH STREET
NEW YORK, N.Y. 10036

OXFORD 7-6760

14 November 15, 19--

Mr. Robert Ferguson
250 East 39 Street
New York, New York   10016

Dear Mr. Ferguson:

    Re: Ferguson vs Kane

    We filed the complaint today in your case asking
for damages as follows:

    1. General damages in the amount of $5,000.
Please note that this is merely the maximum amount
that you may receive and is no indication of the actual
amount which you may be awarded.

    2. Special damages for loss of earnings and medical
expenses.

    We will keep you informed of any developments and
will get in touch with you in sufficient time to prepare
you thoroughly for trial.

    Please call or write me if you have any questions
about this letter.

            Yours very truly,

            George Blake

ad

Monarch stationery measures 7¼ by 10½ inches. Using a 4-inch line, this size stationery will accommodate 150 words; using a 5-inch line, a 250-word letter can be accommodated. Longer letters will require a second page. The date is typed on line 14 and the inside address begins five lines below the date.

MARKING AND COUNTING ERRORS

 $\overset{1}{(\text{S}}he)$ likes $\overset{2}{(\text{thes})}$ life$\overset{3}{.}$He left his $\overset{4}{(\text{h t})}$. It $\overset{5}{(\text{he is})}$.

He likes fast hits $\overset{6}{(.)}$ Set it $\overset{7}{(\text{it})}$ at $\overset{8}{\wedge}$left. Hit it.

1. Faulty capital.
2. Incorrect stroke.
3. Spacing incorrect.
4. Letter does not print.
5. Words transposed.
6. Spacing incorrect.
7. Word repeated.
8. Word omitted.

Only one error is charged to any word, no matter how many errors it contains.

ERASING

Accurate typing is the goal of every typist. The most experienced typist, however, will occasionally make an error; it is therefore essential to learn the proper methods for correcting these mistakes.

1. If your error is on the left side of your paper, use the margin release key to move your carriage to the extreme left side of your machine. If your error is on the right side of your paper, use the margin release key to move your carriage to the extreme right side of your machine. This step is important, so that the erasure particles will not drop into the "well" or basket of the machine and clog the keys.

2. Raise the paper bail out of the way.

3. If the correction is to be made on the upper two-thirds of the page, turn the paper up to a convenient position. If the correction is to be made on the lower part of the page, turn the cylinder backward so as not to disturb the alignment of the typing line.

4.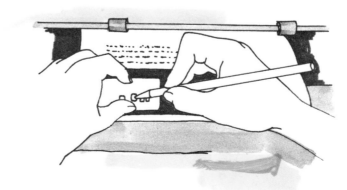

Acme Insurance Company

FOR A SECURE FUTURE

Phone 746-0499

965 HARTFORD AVE. • OMAHA, NEBRASKA 68100

December 1, 19--

Mr. Elliott Travis
Office Specialists, Inc.
64 Monroe Street
Green Bay, WI   53527

Dear Mr. Travis:

Re: Order No. D-6204

The six desks that were ordered on November 1 should have
white formica tops and chrome legs. Please ship them to
the following address:

                American Computer Company
              c/o Nelson Warehousing Service
                    235 Grant Street
                  Omaha, Nebraska   68106

We appreciate your cooperation in the handling of this order.

Very truly yours,

Martin Charleston

ad

An 8½-by-11-inch sheet that has a letterhead more than 2 inches deep needs to be adjusted for date line and inside address placement. Type the date three lines below the letterhead and begin the inside address three lines below the date.

Use an eraser shield to protect the letters surrounding the one to be corrected. These shields, made of metal, paper, or celluloid, are perforated in such a way that the perforations can be placed over the letters to be corrected, thus avoiding any unintentional erasing of the letters around it.

5. Proper erasing technique requires a light, short, downward stroke with an ink eraser. Do not "scrub" or you will suddenly find a hole in your paper. Using a clean eraser, stroke downward lightly. Examine your progress after each stroke of the eraser. The trick is to erase as little as possible. When the erasure is complete, brush or blow any erasure crumbs off the page or typewriter.

6. Return the carriage to the proper position and strike the correct letter. On the manual typewriter, strike the correct letter lightly, then backspace and strike it lightly again. Continue this process until the correction is as dark as the surrounding type. If you have neatly and carefully followed these steps, your erasure will not be noticed.

REINSERTING PAPER

It is possible to remove paper from the machine and then reinsert it in such a way that its removal cannot be detected. The ability to perform this technique enables the typist to continue typing something that was removed from the typewriter before it was finished or to correct an error that was not noticed while the paper was still in the machine.

Type the following sentence:

I can realign my paper perfectly.

Look carefully at how much space you can see between the bottom of the letters and your alignment scale. Typewriters vary, so you must recheck this space whenever you use a different machine.

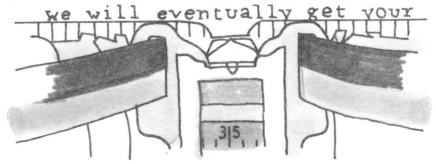

Notice that a line drawn down through an *i* or *l* should go straight down through the calibration marks on your alignment scale.

▶ 1181 St. Catherine West, Montreal, P.Q.
Telephone: 842-3823

▶ J. Paul Morin, B. Com.
National Coordinator

Speedwriting

abc shorthand
8 languages

Secretarial Typing
Business English
Business Correspondence
Business Spelling
and Word Power

25 — 57 + 25

51 + 6 > 57

December 15, 19--

Nancy Taylor

Charm and Finishing Course
Nu Tau Sigma Sorority

MR. EXECUTIVE

Management Training
Program

AATA

American Accountants
Training Association

BCAT

Business Career
Aptitude Test

Mr. Howard Bates
82 Palmer Drive
Buffalo, NY   14203

Dear Mr. Bates:

Christmas is the time to forget work and
remember you--our old friends--who, through your
loyalty and friendship, have made this a better
year.

The happy associations with you are recalled
with satisfaction and pleasure. Each passing year
brings us a higher evaluation of the bonds we have
forged.

Merry Christmas--Happy New Year!

Sincerely yours,

JPM:ad

Left-weighted standard stationery is handled in the same manner as any
other 8½-by-11-inch stationery except that the center point is moved
½ inch to the right.

Variable Spacer (button in left cylinder knob)

Using your variable linespacer, roll your paper up a few inches. Then roll it back and realign it with your typing. Type over the first letter of your sentence. Is it typed exactly on top of your first stroke? If not, readjust your paper until it is lined up perfectly.

Now remove your paper from the typewriter and reinsert it according to the following directions:

1. Insert paper to the approximate position desired.

2. Using the paper release, straighten the paper. At the same time shift the paper sideways until an *i* or *l* in your copy is in perfect alignment with the calibration marks on the alignment scale.

3. Using the variable linespacer, move the cylinder until the original line of typing is even with the top of the alignment bar.

4. Check the accuracy of your reinsertion by putting the ribbon selector in stencil position and typing over one of the original letters. The faint impression that results will indicate whether further adjustments are necessary.

5. When the strikeover indicates perfect alignment, return the ribbon selector to normal position and continue typing.

If you are reinserting the paper to make a correction, do not try to correct both the original and carbon copies at the same time. Instead, insert each sheet separately and make the correction.

SQUEEZING AND EXPANDING

Half-Space Method

Errors resulting from the insertion or omission of a single letter or space can be corrected by a method known as "half-spacing." This method takes advantage of the fact that the space bar on most manual typewriters moves the carriage forward in two half-space movements—one half space when the bar is depressed and another half space when the bar is released. Some typewriters have a special "half-space" key on the keyboard. Check to see if you have one on your machine.

October 15, 19--

Automotive Equipment Company
460 West 24 Street
Trenton, NJ   08610

Gentlemen:

One of our dealers told us that he has sold over five hundred
Arma inner tubes in the past seven months and has not received
any requests for adjustments.

Another dealer wrote to us saying:

> Arma tubes last longer than any other tubes. We
> have a great many users whose Arma tubes are over
> four years old and the rubber is still tough and
> level.

Arma inner tubes are unequaled. Twenty-five thousand perfect
to one imperfect is the record. Why? These tubes are made
from pure para rubber with only enough sulfur to vulcanize.
They do not stretch out of shape and do not deteriorate with
the passing of the years.

Our representative will be in your area within a few days, and
we hope you will consider placing an order with him.

Yours very truly,

Donald Frey, Sales Manager

DF:ad

To insert a single letter with the half-space method:

Example: `They se the typewriter.` (*se* instead of *see*)

1. Erase the entire word that is to be corrected. (In this example erase *se.*)

2. Move the carriage to the space after the previous word. (In this example move the carriage to the space after *they.*)

3. Depress the space bar (this moves the carriage a half space) and, *keeping the space bar in a depressed position*, type the first letter of the corrected word. (In this example strike *s.*)

4. Release the space bar and depress it again and, while the space bar is depressed, strike the second letter, *e*, of the word that is being corrected. Continue in this way until the third letter has been inserted. Remember—the space bar must be in the depressed position while each letter is being inserted.

Result: `They see the typewriter.`

To eliminate an unnecessary letter with the half-space method:

Example: `Tell them about it.` (Change *them* to *her.*)

1. Erase the entire word that is to be corrected—*them.*

2. Move carriage to the point where the first letter had been. (In this example move carriage to the original, *t*, position.)

3. Depress the space bar and, while the space bar is depressed, strike the first letter of the correct word. (In this example strike *h.*)

4. Release the space bar and depress it again for the insertion of the second letter, *e*. Continue in this way until the third letter has been inserted.

Result: `Tell her about it.`

Backspace Method

For manual machines that do not half space with the space bar and do not have a half-space key, follow the steps in the backspace method for squeezing and expanding:

The World Is Our Back Yard

COOPER TRAVEL BUREAU

1449 LANE STREET
SYRACUSE, NEW YORK 13200

Phone 799-5374

July 15, 19--

Mrs. Alma Lassitor
115 Elm Street
Augusta, GA   30904

Dear Mrs. Lassitor:

    Thank you for your letter of July 5. I am sure you will
find the information supplied below of great value to you on
your trip to California this summer. You may be certain that
the staff in each of our offices will be glad for the chance
to help make your trip a successful one.

City	Address	Manager
Columbus	388 Midwood Street	Ronald C. Black
St. Louis	25-05 North Elm Road	Stephen Burns
Kansas City	119 Carroll Place	Albert J. Garret
Denver	690 Third Avenue	Joseph Wellings
Las Vegas	1814 Hudson Street	Harold Richards
Los Angeles	465 Regent Park	Foster L. Lynn

    We hope you have a pleasant, safe trip.

                Very truly yours,

                Joseph H. Norris, President

JHN:ad

1. Erase the entire word that is being corrected.

2. Move the carriage to the point where the first letter of the original word had been.

3. To insert a single letter, space once. To delete a single letter, space twice. Then fully depress the backspace key. Keeping it depressed, strike the first letter of the word that is to be inserted.

4. Release the backspace key and space once. Depress the backspace key again and, while it is depressed, insert the next letter.

5. Release the backspace key and repeat Step 4 until the entire word has been corrected.

Other Methods

On electric typewriters it may be necessary to hold the carriage by hand at the half-space point. The carriage on the IBM Selectric, however, does not move. To make the corrections on this typewriter, locate the horizontal position of the type element by using the black line on the card holder or the red area on the margin scale.

To move back a half space, place the palm of the right hand on top of the front cover, lower the finger of this hand until it touches the carrier position post, press in on this post until the black line is moved back one-half space, hold in position, and type the letter with the left hand.

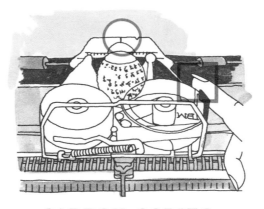

CARBON COPIES

It is customary to make a carbon copy of every letter or form that is typed in a business office. The number of copies required will depend upon the procedures followed by the organization. As a general rule, at least one carbon copy will be made and kept in the company files.

Carbon copies of business letters are never typed on letterhead stationery. Instead, a blank sheet (generally inexpensive yellow paper or onionskin) is used. Carbon copies of business forms—such as invoices or statements—are typed on printed forms similar to the original.

date/miss eleanor crandal/17 chestnut street/philadelphia pa 19112/foster catalog/in accordance with your request, miss crandal, we are sending you full information about the foster school of business. we are glad to learn that you are interested in the courses that we offer and hope that we shall soon have the pleasure of enrolling you as one of our students. (P) as you read our catalog, please notice the following features offered by our school: 1 the tuition rate in the foster school of business is only $70 a month. this means that you can get an intensive course for a very moderate fee. 2 we have courses which vary in length from three months to two years. we offer a short course for the high school graduate who seeks early employment and a longer course for those who wish to prepare for reporting and accounting positions. 3 although we do not guarantee positions (no school is permitted to guarantee), we do have good facilities for assisting our graduates to obtain employment. (P) we shall be glad to talk with you about your future plans why not pay us a visit?/mary 1 kile dean/reference initials

TABLES

A tabulation is centered, preferably with the right and left margins indented three to five spaces.

Single space the tabulation and set it off from the rest of the letter by a double space above and below:

officers were elected:

Martin Miller	President
Alan Walters	Vice President
Harold Watson	Treasurer
Glen Collins	Secretary

May I suggest that, when you wish to make a request, you get

LONG QUOTATIONS

Quoted material that will extend to four or more typewritten lines is indented five spaces from each margin and typed with single spacing. Do not enclose the quoted material in quotation marks.

for word division is as follows:

The division of a word at the end of a line is undesirable, but at times it is unavoidable if the margin is to be justified. When a word is divided, it is essential that it be divided correctly.

May I suggest that you refer to any handbook for the rules to

---

Preassembled "snap-out" carbon packs are available. The sheets of copy paper are often of different colors in order to facilitate the routing of copies.

Notice that there is a dull side and a glossy side to a sheet of carbon paper. It is the glossy side that prints. Therefore, the coated side is placed against the sheet on which the carbon copy is to be made.

To prepare your paper for insertion outside the machine:

Desk Assembly of a Carbon Pack

1. Lay the paper to be used for the carbon copy on your desk. Place the carbon paper over it, with the glossy side down.

2. On top of these sheets place the letterhead, face up. Note in the illustration the arrangement for an original and two copies.

3. Straighten the pack by tapping the edge of the sheets gently on the desk.

4. Check for the proper arrangement of the carbon paper by making sure that its glossy side faces you as the papers are being inserted behind the cylinder.

5. Insert the papers by holding them firmly with one hand while turning the cylinder slowly with the other.

6. When it is necessary to insert a thick pack of several sheets into the machine, the sheets may be kept in alignment during insertion by placing a folded piece of paper, or the flap of an envelope, over the top of the sheets. To start the carbon pack, release the paper release, feed the pack around the cylinder until the sheets appear at the front, and reset the paper release. After the pack is inserted, remove the folded paper or envelope.

FIRST NATIONAL BANK

———————————————————————BROADWAY AND DEEGAN STREET
———————————————————————————AUGUSTA, GEORGIA 30900

September 7, 19--

Mr. Leroy B. Miller
220 High Street
Augusta, GA   30905

SAFE DEPOSIT BOXES

Of all the people who are alive today, few will be alive one
hundred years from today. This is not true of valuable papers.
If the papers are placed in our Safe Deposit Vault, they may
remain undisturbed for centuries to come. Our Safe Deposit
Vault offers the following advantages:

1 The vault is built stronger and with more time-saving devices
   than any other.

2 The vault is built not only to defy time but also fire, theft,
   and accident. It is a steel fortress that time cannot destroy.

3 The rental on a safe deposit box is a very small sum each year.

4 The protection provided offers the cheapest insurance known.

5 Your box can be opened only by you or those whom you give
   permission, and the box is accessible at all times during
   regular business hours.

Let us show you the great convenience and safety of this modern
fortress and stronghold.

J. F. DOWNS, PRESIDENT

JFD:ad

To prepare your paper for a carbon pack in the machine:

1. Assemble the stationery with the original sheet on top.

2. Insert the paper, turning the cylinder until the sheets are grasped slightly by the feed rolls.

Machine Assembly of a Carbon Pack

3. Leave all but the last sheet over the top of the machine.

4. Place carbon sheets between sheets of paper with the coated side toward you.

5. Roll the pack into typing position.

6. Carbon sheets will extend beyond the bottom of the stationery. They can be removed easily by pulling them all out from the bottom simultaneously.

Erasing Carbon Copies

When erasing an original letter with one or more carbon copies, the general steps outlined for erasing must be supplemented by the following:

1. Before making the erasure, insert a stiff card or metal erasing plate immediately behind the original copy at the point where the correction is to be made. Doing this will prevent the pressure used in erasing from smudging the other copies. After each correction is made, remove the card or plate and place it behind the next copy to be erased.

2. Use a hard eraser on the original copy and a soft eraser on the carbon copies. Make certain the eraser is clean before attempting to make a correction with it.

3. To darken a carbon correction after erasing, set the ribbon control lever in stencil position and firmly type over the original copy.

ENUMERATIONS

A series of numbered items is known as an enumeration. This is a display list with the numbers standing out at the left.

When typing enumerations, a period follows the number (except in the simplified letter style which omits the period). Space twice after the period before beginning the first word of the copy.

The numbers and periods must be aligned. If the enumeration contains two-digit numbers, remember to indent one additional space for the numbers one through nine.

The numbers may be typed at the left margin or at the point of paragraph indention. The second line of the enumeration may begin at the left margin or it may be blocked under the first line of copy.

Treat each enumeration as a separate paragraph, double spacing before and after each item.

are as follows:

1. Do your products contain at least 100 pages?

2. What additional charge is made for imprinting the name of
our company?

3. Is a discount granted on orders of 1,000 or more?

are as follows:

1. Do your products contain at least 100 pages?

2. What additional charge is made for imprinting the name of
   our company?

3. Is a discount granted on orders of 1,000 or more?

are as follows:

    1. Do your products contain at least 100 pages?

    2. What additional charge is made for imprinting the name
of our company?

    3. Is a discount granted on orders of 1,000 or more?

PROOFREADERS' MARKS

Sometimes copy is corrected with proofreaders' marks. The typist must be able to interpret these marks when retyping the corrected copy, which is called a rough draft. The most commonly used proofreaders' marks are:

ℛ	Delete	no ¶	No new paragraph
⊃	Close up	=/	Hyphen
∧	Insert	tr or ∿	Transpose
#	Space	lc or /	Lowercase
⌐	Move to left	Cap or ≡	Capitals
⌐	Move to right	sp	Spell out
⌐	Move up	stet	Let it stand
⌐	Move down	ss	Single space
//	Align type	ds	Double space
¶	New paragraph	ts	Triple space

Type this letter, making the corrections as indicated.

June 24th, 19--

Mr. Thomas Abbott
24 Broad St.
Lincoln, New York   Zip Code

Dear Mr. Abbott:

Your application for a mortgage loan on the property located at Columbia turnpike and Mill road has been approved in the amount of 10,000, based on our appraisal and that of the Veteran's Administration. Monthly payments of the amount specified will satisfy principal and interest requirements.

If you find it possible are able to complete the transaction on this basis, bring or send in by Registered Mail your military discharge papers together with the appraisal fee of $20.

You will be notified about of the date on which stet the final papers are to be signed as soon as our attorney completes the titel search and prepares the necessary papers.

Sincerely Yours,

NATIONAL COMMERCIAL BANK

Lawrence C. Young, Pres.

LCY:ts

mr george mason/page 2/march 30, 19—/something does go wrong, you will find our service department ready to serve you as soon as you notify us. (P) just return the enclosed card to find out how this unit can help you with your bookkeeping problems. full information will be sent to you at once. (P) we look forward to hearing from you./cordially yours/manager/reference initials/enclosure

JOB 3

mr william chambers/page 2/september 15, 19—/the difficulty we have had in getting this order together and shipping it to you. (P) now that the flood waters have gone down, we will be able to start production again. this means that your order should be on its way to you shortly. (P) thank you very much for your patience./cordially/gerald pitkin/reference initials

JOB 4

mr edward baker/page 2/june 12, 19—/no doubt that we must do something to straighten out the mix-up that has occurred and do it fast. we cannot afford to antagonize a customer who gives us so much business. (P) in the meantime, duplicate the entire order and send it out at once by air freight. then i want you to thoroughly investigate every procedure in the shipping department and track down the weak link that caused this confusion. (P) i'll expect to hear from you as soon as you discover the reason for this difficulty./sincerely/gerald day/reference initials

JOB 5

brown's novelty store/page 2/april 10, 19—/in all of my years of dealing with your store, i have never had occasion to make any kind of complaint. i find it shocking to be treated as if i were trying to cheat you when my claim for the damaged merchandise is legitimate. your store has had a good reputation in our community—surely you do not want to jeopardize it! (P) all i ask is that you look into the matter. the facts will speak for themselves./sincerely yours/(mrs) max wallace/reference initials

Letters with Special Features

Letters that contain such special features as long quotations, enumerations, and tables may require adjustment in placement. Quotations and tables are usually indented from both sides. Enumerations and quotations are usually typed in separate paragraphs. To allow for the additional space needed, follow the procedures suggested for condensing letters on page 208.

TYPING ON RULED LINES

To type on a ruled line, use the variable linespacer when rolling the paper to the correct typing position. This correct position will be found by rolling the cylinder until the ruled line is slightly below the alignment bar. In this position, the letters to be typed will not cross the ruled line or be too far above it.

EXAMPLE: <u>Proper typing on ruled line.</u>

DATE <u>May 23, 19--</u>

NAME <u>Lynda Gold</u>
ADDRESS <u>1952 Davidson Avenue</u>
CITY <u>Bronx, New York 10400</u>

INVOICE NO. <u>AJ4087</u>

| SALESMAN |
| R. Roberts |

DUPLICATING PROCESSES

The three duplicating processes available in most offices are the direct-copy process, the spirit process, and the stencil duplication process. After determining which process is to be used, the master copy must be prepared properly.

The first step in typing on any type of master is to clean the type bars on your machine thoroughly so that your typing will be clear.

The second step is to prepare a layout of the material to be duplicated.

Direct-Copy Process

This process is used to make from one to ten copies. Copy machines are especially useful in making extra copies of documents, business forms, or correspondence.

When preparing material for copy machines, follow these procedures:

1. Type the material on plain paper, letterheads, or printed forms.

2. Make corrections neatly, using either an eraser or opaque white ink.

Type the following two-page letter in full-block style with open punctuation and a block-style heading for the second page.

date/mr j a mattewson manager/mattewson manufacturing company/139 rawson street/rahway new jersey 07065/dr mr mattewson/i was rather surprised to get your letter of december 21 in which you state that payment on our account is long overdue and that you would like to have us remit our check. (P) apparently my letter of december 6 to your firm has not been brought to your attention. unfortunately, i wrote the letter to the firm without mentioning your name; and it is possible that my letter was misplaced. in that letter i mentioned that we had bought three motors from you and that one motor, model A6032, has been unsatisfactory since it was delivered here on november 25. (P) there is nothing more aggravating than trying to get along with two motors when three are absolutely necessary to have our plant in good running order. in my letter of december 6, i wrote that this particular motor apparently has some defect. we don't want to have our servicemen tinker with it because it is not yet our property. i therefore wrote to you asking that you do one of two things. either send your serviceman around to see what is the trouble with the motor and perhaps make the necessary adjustments, or ship us a new motor and take the defective one back. (P) as i said before, i am confident that my letter has not been brought to your attention. during our many years of good business relationships, this is the first time that i have found cause for any complaint. you usually reply promptly and give us exceptional service. it may be of mutual advantage to have you trace my letter to find out just who has been negligent in this matter. (P) what is rather surprising to me is the tone of your letter—the rather peremptory manner in which you request an immediate settlement of our account. it is just 30 days since we received the shipment, only 20 since the motors have been installed, one of which has been giving us a great deal of trouble. if anybody has cause to complain, it is i, not you. you can readily imagine that there have been many delays in our operation owing to this defective motor, and we have not been able to turn out our products with our usual efficiency. (P) we are, therefore, returning your bill for adjustment. it is my purpose to withhold all payment until you have taken care of this matter to our complete satisfaction. the least you can do is to rush either a motor in exchange or some substitute until the right motor is satisfactorily installed so that we again will be functioning efficiently./very truly yours/purchasing agent/reference initials

The next four jobs represent the second page of two-page letters. Type a second page for each of the jobs using the letter styles and the second page headings you prefer.

Spirit Process

This duplication process is usually used for from 10 to 100 copies, although more may be run.

Remove the tissue between the master sheet and the attached special carbon sheet; do *not* separate the master sheet from the carbon sheet. Insert the master set into your typewriter with the open end first. A heavy backing sheet used behind the carbon will improve the type impression.

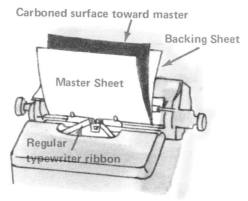

Carboned surface toward master

Backing Sheet

Master Sheet

Regular typewriter ribbon

Leave the ribbon in the regular position and type with a sharp, smooth touch. Reduce the pressure on the electric machine two or three points.

The carbon prints on the *reverse* side of the master. To make a correction, follow these steps:

1. Roll the pack forward and bend the master sheet forward so that you can see the error.

2. Using a razor blade, a fiberglass eraser, or a desk knife, lightly scrape the error off the back of the master.

3. Tear off a corner of the carbon sheet and place it over the spot where the correction is to be typed with the greasy side facing you.

4. Roll the pack back slowly and use the ratchet release to position for typing.

5. Type the correction over the error and remove the torn pieces of carbon.

6. To correct a whole line of typing, write the line in an unused part of the master. Cut out the correct and incorrect lines. Tape the corrected line into position.

Stencil Duplication Process

The stencil duplication process can be used to reproduce a thousand or more copies.

A stencil has a wax, plastic, or gelatin surface. The typewriter cuts openings in the stencil, and the duplicating machine feeds ink through these openings onto the paper.

Mr. William A. Hodges   2   August 12, 19__

and utilizing close to the full capacity of the press. Since
this press will sell at a lower hourly rate than the 54 x 78-
inch Crabtree, it could show considerable savings on 7 x 10
and 8 x 10 sizes.

I will keep you informed on all our new developments, especially
the new 4- and 5-color Web-fed presses we are planning to
install; and I do hope we will have the opportunity to get
together again soon. The next time I might be able to take
you to visit some of our plants, particularly our Web-fed
operation in Saddle Brook. It is evident that we are developing
our equipment along the same line as your production requirements. Because of this, I am encouraged to feel that you will
find our services and facilities an aid to you.

                              Sincerely yours,

                              Edward Taylor

AMD

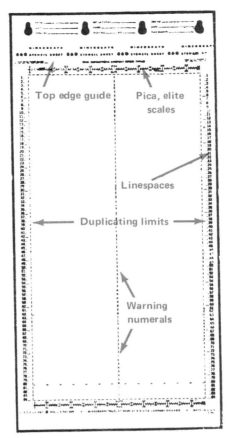

Top edge guide

Pica, elite scales

Linespaces

Duplicating limits

Warning numerals

Read the instructions that accompany the package of stencils and follow these steps:

1. Set the ribbon control at the stencil position.

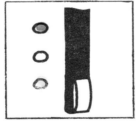

2. Insert the stencil pack into the typewriter. If the pack does not feed easily, depress the paper release to insert. Be sure the stencil is not wrinkled.

3. Straighten the stencil.

4. Push the paper bail rollers to the extreme left and right sides so that they will not roll on the stencil sheet.

5. Compare the typing layout and the markings on the stencil to determine at what points to set margins and tab stops and on what line to start typing.

6. On a manual machine, type with an even touch and at a rate a little slower than normal speed. Type punctuation

FREEMON-ENSON LITHOGRAPHERS, Inc.

Phone 61-1144

37½ SOUTH MADISON STREET, MIDDLETOWN, OHIO 45042

August 12, 19__

Mr. William A. Hodges
Allison Publishing Company
25 Walnut Street
Philadelphia, PA   19123

Dear Mr. Hodges:

I enjoyed my visit with you last week, and I felt that our
conversation and exchange of information was very worthwhile.

As you suggested, I am altering one of the categories of
educational titles to fit your requirements. You will remember
that I submitted two sets of prices on two sizes. My object,
of course, was to prove how competitive we are in addition to
being capable of meeting your quality standards and filling
your production needs.

The two enclosed estimates are for typical 8 x 10 books, one
for a 320-page side-stitched book, plus glued cover, on which
we had figured a basic estimate from flat sheets and will give
you an allowance for folded signatures. I am most interested
in your reaction to these prices.

We had an opportunity to discuss a recent quotation with you
on a history book, in which we quoted you for the black and
white text on a 6½ x 9½ to be printed on our sheet perfecting
press. You then stated that a larger trim size would probably
be required.

Since the basic text printing is going to be just black and
white, you may be interested in a new pressroom development.
Within the next two months, we will have a 42 x 65-inch Crabtree
perfecting press in operation. This press will produce 64 pages
of an 8 x 10 book at one time, printing both sides simultaneously

marks and letters such as *o* and *e* with a light touch and capital letters with a heavy touch. On an electric machine, set the pressure dial two or three points lower than usually used.

To make corrections on a stencil, follow these steps:

1. Roll the stencil forward two or three lines.

2. Use the glass burnisher or a paper clip to rub over the error lightly. Do not tear the stencil.

3. Apply a *thin coat* of correction fluid and let it dry.

4. Roll the stencil back to the error with care to avoid wrinkling. Use a light touch in making the correction.

Offset Process

The offset duplicator is not used in many offices because it is quite expensive. Because of the high quality of the printing and the long runs of which such a process is capable, the master may be typed in the office and sent out for offsetting.

To prepare a master for offsetting, follow these steps:

1. Use a carbon ribbon, not a cloth one.

2. Use special offset master paper.

3. Type with an even, sharp touch.

4. Make corrections by applying a thin coating of opaque white ink.

5. Handle the master with care to avoid smudging. White out all fingerprints, smudges, and other marks that may appear on the sheet. To protect the copy, lightly coat it with a plastic spray or place a piece of tissue paper over it.

date/charles crane & company/28 broad street/newark new jersey 07162/ gentlemen/we thank you for your check, dated june 27, for $196 to cover our invoice no A4831 of may 13. (P) the discount period, during which 2 percent may be deducted on this invoice, expired on june 12; and your check was received june 30. we are crediting you with the amount of your check, which leaves an unpaid balance of $4 in your account. (P) you may feel that the small amount involved in this particular case does not warrant our action. we wish to assure you, however, that the same fair policy is pursued with all our customers, regardless of how large or how small the account may be. (P) may we request your cooperation?/yours truly/william a chester manager/reference initials

Two-Page Letters

Use plain paper of the same quality and color as the letterhead for the second and each succeeding page of a long letter. Begin typing the heading for the second and succeeding pages on the seventh line from the top of the page. This heading consists of the name of the addressee, the page number, and the date. Either of the following styles may be used for the heading:

Mr. Mark Branding 2 July 22, 19—

Mr. Mark Branding
Page 2
July 22, 19—

Begin typing the message on the third line below the last line of the heading, using the same margins as were used on the letterhead sheet.

Never divide the last word of a page. Always leave at least two lines of the paragraph at the bottom of a page and always type at least two lines at the top of a continuation page. Do not divide a paragraph of three or fewer lines. The page can be one blank line shorter or longer to compensate for a shorter paragraph. The complimentary close appearing on a continuation page should always be preceded by at least two lines of the message.

Keep the bottom margin of each page uniform except for the last page.

Section 5
BUILDING COPYING SKILLS

Type the following letters in indented style with double spacing and closed punctuation.

JOB 1

date/mr edward lowell/17 east park grove/ramsey new jersey 07446/dear mr lowell/thank you for writing to us about your account. we understand the trouble you have had in meeting your payments and are happy to cooperate by changing the due date from the 15th to the 30th of the month. (P) we hope this arrangement will prove satisfactory./sincerely yours/ barrett furniture company/credit manager/reference initials/cc mr roger collins

JOB 2

date/miss sarah greenville/23-07 hopewell avenue/south bend indiana 46624/dear miss greenville/this is just a note to tell you how pleased we were to receive your fine order of august 7. the pins are now on their way to your shop and should reach you in time for your sale on august 19. (P) a copy of our latest fall catalog has also gone out to you. we know it will prove valuable whenever you wish to place an order in the future./yours truly/harold singer/shipping department/reference initials

JOB 3

date/mr carl thomas/298 cottonwood avenue/tucson arizona 92327/dear mr thomas/it is a pleasure to tell you that our business relations with starr brothers have been very pleasant during the six years that we have been dealing with them. (P) their bills have always been paid promptly; at no time have we had to send so much as a reminder. we wish that all of our customers were as prompt with their payments as starr brothers. (P) incidentally, we understand that a branch store is now being built in the suburb of greenville./sincerely yours/wentward paper products/jacob jones/ reference initials

JOB 4

date/baker brothers inc/26 market street/philadelphia pa 19103/gentlemen/because of the rising cost of raw materials, we are obliged to increase the prices of our leather products. the higher prices will apply to all orders received on or after march 1. (P) this advance notice is being sent to you so that you may take advantage of the opportunity to save money. we suggest that you place your order while the current lower prices are still in effect. (P) a large volume of business will, no doubt, reach us before the end of next month; and there may be a delay in some of our deliveries. we therefore urge you to determine your requirements within the next ten days and let us fill your needs at once/yours truly/ronald barnes president/ reference initials

PREPARATORY DRILLS

Set margins for a 70-space line. Indent paragraphs 5 spaces. The first 16 — 86. sentence in each group is alphabetic; the second, a number and symbol review; the third, a fluency drill; and the fourth, a paragraph of unarranged copy.

Words

```
....1....2....3....4....5....6....7....8....9....10....11....12
```

1a A squad of sixty men braved the fury of the blaze to rescue
    three injured women on the jagged peak.

1b Lee & Harts' check #92754 for $1,103.68 is lost!

1c Not one of us was on time for the class meeting this morning.

1d   Our club wants to obtain enough cash to send six members   12
    of our class to Mexico and Brazil for the big games being held   25
    next month. We realized from the very beginning that we can-   38
    not collect so vast a sum unless each citizen in town gives   50
    us a hand. May we count on receiving your check soon?   62

2a The object of my talk will be to explain that new zoning laws
    have been requested by our merchants.

2b Model #2498 sold by Hyde & Sons costs $10,376.50. *Tono.*

2c Did the teacher request her students to make out the reports?

2d   I am writing this letter to thank you for the kindness   12
    you showed our agent when he visited your firm last week.   24
    The order you gave him will be filled in a few days, and the   36
    shipment should reach you no later than July 18. May I take   49
    this opportunity to assure you that we will always do what-   61
    ever we can to give you immediate service.   70

3a The lazy boy worked diligently because he expected me to give
    him a quart jar of fresh milk.

3b They quoted prices as follows: Lots of 100 @ 75¢; 500, 70¢. ⟵

3c Please quote us the price of the heating unit you mentioned.

3d   It is with great pride that we send this letter announcing   13
    our big sale of winter coats and suits. This is the best time   26
    to take care of your needs for the cold months ahead, but you   38
    must act at once because we cannot guarantee how long our stock   51
    is going to last. Once the public learns of the values to be   64
    found in our store, we are sure our entire line will quickly   76
    disappear.   79

4a Just before dawn, an extremely thick haze spread quickly over
    the peacefully sleeping village.
    ....1....2....3....4....5....6....7....8....9....10....11....12
```
```

PORTER CABLE
•
BLACK AND DECKER
•
STANLEY-DEWALT

HOUSEHOLD APPLIANCES

BLAKELY HARDWARE COMPANY

Starr & Borden Avenues
•
Albany, New York 12200
•
Phone 764-2200

PAINTS — WALLPAPER

August 10, 19__.

Mr. George Stockholm,
　Barrow Novelty Company,
　　62 Pleasant Viceo Avenue,
　　　Lima, OH　45802.

Dear Mr. Stockholm:

　　We are happy to respond to your request for literature about our products.　Our latest catalog and price list will be sent to you in a few days.

　　May we ask a favor?　Would you be good enough to furnish us with the names of others in your organization who might be interested in receiving our catalog.

　　Thank you for your cooperation.

　　　　　　　　　　　　Sincerely,

　　　　　　　　　　　　Thomas J. Kreff.

TJK:ad

4 b   The asterisk (*) in paragraph 9 referred to a footnote.

4 c   The manager of the store decided to refund the entire price.

4 d   As a stamp collector, you know that there is no limit   12
to the amount of money that can be spent on this type of hobby.   25
On the whole, however, it is impossible for an average person   38
to attempt to keep up with the many hundreds of stamps that   50
are minted every year; and the person who buys wisely is the   63
one who will get the most joy out of stamp collecting. If   75
you spend only a small sum yearly on your stamp album, and   87
you want to know how you can do it wisely, we shall be happy   99
to supply you with a copy of a fine pamphlet that contains   111
many useful hints designed to improve your collection.   122

5 a   Jill was amazed at the sight of so many exquisite birds provided
by the city for the zoo in the park.

5 b   The seating capacity of Room 214 was 63 students.

5 c   We looked out of the window and saw that it snowed last night.

5 d   This brief note is being written to tell you that we have   13
again contacted our factory and have been told that they will   26
be unable to deliver the ebony bridge set and bench you ordered   39
a week ago for about five months. We hoped we would be able   51
to obtain these pieces by December at the latest, but it is   63
obvious that production is lagging very far behind. We do   75
not doubt you are probably unhappy over the long delay, and   87
we are exceedingly sorry we cannot give you better delivery   99
service.   101

6 a   Many express trains that were bound for the city whizzed down
the tracks along the jagged bank of the quiet river.

6 b   The interest at 5% amounted to $150 at maturity.

6 c   We stood on the pier and waved our hats as the liner sailed.

6 d   We regret the fact that your staff cannot be present for   13
the meeting we are holding at the end of August. We called   25
this meeting because we are worried about sales this summer   37
and are sure that we must act quickly or suffer greater losses   50
this winter. Over a hundred stores have decreased the size   62
of their orders as a result of this decline. Surely these   74
conditions suggest how important our meeting is for anyone   86
interested in higher sales.   92

7 a   The audience enjoyed the meeting, but some of them were puzzled
by the queer views expounded by the speaker.

....1....2....3....4....5....6....7....8....9....10....11....12

and have consistently found them able to cut the grass on our 18-hole golf course in one-half the time it took with our former mower." (P) try a west-chrome mower—then make up your mind. i'm sure you will be delighted, too./lawrence ballard sales manager/reference initials

JOB 4

date/mr george a stockholm/bentley high school/danbury ct 06811/modern dictation/we have not heard from you, mr stockholm, and we are wondering whether you received the copy of modern dictation that we sent you at your request several weeks ago. please drop us a line if you did not receive it. (P) if you did receive your copy, we hope that you have had a chance to give it careful examination. the preface explains the purpose underlying the planning of each division and makes some excellent suggestions for the successful use of the book. (P) a teacher from springfield has been using this book for almost six months and has the following to report: "modern dictation should be placed in the hands of every advanced pupil and used for daily homework and classroom drill. it increases the efficiency of the commercial department by helping to develop even more shorthand writers of the highest type. this is the type of book i have wanted to use in my classroom for many years." (P) if you will mail your order now, you can begin the fall term with the feeling that your dictation troubles are over./ s.g. lyons sales manager/reference initials

JOB 5

date/miss mary hill/54 state street/troy new york 12181/free gift/it has always been the policy of this bank to encourage systematic thrift, miss hill. in furthering this idea, we are introducing a new dime carrier, which we should like you to try. (P) it may seem a small matter to put in only a dime a day, but the power of dimes is almost beyond belief. dimes grow to dollars before you realize it. the woolworth building was built with dimes!! (P) what we should like to have you do is to start the foundation of a woolworth building and watch it grow. if you will return the enclosed card, we will send a carrier to you at once./joseph h. norris president/reference initials

Indented Style Letter

The indented style letter is a conservative style that may be single or double spaced. Although mixed punctuation may be used, this letter style is often typed with closed punctuation. The inside address, paragraphs, and closing lines are indented.

This style is not used extensively today.

....1....2....3....4....5....6...,7....8....9....10....11....12 Words

7b The sales tax is 5¢. It may be 6½¢ next year.

7c A meeting was held to discuss the merits of the proposed plan.

7d   We were glad to have your opinion of our new policy and   12
will certainly give serious thought to the excellent ideas   24
you put forth. As you are no doubt aware, we talked with   36
many buyers before we drew up this plan, and we feel that   48
this decision will result in the opening of a new and exclusive 61
market for our silk suits. We are going to issue a report   73
covering the points discussed last week, and we hope you will   86
read it with great interest.   92

8a They judged it very unwise to minimize the danger of his plight
because he knew what to expect.

8b The window envelope measures 6 3/4 inches by 3 1/2 inches.

8c We talked about the picnic that our club is planning to have.

8d   I think you will be glad to know that we now have in   12
stock the type of oak bench for which you asked when you came   25
to our shop last week. It is sold as part of a set; but if   37
you would like just the one piece, I feel sure we can get it   49
for you. Will you please call our store by the end of this   61
week so that we will know if you wish to have it.   72

9a Jack was extremely awkward on the stage, but he fought back
the impulsive urge to quit.

9b Never use the cent sign (¢) nor the percent sign (%) for "In
care of."

9c Her father said that the bridge over the river was not safe.

9d   Once you know what you can do and what type of work you   12
want, it is a good idea to let your friends know of your plans. 25
Talk with them and let them help you if they can. You will   37
find that most of them will be glad to help you to find the   49
kind of job that will make you happy.   57

10a I know that the junior squad was expected to give a new horizontal
bar for the school gym.

10b The diagonal mark (/) is sometimes used to separate reference
initials in a letter; as, AGS/BLR.

10c Throughout the whole evening, the old dog sat near his master.

....1....2....3....4....5....6....7....8....9....10....11....12

BUILDING COPYING SKILLS   78

Type the following letters in the simplified style estimating the number of words in each letter using open punctuation.

JOB 1

date/ mr robert foster president/ingham trust company/40 north michigan avenue/lansing michigan 48774/cable services/we are delighted to comply with your request for monthly cable service, mr foster. (P) your cable name will be INGTRUSTCO, and the address will be as listed above. you may begin using the service on monday, september 4. (P) the enclosed list of rates is the most recent used throughout the world. full instructions on how to place calls are also included. should you need any additional information or advice, please call me. our services are at your complete disposal. (P) we are certain, mr foster, that you will find this service convenient and worthwhile/douglas phillips account manager/reference initials/enclosures (2)

JOB 2

date/mr herman lynch/motor express company/910 weber avenue/ogden ut 84193/training conference/we should like to invite your staff, mr lynch, to our training conference. it will be held at the statler hilton on november 3 and 4. (P) all aspects of a secretary's many duties will be thoroughly covered. in addition there will be direct participation in workshops on human relations and office supervision. our methods have been tested and proved. (P) do you have people in your organization, mr lynch, whom you would like to groom for executive or supervisory positions? our training conference will do it for you./david burns training director/reference initials/a postage-paid reply card is enclosed for your convenience in registering

JOB 3

date/mr l gregory/1180 lester place/ames ia 50010/beekman catalog/on june 23 we received a request from you, mr gregory, for a catalog describing our products. that catalog was sent at once, and i hope you have had time to examine it thoroughly. if you have, then you no doubt noticed that our stock is complete and our prices are the lowest you will find anywhere. as for quality, i know of no company whose products can equal ours in material and workmanship. (P) just listen to what one of our dealers said in a recent letter: "i have been ordering supplies from westchrome for over 18 years, and i have never had occasion to complain about the quality of their tools or the service they render." (P) another delighted customer writes: "your lawn mowers are tops! we have been using them at our country club

10 d
It is a sad fact that there are many young boys and girls 13
leaving school each year who do not know where or how to look 26
for a job. Some of them may have spent a long time building 38
the skills needed to fit them for a job, but they had never 50
learned how to sell those skills to the world. Do not let 62
this happen to you. When the day comes that you are ready to 75
look for a job, you should be armed with a plan of action 87
that will make your job hunt an easy and happy event. 98

11 a
Many were dazzled by the sight of the exquisitely fine jewels
which sparkled on the shelves.

11 b
I saw the advertisement in the Thursday's Post on page 27.

11 c
Ask the bank clerk also to fill in every item on the paper.

11 d
The first step you should take before you go out to look 13
for a job is to make up your mind as to the type of job you 25
wish to find. Of course, what you want to do must depend on 37
what you are able to do, and you should not set your sights 49
on any job for which you do not have the skill. True, you 61
might be able to land the job; but you will find that you 73
will not be able to hold it for very long. 82

12 a
They wanted the quartet to begin their evening program by
harmonizing ballads from the back country.

12 b
America--the bastion of democracy--has an obligation to all
human beings.

12 c
You may remain with my cousin until I return from the country.

12 d
We think we have found the type of house for which you 12
and your wife have been hunting for the past two months. It 24
is a fine house with a great deal of land around it, and we 36
feel that it would be a very good buy for you. The man who 48
now owns it is ready to make a quick sale, and it would be 60
a good idea for you to drive out to see it before the end of 72
this week. If you call our office, we will give you the name 85
of the owner and tell you the best road to use in order to 107
reach the house. 111

13 a
Dazed and exhausted by his victory, the prize fighter came
from the ring and walked quickly through the jostling crowd.

13 b
We want no ifs, ands, nor buts.

13 c
Will you check each carton of the shipment as soon as you can?

....1....2....3....4....5....6....7....8....9....10....11....12

ARMA RUBBER COMPANY

administrative management AMS simplified style

15   July 27, 19--

16
17
18
19
20   Mr. Fred Martin
21   736 Euclid Avenue
22   Cleveland, OH   43551
23
24
25   PURCHASE AGREEMENT
26
27
28   It was a pleasure, Mr. Martin, to speak to you today.
29
30   As we discussed, I am sending you an outline of our
31   new purchase agreement form as well as some up-to-
32   date literature.
33
34   You will notice that there are two types of purchase
35   agreements enclosed.   One is the noncancelable
36   agreement and the other is the agreement that includes
37   the 10 percent down payment.
38
39   These contracts supersede the ones that you are
40   presently using, Mr. Martin.
41
42
43
44
45   FREDRIC WALDMAN, MANAGER
46
47   st
48   Enclosures
49
50
51
52
53
54
55

13 d
　　　　Our firm is proud of the fact that agents in every part　12
of the state have been writing to tell us that sales are now　24
higher than ever before and will no doubt rise even higher　36
by the end of this year.　To tell the truth, we were quite　48
sure that this would occur.　We knew that if we gave people　56
the kind of motor they wanted, they would rush to buy it　68
from our many dealers.　The sales that are made each day of　80
the week show how right we were.　87

14 a
After a very exciting day, the boy came home, took out a jigsaw
puzzle, and played quietly until bedtime.

14 b
The totals are 3,728; 2,142,607; and 42,429.

14 c
I shall certainly thank the man when I go into town on Friday.

14 d
　　　　Do you ever think about the type of work you would like　12
to do when you leave school?　Have you thought about the field　25
you wish to enter?　To be able to make a wise choice, you　37
should first know what talents you have and where these talents　50
can best be used.　In other words, to be happy with a job, you　63
must choose one that suits your ability.　82

15 a
The citizens requested the government official to make the
topic of Social Security the subject of his next talk.

15 b
I paid $453.70 for a 12 by 15 Broadloom rug for our home.

15 c
If you wish, they will gladly inform you of my decision now.

15 d
　　　　This note is to tell you how sorry I am that I will not　12
be able to come to the dinner that our club is holding this　24
month.　I have attended these dinners for many years, and I　36
was looking forward to this one.　However, my firm is opening　49
another branch store next week; and I have been chosen to take　62
charge of that store for about three months.　72

16 a
After having heard the lawyer's eloquent plea, the jury retired
to a back room to analyze the perplexing case.

16 b
The chairman shouted, "Order! Order in the house!"

16 c
The sky had grown dark when the children ran from the beach.

16 d
　　　　There is a slight chance that I will be able to come back　13
to town for the dinner, but I cannot be sure until I go to the　26
branch store to see what must be done.　Should I find I am able　49
to do so, I shall take the evening off and drive in for the　61
dinner.　63

17 a
Queen Elizabeth, wearing her famous jewels, went very slowly
to the ship and extended her hand to the captain.
....1....2....3....4....5....6....7....8....9....10....11....12

date/airmail/mr roger adams/talbout & adams/64 anthracite building/ harrisburg pa 15908/dear mr adams/you wrote to us some time ago to request the exclusive sales agency for our products in the city of harrisburg. as we wrote you at that time, we had already committed ourselves to another dealer. (P) however, things have not worked out well; and we have found the arrangement unsatisfactory. we need a dealer who will be aggressive in actively promoting our products. the franchise will be exclusively his, and he would have complete freedom as to local policy and prices. (P) are you still interested? if so, contact us at once and we will make the arrangements./very truly yours/national oil company/theodore barnes/ reference intials

JOB 5

date/mr otto c simon/615 west main street/pittsburgh pa 15096/ dear mr simon/re policy no 13-471-293a/we wish to thank you for the patience you have shown in waiting for our agent to get to your property to assess the damage done by the flood on may 23. this disaster created more claims than any other flood in insurance history. as a result, it was impossible to get to all of the homes involved within the usual time required for inspection. (P) we must ask you to be patient just a little longer. our agent should reach your area by the end of next week; and once he has assessed the damage, your claim will be processed quickly. (P) in order to facilitate his task, will you please fill out the enclosed damage form and return it to us in the post-paid envelope. (P) again, thank you./sincerely yours/ mutual insurance company/thomas many/claims division/reference initials /enclosures (2)

AMS Simplified Style Letter

The AMS simplified letter is a variation of the full-block style letter that is recommended by the Administrative Management Society.

This letter uses the block style and open punctuation, but the salutation and complimentary close are omitted. A subject line is always included and is typed in solid caps a triple space below the inside address. A triple space separates the subject line from the body of the letter. The word *subject* may be omitted.

The writer's name and title are typed in solid caps and this line is preceded by at least four blank lines and is followed by a double space.

In the reference initials line, only the typist's initials are used. They are typed a double space below the writer's name and title.

Note that the addressee's name is used at least once in the body of the letter to maintain a friendly tone in what might be considered a cold letter.

This style has not been popular except among those who consider efficiency especially important.

17 b   The new office building will be 50 stories high.

17 c   Ten weary men fell asleep in the back of the broken army truck.

17 d   As you are aware, we regard you as a friend, and you are   13
       looked upon as a leader in our trade. For this reason, we   25
       advise you to join us in July when we start our pull for   37
       increased sales of our nylon bags. It is a fact that we   49
       averaged over a million sales last July, but in my opinion,   61
       I expect a million extra sales when you join with us.   72

18 a   The six squads of weary men climbed into the jeeps and drove
       back to camp through the freezing rain.

18 b   I know--or should I say, I feel--that you will do well.

18 c   Ask the chairman to stop at my desk on his way to the office.

18 d   Ask them to check to see if the silk suit I ordered is   12
       on the truck. If it is not, I will call the shop and speak   24
       to the clerk who said it would reach me in time for the dance   37
       given by the country club.   43

19 a   The woman quickly sealed the five dozen glass jars of straw-
       berry preserves with wax.

19 b   The present work force of 720 men will be increased to 851.

19 c   It is the duty of a man to do me a good turn, and he will if
       he can.

19 d   Ruth hurt her foot while jumping from the bar in the gym.   13
       She would not have been hurt in this manner if someone had not   26
       moved the huge rubber mats that should have been left on the   39
       floor under the bars.   54

20 a   The foreman was expecting delivery of benzene and liquid glue
       by the first week in January.

20 b   If a man has freedom enough to live healthy . . . he has enough.
       --Goethe

20 c   Your aim is to keep an even typing rate in all practice.

20 d   If you wish to know the joy of being a truly expert typist,   13
       it is vital for you to seize every chance to develop proper   25
       techniques and good work habits. Doing this will insure your   37
       success.   39

21 a   Sixty zebras were brought back by the museum's well-equipped
       expedition into the African jungle.

       ....1....2....3....4....5....6....7....8....9....10....11....12

Type the following letters in full-block style with open punctuation.

JOB 1

date/mr. frederick parks/smith enterprises inc/room 221/jackson building /denver colorado 76924/gentlemen/subject july conference/thank you for your invitation to the coming conference. the outline was very interesting, and i am sure that several members of our organization will wish to attend. we will send you the exact number just as soon as our plans are completed. (P) you are most welcome to a full report on our safety procedures at the plant for use at the conference. it will be sent out to you within the next few days. as you will see when you read this report, our improved safety standards have greatly lessened our accident rate. this has not only improved worker morale but has also lowered our insurance rates. (P) if you have any questions, please feel free to contact me./very truly yours/brown manufacturing company/robert wells/general manager/reference initials

done but to be redone.

JOB 2

only a space between initials

date/william t. barton m d/medical arts building/main street and worth avenue/salem oregon 97302/my dear dr barton/may i thank you for your prompt reply to my request for information about the medical record for mr george hall, who was injured in our plant on december 15. as i explained, such information was necessary to insure that mr hall is assigned to tasks that will not be detrimental to his complete recovery. (P) i understand that he will be examined periodically by you during the next two or three months. may i ask that you keep me informed about his physical condition. (P) i will see to it that mr hall is kept on light duty until i have been advised otherwise by you./sincerely yours/arthur watkins/reference initials/cc mr rawlins

JOB 3

date/mr paul t jones manager/mcneill & johnson inc/34 tilden street/ milwaukee wi 53221/dear mr jones/time passes so quickly that you may not realize it is now three months since we first billed you for the supplies you purchased from us in november. we wrote to you in december and january. we have waited patiently for a check from you, but we have had neither a payment nor an explanation as to why you have delayed settling this account. (P) you can surely understand that it is not possible for us to carry this account indefinitely, and we must therefore insist that you take care of this matter by the end of the month at the latest. if we do not receive your check by that time, we shall be forced to place the matter in the hands of our collection agency./very truly yours/vincent 1. moore/accounting department/reference initials/cc robert allbright

21 b   The #10 envelope measures 9½ by 4¼ inches.

21 c   We assure you that we are happy with what he did.

21 d   Few of the things that come to the man who waits are the   13
        things he has been looking for. The more work a man has to   25
        do, the more he is able to accomplish. He learns to make every   38
        moment count. A man should never be afraid to admit that he   50
        has been in the wrong.   55

22 a   Dazed and frightened, the quivering boys limped to join the
        crowd of shrieking citizens.

22 b   "This job," he said, "must be improved upon."

22 c   Will you please write a full report of this fire.

22 d   There is nothing more gratifying than self-approval.   12
        You may cheat others, but you cannot cheat yourself. Many   24
        of those who praise you might condemn you if they knew you   36
        as you know yourself.   41

23 a   The red fox jumped over the wall as the very excited man came
        into view brandishing a shotgun.

23 b   Carbon copies are easier to read if you type 1/4 and 1/2 rather
        than ¼ and ½.

23 c   I was happy to hear that he did the work so well.

23 d   There is a difference between talent and genius. Talent   13
        does what it can; genius does what it must. It is doing that   26
        little bit more that makes the difference.   35

24 a   The impoverished quartet finally signed a contract to play
        with the newly organized jazz band.

24 b   Washington's "Farewell Address" was his greatest speech.

24 c   Keep your desk clear of papers and books you do not need.

24 d   The ability to write a good business letter is a valuable   13
        asset. Placing the correct estimate on the power of letter   25
        writing is a big step toward business success. To develop   37
        this ability: write important letters by hand before dictating, 50
        evaluate incoming correspondence, study grammar, and use extreme 63
        care in every letter you write.   70

25 a   From the back porch, I could see the extremely lovely sight
        of the yellow jonquils swaying in the morning breeze.

25 b   Address the letter to Mrs. William Elton, 490 Park Avenue,
        New York, New York 10015.
        ....1....2....3....4....5....6....7....8....9....10....11....12

Phone 452-4100

Chambers-Sanderson Company

450 Wabash Ave., Chicago, Illinois 60600

April 21, 19__

Mr. Thomas Dumas
Madison Furniture Company
879 South Peters Street
New Orleans, Louisiana   70130

Dear Mr. Dumas:

SUBJECT: Executive Conference Desk

We are writing in response to your letter of March
10 concerning the Executive Conference Desk in which
you expressed an interest.

The price of this desk is $295 with a 10 percent
discount for payment in full within ten days of
delivery.

We are sorry we do not have a color photograph of
the desk, but the enclosed photograph shows the details.
Note that the direction of the grain runs from side
to side and thus conforms to the other pieces you
now have in your conference room.

Current delivery on the desk is approximately eight
to ten weeks.

Sincerely yours,

Martin Biggs, Sales Manager

TSW
Enclosure

```
....1....2....3....4....5....6....7....8....9....10....11....12
```
Words

25 c   It will take at least two days for you to get it.

25 d   Start the day with a smile and be a friend to everyone.   13
No one likes a grouch. Be kind to people if you would have   25
them be kind to you. Treat others as you would wish to be   37
treated.   39

26 a   The officer quizzed the taxi driver who, in attempting to avoid
injuring the boy, had driven his cab on the sidewalk.

26 b   Walter's company now has 73 outlets, located in 38 cities.

26 c   Set a goal of at least one additional word a day.

26 d   Hotels are operated on one of two plans--the American   12
plan or the European plan. The American plan includes the   24
cost of meals while the European plan does not. Most hotels   36
in cities follow the European plan. Resort hotels, however,   48
often follow the American plan.   55

27 a   The junior executive requested an itemized account of all
expenses during the trip from New York to Baltimore.

27 b   Refer to pages 29, 45, and 73 in our catalog.

27 c   This is the usual form, and he should sign it at once.

27 d   A new five-year passport law went into effect in August   12
1968. Renewals are abolished, subsequent passports may be   24
obtained by mail, and the fees are changed.   33

28 a   The very dazed explorer, wandering by chance in the quiet
jungle, found tusks of many elephants--their burial ground.

28 b   The C.O.D. shipment was delivered at 2 p.m.

28 c   I am glad to learn that the bill has been paid.

28 d   Glass is made by heating sand with other substances such   13
as soda, salt, and potash. The molten mass may be rolled or   25
formed into desired shapes as it cools. It can even be drawn   38
into long threads.   42

29 a   Sixty blazing fires were started by the earthquake that completely ruined the Javenese city. Hundreds were injured.

29 b   The airlines use codes for cities; for example, ORD, LAX, and
NYC.

29 c   Ask them how long it will take to complete the work.

```
....1....2....3....4....5....6....7....8....9....10....11....12
```

Lincoln Sport Shop
Attention: Mr. John Parker, Jr.
529 Magnolia Street
Royal Oak, Michigan 48073
Gentlemen:

Thank you very much for the letter in which you expressed an interest in handling our line of sporting equipment. It will be a pleasure to add your name to our fast-growing list of satisfied dealers in this part of the country.

Mr. Robert Moore, our agent in your area, has been asked to stop in to see you on his next trip to your city.

Cordially yours,

Thomas Seamon

cc Martin Crake

Full-Block Style Letter

The full-block style is efficient because it requires fewer machine adjustments, resulting in the saving of time for the typist. The date, inside address, salutation, paragraphs, and closing lines all begin at the left margin. It is customary, although not necessary, to use open punctuation with this style of letter.

29 d   There are six principal organs of the UN: the General   12
Assembly, the Security Council, the Economic and Social Council,   25
the Trusteeship Council, the International Court of Justice,   37
and the Secretariat. The official languages in all except the   50
International Court of Justice are Chinese, English, French,   62
Russian, and Spanish.   67

30 a   Jack, in a quiet voice said, "By fighting a war, man may well
expect to destroy his civilization."

30 b   Have you ever seen the painting "The Blue Boy"?

30 c   You will find your work easy if you really like to do it.

30 d   Modern history shows a shift from crude to more sophis-   12
ticated kinds of money. Within countries, the change has been   25
from copper, gold, and silver coins to paper bank notes and   37
checks. Within the international monetary system, the trend   49
has been to rely less upon gold and more upon deliberately   61
created credit among nations.   67

31 a   When I realized that my fur jacket was exceptionally tight
and quite beyond repair, I gave it to her.

31 b   Use the quotation (") for inches: 12", 25", 60".

31 c   He must sign the paper in the presence of a notary.

31 d   New words and phrases and new meanings for older, estab-   13
lished terms constantly acquire widespread usage. When they   25
pass the test of time, they are entered in the dictionaries.   37
Many, however, are merely a passing vogue.   46

32 a   The angry boy jumped up and seized his ax when he saw the
squealing pigs chewing the vegetables in back of the house.

32 b   Flight 315 leaves at 8:45 a.m.; Flight 79, at 8:55 a.m.

32 c   Some bills for small amounts may be paid more easily by check.

32 d   The U.S. Post Office Department is the largest single   12
business organization in the world. It conducts the greatest   25
communications system ever known to man. For example, business   38
mail represents roughly 80 percent of its total mail volume.   50

33 a   Just when her bookkeeping average was extremely high, my friend,
Hazel, was forced to quit school.

33 b   Legal-size paper is 14 inches long; it has 84 writing lines
rather than 66.

....1....2....3....4....5....6....7....8....9....10....11....12

Estimate the length of the letters in the following jobs and type each letter in the modified-block style with indented paragraphs and with mixed punctuation.

JOB 1

date/mr. leroy b. miller/roger goodwin enterprises/4830 mcdonald street/ canton OH 44706/dear mr miller/subject special summer offer/this is the time of the year when the work in our shop comes almost to a standstill, and we become so desperate to provide work for our men that we are willing to reduce our prices in order to bring in some extra business. (P) therefore, if you will place your printing order within the next 30 days, we will give you an opportunity to receive a 15 percent discount on all letterheads envelopes and business forms. (P) if you are interested in taking advantage of this offer, simply send us the enclosed order form before july 19./cordially yours/freeman-enson lithographers, inc./assistant sales manager/reference initials/enc

JOB 2

date/registered/mr. william handy/martin hotel/denver, colorado 80202/ dear bill/i am enclosing a special report that contains a detailed study of the problem we have had in the denver area. if you will go over it carefully, you will begin to see why we sent you out there and what needs to be done. (P) paul manning of acme sales is one of the best contacts you could make. i know he will gladly give you whatever help you need. (P) i'll call you on wednesday at 3:30./sincerely/h. conlon/reference initials/enclosure /ps needless to say, the report i am sending should not be shown to anyone outside our organization.

JOB 3

date/airmail/teenage fashions/one north 16 avenue/austin texas 78741/ attention mr 1 thomas/gentlemen/on september 1 we sent you an order for goods which should have reached us by this time. (P) what is the reason for the delay in this shipment? this is the first time in our experience that orders from your company have been delayed. (P) we need these goods for a special sale that we are having at the end of the month; and if we do not receive them in a few days, we shall be forced to cancel our order./ yours truly/smith, king & company/manager/reference initials

```
....1....2....3....4....5....6....7....8....9....10....11....12    Words
```

33 c Dates are one of the most important features on all business papers.

33 d
```
        Two weeks ago, at your request, we forwarded an itemized     13
statement of your account showing the balance due.  We have had      26
no word from you since.  We wish it were within our power to         38
extend the date of payment, but it is the policy of this company     51
not to relax its rules in such matters.  We must therefore urge      64
you to pay the balance at once.  We realize the difficulties you     77
have encountered, but we feel that we have been quite fair in        90
allowing you sixty days in which to make payment.  We are ex-        103
tremely sorry that we cannot give you the extra time you             115
requested.                                                           118
```

34 a At her job the lazy girl was required to check all tax forms and then give them to her employer for signature.

34 b This offer (and it is our final offer) is too good to be refused.

34 c It is a steady, even, errorless rate of speed that counts.

34 d
```
        As requested in your letter, we are enclosing a folder       12
giving the rates at our hotel for the months of June and July.       25
Now that summer is coming, many people are beginning to make         37
plans to leave the city for weekends and vacations.  We expect       50
that the rooms which are now available will be quickly rented.       63
We know that you will like it here.  Every room was designed         75
and equipped by experts to insure that you will be comfortable       88
during your stay.  The six experienced cooks in our kitchen          100
specialize in preparing food that will certainly please and          112
delight you. Make your reservations in advance.                      122
```

35 a Six years of valuable experience should qualify him to judge whether Jack deserves the prize.

35 b Capitalize and center this heading: TABULATION.

35 c When stapling a letter and its answer together, always put the answer on top.

35 d
```
        West Germany has several reconditioning centers where tens   13
of thousands of workers are reconditioned during periods of          25
four to six weeks.  Workers selected are prone to heart disease.     39
These centers are operated by insurance companies and large          51
industrial enterprises.                                              56
```

36 a A bronze plaque was given to the jockey to commemorate the extremely fine record he had established.

36 b He swam in the 50-, 100-, and 220-yard free-style races.

36 c It is often necessary to use a backing sheet to produce clear carbon copies.
```
....1....2....3....4....5....6....7....8....9....10....11....12
```

SMITH, KING & COMPANY

January 6, 19__

Niagara Prospect Company
105 32d Street
Niagara Falls, NY   14305

Attention: Mr. Norman Chambers

Gentlemen:

SUBJECT: Care of typewriters

I am glad to learn that the trouble you have
had with your new machines has been corrected and
that they are now in good working order.

May I suggest that you consider our annual
maintenance service. This contract not only covers
emergency calls but also provides for periodic
inspection by one of our factory-trained men, who
will clean and oil your machines and maintain them
in tiptop condition.

A booklet describing this plan is enclosed.
If you have any questions after reading it, please
feel free to call.

Sincerely yours,

SMITH, KING & COMPANY

L. R. Barnum, President

LRB:ad
Enclosure

36 d   All articles acquired abroad and in your possession at   12
the time of your return must be declared to U.S. customs, either   25
orally or in writing. Declaration lists are distributed on   37
planes and ships and should be prepared in advance. Wearing   49
or using an article acquired abroad does not exempt it from   61
duty.   63

37 a A sly brown fox quickly jumped over the lazy dog.

37 b A burning meteor is called a "shooting star" or "falling star."

37 c In modern business practice very few numbers are written out.

37 d   Pewter is a metal that has always led a double life. It   13
is a tin alloy, but its color and texture are appealing. It   25
was used for decorative tableware in the 18th and early 19th   37
centuries.   50

38 a The public was amazed to view the quickness and dexterity of
the juggler.

38 b "To be or not to be . . . "--Shakespeare.

38 c Two-letter abbreviations of state names are authorized for
use with ZIP codes only.

38 d   Stamp values are based on an internationally established   13
market and are as carefully determined as that of any blue-   25
chip stock listed on a securities exchange. Owners of good   37
collections have found themselves in command of a readily   49
convertible commodity when currency, stocks, and bonds have   61
been wiped out by inflation.   67

39 a A quart jar of oil mixed with good zinc oxide makes a very
bright paint.

39 b The dollar sign ($) should appear only at the beginning of
each column and before the total.

39 c They can show all of the items during the annual sale.

39 d   During the last week of November, our store is going to   12
move from its present location on Main Street to Broadway.   24
For this reason, we are going to hold our annual leather and   37
luggage sale at an early date. We are, therefore, sending you   50
this invitation to inspect our stock of beautiful traveling   62
bags. Every item in our large department is going to be dras-   75
tically reduced, and we know that you will be able to obtain   87
valuable leather pieces at bargain rates. We want our charge-   100
account customers to have first choice, so come in soon.   112

....1....2....3....4....5....6....7....8....9....10....11....12

POSTSCRIPTS

A postscript is a sentence or paragraph added at the end of a letter. It can be very effective when it is used to emphasize an important idea. Avoid using the postscript to express an afterthought.

Start the postscript a double space below whatever notation was typed last. If the paragraphs of the letter are indented, indent the postscript; otherwise begin it at the left margin.

PS: or *P.S.* is used before the first word of the postscript.

```
TRS/vmj
Enclosure

PS:  Treat the postscript in the same way that any other
paragraph is treated, except that it is preceded by
PS: or P.S.
```

MAILING NOTATION

Type any mailing notation, such as *SPECIAL DELIVERY*, on the second line below the date, starting it at the same point as the date. This is a reminder for the secretary or typist to type the notation on the envelope and to see that additional postage is affixed. It may also be needed for future reference.

PERSONAL NOTATION

When a personal notation is needed, type it in solid caps three lines above the inside address. Such notations might be *CONFIDENTIAL* or *PERSONAL*.

REFERENCE LINE

If a firm files letters numerically, there is usually a reference line printed on the letterhead for the reference number. If no reference line is printed, type the file number four spaces below the date line. This line need not be underscored nor need it be typed in solid caps.

Modified-Block Style Letter with Indented Paragraphs

A semiblocked letter is simply a modified-block letter with the paragraphs indented. The following illustration is typed with five-space indentions, but it is not uncommon to indent ten or even more spaces. The letter may be single or double spaced.

As in the modified-block style, the date and closing lines begin either at the center of the page or at the right margin.

```
....1....2....3....4....5....6....7....8....9....10....11....12    Words
```

40 a Whenever the big black fox jumped, the squirrel gazed very
suspiciously.

40 b The meeting will be held Saturday, March 11, at 10 a.m.

40 c This is a good day for her to go to the city to see a show.

40 d
```
      Our records indicate the fact that we have not received     12
an order from your company in recent months.  Have you had        24
cause to find fault with our stock or our service?  If such       36
is the case, I would consider it a favor if you would be kind     49
enough to mail a note to me informing me what we have done to     62
displease you.  I am sure that whatever the difficulty might      74
be, it can be ironed out promptly.  Because we have always        86
looked on you as one of our most valuable customers, I hope       108
to have word from you within a very short time.                   118
....1....2....3....4....5....6....7....8....9....10....11....12
```

PUNCTUATION DRILLS

Spacing

1. Two spaces follow the period, question mark, and exclamation mark at the
end of a sentence.
2. Two spaces follow a colon when it is used as a mark of punctuation.
3. One space follows the comma and semicolon.
4. One space follows a period at the end of an abbreviation such as Mr. T.
Small; no space follows a period within an abbreviation such as U.S.

*Set margins for a 70-space line. Indent paragraphs 5 spaces. Strike the
space bar with a sharp stroke, releasing it immediately.*

```
....1....2....3....4....5....6....7....8....9....10....11....12
```

1   No more; until tomorrow; as of now; please wait; if not;
2   Did you? May we? Can they tell? Is it here? Are they not?
3   This list: the following: as given: Here are all the facts:

4   She is ill. Do not yell. She can call. See the white sail.
5   They fail. Your doll. Old mill. Their mail. Mr. T. Small.
6   you look, can talk, lack, take back, deep dark, break, brick,
7   Be still! Yes, it is. No, not me. Oh, I know! True, I am.

8   Here is the bill. It is hers. Give it to me. It is not mine.
9   Ask her for it. Please do it now. This is the one.

10 Give me the book, pen, and the ink. I sold the balls to Mary,
Jane, and Jack; of course, they all paid for them.

11 All work, so they say, is bad. At last, we are at home. Yes,
I have it. She bought yellow, black, and green paint.

```
....1....2....3....4....5....6....7....8....9....10....11....12
```

BUILDING COPYING SKILLS   87

ENCLOSURE NOTATION

If any item is to be enclosed in the envelope with the letter, indicate this by using an enclosure notation. The purpose of this notation is to remind the person who puts the letter into the envelope to insert the enclosures too. It also aids the person who opens the envelope by reminding him to look for the enclosures.

The older practice is to double space after the reference initials before typing the enclosure notation. The common practice today is to place the enclosure notation at the left margin on the line below the reference initials.

There are many different forms used for this notation:

Enclosure	Enclosures (3)
Encl.	Enclosures—3
Enc.	Enc. 3
Enclosure: Check	3 Encs.
Check Enclosed	3 encls
2 Enclosures	Enclosures
2 enclosures	Check
Enclosures 2	Card
	Brochure

NOTE: The word *Inclosure* and the abbreviations *Inc.* and *Incl.* are used in military correspondence.

CARBON COPY NOTATION

If the writer is sending a copy of the letter to another person and wishes the addressee to know that it is being sent, make a carbon copy notation at the left margin on the line below the reference initials or below the enclosure notation if it is used.

If more than one person is to receive a carbon copy, the names should be listed alphabetically.

CC Mr. R. A. Austin	CC: Mr. R. A. Austin	cc: Miss Albert
Mr. J. C. Smith	Mr. J. C. Smith	

BLIND CARBON COPY NOTATION

When the writer does not intend to let the addressee know that anyone else is receiving a copy of the letter, type *bcc* (Blind Carbon Copy) on the upper left corner of the *carbon copies only. This notation is never typed on the original copy.*

12   By doing, not saying, it is done.   Say what you will, the pen,
the pencil, and the box are gone.   Will you find them?

13   All, not part, is required.   Does he want eight, nine, or ten?
14   You may, if you must, leave now.   Are you ready to go?

15   Helen, not Mary, cooked breakfast, lunch, and dinner for us.
16   If, when I come, you have not arrived, I will not wait.

17   Did you, while at home, read the book?   If not, then take it
now.   Oh, did you say you bought a copy?   Where is it?

18   The motto of the U.S. Corps of Engineers is "The difficult   13
we do at once.   The impossible takes a little longer."   And   25
speaking of the impossible brings to mind a story about Daniel   38
Webster.   As he sought to speak on Bunker Hill, the crowds   50
pressed upon him.   When he asked them to stand back, someone   63
said, "It is impossible, Mr. Webster."   He replied, "Nothing   76
is impossible on Bunker Hill."--Beam   84

....1....2....3....4....5....6....7....8....9....10....11....12

CAPITAL LETTER DRILLS

*Set margins for a 70-space line. Indent paragraphs 5 spaces. Hold the
shift key down until the capital letter has been struck and released; then
release the shift key, returning the finger to typing position quickly.*

1   A b C d E f G h I j K l M n O p Q r S t U v W x Y z A b C d E
2   a B c D e F g H i J k L m N o P q R s T u V w X y Z a B c D e
3   A b C D E f G H I j K L M n O P Q R S t U V W x Y Z a B C d E

Words

4   I came in.   He saw Bill.   Where is Main Street?   Call Dr. Lake.
5   She told Jack.   Give it to her.   Did you visit Salt Lake City?
6   Put it there.   Do it now.   Meet me on Tuesday in Bryant Park.

7   Last April, Paul and Mary Burke left Salt Lake City and   12
took a train to New York.   Arriving at Grand Central Station,   25
they hailed a taxi and drove to the Waldorf Astoria Hotel on   37
Park Avenue.   After lunch, Mary and Paul took a sightseeing   49
bus.   During their trip they saw the Empire State Building,   61
Wall Street, Grant's Tomb, Radio City, and the Central Park   73
Zoo.   Paul and Mary stayed in New York until Friday and then   86
returned to Salt Lake City.   92

8   George Gershwin, Tin Pan Alley's own, was one of the great   13
creative figures in American music.   It was his "Rhapsody in   25
Blue" that established jazz as a true form of American music.   38
The public's love for the "Rhapsody" brought wealth and fame   51
to Gershwin.   His "Porgy and Bess" had one of the longest runs   64
in show business.   68

....1....2....3....4....5....6....7....8....9....10....11....12

Beekman Paper Company
180 Park Lane
Fremont, CA 94538

Attention: Mr. Carl Black

Gentlemen:

SUBJECT LINE

The subject line previews the content of the message. The preferred position for the subject line is a double space below the salutation and a double space above the body of the letter. It may be blocked with the left margin or centered.

When the word *subject* is used in the subject line, it is typed in solid caps and is followed by a colon. The word *subject* may be omitted as in the simplified letter style (see page 186). Legal correspondence sometimes uses the terms *Re* or *In Re* instead of the word *subject*.

July 20, 19_____

Mrs. F. D. Walters
199 First Avenue
New York, NY 10021

Dear Mrs. Walters:

SUBJECT: Christmas Cards

Wouldn't you like your Christmas Cards to be so different . . .

COMPANY NAME

The company name may be used in the signature to emphasize the fact that a letter represents the views of the company as a whole rather than just the views of the individual who has written the letter.

If the company name is used, it is typed in solid caps on the second line below the complimentary close.

Yours truly,

NEIL & JOHNSON

Paul T. Jones, Manager

SUBSTITUTION DRILLS

Set margins for a 70-space line.

....1....2....3....4....5....6....7....8....9....10....11....12

1 r-t   Write to the three men relative to the results.

2 m-n   It is important to make a nominal assessment.

3 o-i   Consider a possible joint effort for the collection of
conclusive evidence.

4 a-s   Assist us now by assuring the assembled salesmen of your
satisfaction.

5 e-i   The children believed they had discovered an ancient buried
treasure.

6 s-d   The designs were finished on Tuesday and the dresses were
shipped.

7 r-e   A report will be prepared on replacement parts in the very
near future.

8 v-b   It is obvious to everybody that they were brave.

9 w-e   Few of the women knew that we were wearing a new weave.

10 d-e   I had hoped that a different method would result in increased
dividends.

11 o-l   If you could possibly locate the lot of wool, I would buy it.

12 f-g   Finding the right gift for a friend is difficult but satisfying.

13 i-u   Miss Muir has built a reputation with United as an invaluable
employee.

14 a-e   Our agent is eager to move ahead after he speaks to you.

15 k-l   Mr. Koler talked to the group. They were lucky to hear
such a knowledgeable man.

16 c-d   We have decided to discard requests for a discussion broadcast.

17 u-y   The youngsters are busy filling your orders throughout
the country.

....1....2....3....4....5....6....7....8....9....10....11....12

Special Parts of a Business Letter

In addition to the eight basic parts, a business letter may contain one or more of the following special display parts:

1. Attention Line
2. Subject Line
3. Company Name
4. Enclosure Notation
5. Carbon Copy Notation
6. Blind Carbon Copy Notation
7. Postscripts
8. Mailing Notation
9. Personal Notation
10. Reference Line

ATTENTION LINE

An attention line is a part of the address. The purpose of the attention line is to direct the letter to an individual or a department, and it appears on the envelope as well as on the letter.

Here are two ways in which the letter might be addressed:

Beekman Paper Company
Attention: Mr. Black
180 Park Lane
Fremont, CA 94538

Mr. Carl Black, Credit Manager
Beekman Paper Company
180 Park Lane
Fremont, CA 94538

There are circumstances which make the use of the attention line advisable; for example, when some legal question is involved, when the name of the head of a department is not known, or when there may be a possibility of the letter not being opened because the person is away from the office. Some businessmen, however, fall into the habit of using the attention line far more often than is necessary. There is a growing tendency to address the letter to the individual or a department.

When the attention line is used, type it as the second line of the inside address or a double space below the inside address and a double space above the salutation. The preference for placement when it follows the inside address is to block at the left margin. It may be centered and it may be underscored. A letter addressed to a firm, even though it contains an attention line, should use the salutation *Gentlemen*.

Beekman Paper Company
180 Park Lane
Fremont, CA 94538

Attention Mr. Carl Black

Gentlemen:

```
....1....2....3....4....5....6....7....8....9....10....11....12
```

18 f-d I offered to find a different decorator if he could afford
one.

19 c-v Did you receive the covering letter for the conversion of
the policy?

20 g-h Although he thought Mr. Highman thoroughly knew the subject,
the rough draft lacked expertise.

21 y-t You have yet to improve the style and quality of your factory
products.

22 s-w According to their wishes, a trip to the West was scheduled.

23 d-k I asked them to cover the desk so that nothing could skid.

24 f-r Our firm offers information about different forms of insurance.

25 p-o Every important sporting event will be photographed by our
reporters.

26 j-h John thought he should join Mr. March in the project.

27 r-u During the past four years, he had had innumerable opportunities
for an assured future.

28 s-e A series of science books was published to stimulate interest
among students.

29 g-t I suggest that you take advantage of the great decrease in
freight rates.

30 e-t He sent the letter with return postage guaranteed.

31 z-a We were amazed when we realized that the zigzag trail was
so hazardous.

32 s-c The case was closed until necessary inspection could be made.

33 x-c/s Anxious to please, the six boys did the exact number of
exercises.

34 b-n Nobody began the binding. Will you obtain the material
to do it?

35 g-b Mr. Billings began the project by bringing in big men to speak.

36 i-k I was thinking about making a skirt with a kick pleat.

37 q-a She has acquired a stock of quaint antiques not to be equaled
anywhere.

```
....1....2....3....4....5....6....7....8....9....10....11....12
```

Type the following letters in modified-block style. The number of words in the body of the letter is given for Jobs 1 and 2. Estimate the words in the body for Jobs 3, 4, and 5. Use the current date and insert capitalization and punctuation.

JOB 1

Date/miss anna leeds/28-06 court street/trenton NJ 18619/dear miss leeds/ we are happy to inform you that you have won first prize in our contest. (P) plans for a wonderful three-week vacation have been made through the acme travel agency in your city, and I suggest that you contact them for details. you will soon receive our check for $500 to cover incidental expenses./sincerely/james banning, editor/reference initials *(54 words)*

JOB 2

Date/mrs sarah carlson/248 maywood drive/canton OH 44708/dear mrs carlson/thank you for your check for $132.52. (P) i regret that our new catalog is not yet available. you should receive a copy in a few weeks. (P) if there is any information i can give you on any particular product, please write me again./sincerely yours,/john whitmore/reference initials *(43 words)*

JOB 3

Date/mr ernest dearborn president/mason & carter inc/18-37 65th street/ new york NY 10042/dear mr dearborn/miss anne davis has applied for a position as a secretary with our company and has referred us to you for information regarding her ability. (P) we should appreciate it very much if you would give us your opinion concerning the quality of her work and her skill in handling the various duties of a business office. (P) we assure you that your reply to this inquiry will be kept in the strictest confidence./ very truly yours,/o. r. turner/personnel director/ reference initials

JOB 4

Date/mr samuel a hart jr/assistant manager/beekman paper company/180 park lane/fremont CA 94538/dear mr hart/thank you for the kind invitation to your annual dinner. it would have been a great pleasure to be with you, but a previous appointment makes it impossible for me to attend. (P) the report that you requested is being prepared, and it will be sent as soon as it comes off the press./sincerely/alan c feldman/president/reference initials

JOB 5

date/mr richard mccabe/55 oak avenue/paterson nj 17514/dear mr mccabe /thank you for your letter of january 4. i am happy to learn that you are so pleased with our equipment that you have decided to place an additional order with us. (P) as you requested, we have asked our agent in your area to call on you within the next few days. he will have with him our latest sample catalog. as you will see, model 232 is now selling for $235./cordially yours/john t. barrow, sales/reference initials

DOUBLE-LETTER DRILLS

Set margins for a 70-space line. Indent paragraphs 5 spaces. When typing double letters on a manual typewriter, do not allow a full return of the key between strokes. On an electric allow the key to return to position between strokes.

```
....1....2....3....4....5....6....7....8....9....10....11....12....13   Words
```

1 They quizzed the ragged peddler about those messages he scribbled.

2 They cannot succeed if they attempt to accomplish the impossible.

3 The grinning buffoon puzzled the queen with two different riddles.

4 The crippled man came running from the cottage when the roof fell.

5 The abbot was killed by the bullets that whizzed over the old wall.

6 The merry innkeeper hummed a happy tune while he chopped the wood.

7 The man admitted having seen the terrible accident occur at noon.

8 A committee meeting was suddenly called to discuss the tragic affair.

9
```
     I am attaching a list of the suggestions and comments      12
made by my staff in regard to the matter we discussed at our    24
meeting.  As you see, they do not feel that what has occurred    37
will affect sales this summer, but they appear to agree that     49
unless something is done, sales will suffer in the fall.  In     61
view of this, I think it would be an error for you to over-      73
look any opportunity that would surely lead to additional        85
annual sales in the territory.                                   91
```

10 The sobbing boy confessed that he had shattered the new hall mirror.

11 It took them less than an hour to paddle across the silent lagoon.

12 Booming cannons announced the arrival of the new Yankee Clipper ship.

13 A robbery was committed on a sunny afternoon during the early summer.

14 While carrying the baggage, the struggling porter tripped and fell.

15 I cannot exaggerate her efforts to gain the support of the community.

16 I suggested the plan to the office staff but they did not accept it.

17
```
     I am happy to send you a booklet that tells all about the   12
many uses of mirrors in your home.  As you will see from the     25
illustrations, a mirror will add to the attractiveness of any    37
room, and the prices at which our mirrors are offered will       49
surely please you.  May I call to your attention the fact        61
that we give a full guarantee with every one of our mirrors      73
that we sell, and it is possible to buy from us with a great     85
degree of confidence.  I suggest that you accept this invitation 109
to visit our show room as soon as possible.                      118
```

```
....1....2....3....4....5....6....7....8....9....10....11....12....13
```

Collins, Bradley & Fox

9 Purchase Street
Boston, Massachusetts 02100

June 18, 19__

Mr. Howard McGrath
Mark Supplies, Inc.
18 Emerson Avenue
New York, NY   10042

Dear Mr. McGrath:

Thank you for your letter of January 17.

We are delighted to know that you are pleased with
the manner in which we handled your recent order.
Such praise is most welcome because it indicates that
our customers are aware of the effort we put forth
to provide the service they want.

I am confident that your satisfaction with us will
continue in the future.

                         Sincerely yours,

                         Roger P. Simmons

AMD

SENTENCES WITH HIGH-FREQUENCY
BUSINESS PHRASES

Set margins for a 70-space line and tab key for 5-space indention.

```
....1....2....3....4....5....6....7....8....9....10....11....12
```

1   Our service department is always ready to work with you on your own particular office needs.

2   We regret that we cannot fill your order at this time, but we will do so as soon as possible.

3   We should like to inform you that we have made it more convenient for you to buy on credit in our store.

4   Our men now have a copy of your new plan, and they will be glad to put it into use by the first of the year.

5   In bringing my accounts up to date, I have prepared for you a statement of your account. This statement is enclosed.

6   We should like very much to receive an order from you, and we will do our best to satisfy you with our goods and service.

7   We hope you give this letter immediate attention and that you will favor us with a check to cover the amount of your bill.

8   We do not have in stock the material you requested in your last order. We are therefore returning the check you enclosed.

9   Your account still shows an unpaid balance. Under the circumstances, we cannot extend to you further credit at this time.

10   Will you please let us know by return mail if you would like to have a copy of our book. We shall appreciate an early reply.

11   If anything did not satisfy you in our last shipment, kindly let us know. We wish you to be pleased with everything we offer.

12   It will take a day or two before we can make up your order in full, but I am sure you will understand the cause of the delay.

13   I am sending you this information so that you will know the present state of your account in the event that you should need it.

```
....1....2....3....4....5....6....7....8....9....10....11....12
```

July 8, 19__

Mr. Howard Bell
482 Eden Road
Dallas, Texas   75208

Dear Mr. Bell

Sincerely yours

Arthur Martin

July 8, 19__.

Mr. Howard Bell,
482 Eden Road,
Dallas, Texas   75208.

Dear Mr. Bell:

Sincerely yours,

Arthur Martin.

Modified-Block Style Letter

In the modified-block style, the date, complimentary close, and writer's name are started at the center of the line. Set a tab stop at this point. The inside address, salutation, and body begin at the left margin.

The following letter is typed in modified-block style with mixed punctuation. There are 72 words in the body of the letter. Check the letter-placement chart on page 163 to determine the margins.

```
....1....2....3....4....5....6....7....8....9....10....11....12
```

14   You will be glad to know that the material for your catalog
will be prepared and mailed to you today. Please let us know
when it reaches you.

15   This is to advise you that the material you ordered a few
weeks ago is now ready for shipment and will reach your office
in a week or ten days.

16   This is in reply to your letter of March 1. The goods
you ordered were sent from here a few days ago and should arrive
at your office in the very near future.

17   We are in receipt of your letter of April 11, in which
you inquire about your account. We shall be happy to forward
a statement to you by return mail.

18   We have written to you several times, but we have not
received a reply. Please let us hear from you in the near
future so that we may balance your account on our books.
```
....1....2....3....4....5....6....7....8....9....10....11....12
```

SPEED-FORCING DRILLS

Set margins for a 70-space line. When returning the carriage on a manual typewriter, use a quick wrist and hand motion. Drop the hand to typing position without letting it follow the carriage across. When using the return key on an electric, flick the key, release it quickly, and return the finger to typing position.

		Seconds		
		15	12	10
			Words	
1	Ask the man to do it now.	20	25	30
2	They will check their work.	21	27	32
3	She will speak to them soon.	22	28	34
4	He raised money in the drive.	23	29	35
5	He did not know that she went.	24	30	36
6	Quote a price for the curtains.	25	31	37
7	Make a list of all of the names.	26	32	38
8	I told them not to take the test.	27	33	40
9	Let us ask the girl to do the work.	28	35	42
10	She said she would buy the logs today.	29	37	44

REFERENCE INITIALS

Reference initials are useful whenever a question arises about who did what. These initials usually consist of the dictator's initials followed by the typist's initials. If the dictator's name is typed under his signature, the reference initials may be those of the typist only. Do not include reference initials in a personal letter. Here are several forms that are commonly used:

hlf	lwl: hlf
HLF	LWL/hlf
LWL: HLF	LWL hlf
LWL: hlf	L Lawson/hlf

Letter Punctuation

There are three forms of punctuation: mixed, open, and closed. The mixed style is the one most often used today. The open style has a clean, modern look and is used with the full block and simplified styles. The closed style was once widely used in the United States and is still widely used in other countries.

MIXED PUNCTUATION

July 8, 19__

Mr. Howard Bell
482 Eden Road
Dallas, Texas   75208

Dear Mr. Bell:

Sincerely yours,

Arthur Martin

#		15	12	10
11	Will you tell me which way I should go.	30	38	45
12	We plan to rent the house near the lake.	31	39	47
13	If you like the job, you will do it well.	32	40	48
14	She did not come to see us when we called.	33	41	49
15	Ask the old man to tell you about his trip.	33	42	50
16	One day I went to the park to hear the band.	34	43	51
17	Each of you can do this work if you will try.	35	44	53
18	Give them to the boys when they come to lunch.	36	45	54
19	After you left, I found these books on the bus.	37	46	55
20	Try to stay with us until the end of this month.	37	47	56
21	We will be glad to have you go with us next time.	38	48	57
22	He was away from the office when his brother came.	39	49	59
23	It has been only two months since he took this job.	40	50	60
24	Look over the new list and check the items you want.	41	51	61
25	I know that they will be here in less than two hours.	41	52	62
26	They told me that she would be at the shop to meet us.	42	53	63
27	It may be that we shall not be able to return tomorrow.	43	54	65
28	Please send me the name of the city in which they lived.	44	55	66
29	I was sorry that she had to leave before the job was done.	45	56	67
30	They should have told you about the fire before this time.	45	57	68
31	We want to know if the boy broke his leg when he fell down.	46	58	69
32	We all think it would help to have you talk to our teachers.	47	59	71
33	It is hard to tell whether the plan they made today was wise.	48	60	72
34	We are able to offer you the very best price for your old car.	49	61	73

COMPLIMENTARY CLOSE

The complimentary close is typed on the second line below the last line of the body of the letter. Start the closing at the left margin if the full-block or simplified style is used; otherwise start the closing at the point at which the date line begins (see page 180).

Capitalize the first word of the complimentary close. It may be followed by a comma or no punctuation, depending upon the punctuation style being used.

DICTATOR'S NAME AND TITLE

Type the name of the writer of a letter and his official title on the fourth line below the complimentary close or on the fourth line below the company name when it is used (see page 180). If the name or title is long, type the title on the fifth line. The space above the typewritten name and title is used for the penwritten signature of the writer.

Never type *Mr.* or any other title before a man's name in the closing lines. If there is no title before a woman's name, assume that the title is *Miss*. *Mrs.* may be typed in parentheses before the typewritten name.

Yours very truly,

Charles T. Naylor
Director of Personnel

Sincerely yours,

Charles Grey, President

Sincerely,

(Mrs.) Mary Willis

Cordially,

Mary Willis

A secretary who is asked to sign mail for her employer may use either of the following styles:

Sincerely yours,

Secretary to Mr. White

Sincerely yours,

Louis L. White, Manager

MINUTE SPEED DEVELOPMENT
AND ACCURACY

Set margins for a 70-space line and tab key for 5-space indention.

25 WORDS

All of us wish that we could have more free time; but the free time we have will not count for much if it is not used wisely.

30 WORDS

It is good to set a high goal in life, but do not make that goal so hard to reach that you find you are not able to climb high enough to grasp at it.

35 WORDS

No firm wishes to hire a man who is unable to get to work on time. If he does get the job, you may be sure of the fact that he will not keep the job for more than a few days.

40 WORDS

Be sure that you have both feet flat on the floor when you type, and do not let your eyes look away from your copy. Follow these two rules and watch your typing speed begin to rise to higher levels.

45 WORDS

Accurate repetition is the very best means you can use to build up your speed in typing. This applies to both word and sentence practice. When words are selected for repetitive practice, they should be very carefully chosen.

50 WORDS

The selections for speed practice that you find in this book will furnish sufficient material to enable you to develop more than an average speed. The selections may also be used for speed tests in order to determine your speed over a period of time.

55 WORDS

Punctuation marks are not used to make a page look pretty but to add expression and meaning to our writing. They are the signals that a writer uses to make his meaning clear to the reader. They are the substitutes for the pauses and voice changes that are used in speech.

60 WORDS

The efficient secretary is one who is not only fully capable of taking dictation and transcribing but has acquired the skills involved in office procedures. She must be acquainted with correct grammar, must be proficient in the use of office machines, and must also present an attractive appearance.

65 WORDS

Punctuality in keeping every one of your appointments is one of the most insistent demands of business etiquette. If your working day begins officially at nine o'clock, then you have an appointment to keep every day at that hour, and not only business etiquette, but also prudence, indicates that you always be there on time.

SALUTATION

Type the salutation flush with the left margin on the second line below the inside address. The salutation may be followed by a colon or no punctuation, depending on the punctuation form being used (see page 172).

Capitalize the first word and any nouns and titles in the salutation; for example, *Dear Sir*; *My dear Mr. Wright*; *Dear Miss Matson*.

Set the margins on the typewriter for a five-inch line and set a tab stop at the center of the page. Insert a sheet of paper in the machine and space down 15 lines. Move the carriage to the center point. At the signal to begin, start typing the following headings, using the current date, spacing down five lines, typing the inside address, double spacing, typing the salutation, spacing down five lines, and following the same procedure for the next heading. Only two headings can be typed to a page so continue the drill on the next sheet of paper. If you finish the drill before time has been called, begin with the first heading again. Do not type the numbers preceding each heading.

1. (Current date) Mr. Charles Brown/259 Oregon Avenue/Austin, TX 78716/Dear Mr. Brown:
2. (Current date) Miss Lillian King/10 Woodlawn Avenue/Atlanta, GA 30303/Dear Miss King:
3. (Current date) Trade Manufacturing Company/13 West 15 Street/ Albany, NY 12204/Gentlemen:
4. (Current date) Mr. George H. Reynolds, President/Martin Manufacturing Company/15 South Wabash Avenue/Chicago, IL 60614/Dear Mr. Reynolds:
5. (Current date) Baker Brothers, Inc./42 Water Street/Dayton, OH 45428/Gentlemen:
6. (Current date) Mrs. T. Cole/606 Wilmington Drive/San Diego, CA 92110/Dear Mrs. Cole:
7. (Current date) Dr. James Mathewson/710 14th Street NW./Washington, DC 20018/Dear Dr. Mathewson:
8. (Current date) Mr. George Press, Jr./21 River Street/Avon, CT 06001/ Dear Mr. Press:
9. (Current date) Mr. Leo Glenn II/1180 Lester Place/Ames, IA 50010/ Dear Mr. Glenn:

BODY

Begin the body of the letter on the second line below the salutation or on the second line below the subject line (see page 177) in all styles of letters except the simplified (see page 186). Start each paragraph at the left margin except for the semiblock and indented styles (see page 180) or for a double-spaced letter. Paragraphs may be indented five or ten spaces.

Use single spacing in all except very short letters and leave a double space between paragraphs.

70 WORDS

A secretary owes her employer loyalty. Since she is closely associated with him, it is logical that she should know more than the other employees about his little eccentricities, his temperament and possibly its unpleasant phases, and his private affairs. However, loyalty forbids that she should discuss any of these things with other employees.

75 WORDS

Tact is difficult to define, but it is not hard to recognize, and it is always appreciated. Probably the best way to describe it is to say that it is the "shock absorber" in human contacts. By it we avoid the jars of harsh contacts and make smooth our social relationships. More than most other components of personality, it is not inborn but is developed from experience.

80 WORDS

Etiquette, whether in social life or in business, is always based on the same principles: courtesy and consideration for others. No matter what the situation, if you are courteous and considerate of the other person, you cannot go very far wrong. However, since life in a business office presents situations not encountered in other fields, it may be helpful to discuss some of them in more detail.

85 WORDS

To be a valuable secretary, you must offer your employer more than your skill in typewriting and shorthand. Your disposition is almost as important as your secretarial abilities, and you must cultivate a pleasant manner in your dealings with everyone in the office, particularly your boss. In the office, you should have just one mood—fair and sunny—and it will help to have a sense of humor that shrugs off minor irritations.

90 WORDS

If you want to achieve success as a secretary, you must develop a keen sense of diplomacy and tact. Very early in your secretarial career, you must learn to be tight-lipped about everything that goes on in your employer's office; and you must never discuss his personal affairs with even your most intimate friends. Every employer likes to feel that his secretary can be trusted, but this confidence will come only after you have proved yourself to him.

PACING DRILLS

Set margins for a 70-space line. Each number represents 5 words.

1 Our annual hardware catalog was sent by mail today and should reach you in a day or two. We also sent our latest price list to replace the one you already had. All items in the catalog can be purchased at any local hardware dealer in Albany, and each purchase carries a two-year guarantee that assures your satisfaction. As I am sure you are aware, we take great pride in the fact that so many contractors agree with our claim that our hardware products are the finest that can be found anywhere on the market today.

title, use the courtesy title *Mr.*, *Mrs.*, or *Miss*. If there is no way to determine the marital status of a woman, use *Miss*. (The abbreviation *Ms.* meaning either *Miss* or *Mrs.* is acceptable.)

When *Jr.*, *Sr.*, or a roman numeral such as II is typed after a name, you may or may not use the comma before the *Jr.* or *Sr.*, but no comma is used before the roman numeral.

Never use two titles that mean the same thing. Use *Dr. Harold Abbott* OR *Harold Abbott, Ph.D.* The modern tendency is to omit business titles in addresses. If a business title is used, it may be written on the line with the personal name, on the line with the company name,. or on a line by itself. Choose the arrangement that gives the best balance.

Mr. Howard Bell, President   Mr. John C. Hallman
The Short and Watson Company   President, Lee Associates

Mr. James Trevor
Superintendent of Education

STREET ADDRESS

If the name of a building is to be indicated in the address, type it on a line immediately above the street address. If a post office box number is given in the address, do not use the street address.

Always type the street address on a line by itself. Refer to page 158 for rules for typing house numbers and numbers used as street names.

Do not abbreviate *North, South, Northeast*, or a similar word when it appears before the street name; for example, 55 West 42 Street. Do abbreviate the section of the city after the street name, using a comma before it; for example, 710 14th Street, NW. A dash may be used between a house number and a street name with numbers; for example, 710—14th Street, NW.

Room numbers and apartment numbers follow the street address.

CITY, STATE, AND ZIP CODE

Refer to page 158 for rules for typing this line in the inside address.

Never use an abbreviation for the city nor for the words *Fort, Mount, Point*, or *Port*. Do abbreviate the word *Saint* in the names of American cities.

In foreign addresses, type the name of the country in full (except for U.S.S.R.) on a separate line in solid caps:

Mr. Howard Scott
The British Schools S.R.L.
Viale Liegi 14
Rome
ITALY

2. You will probably be glad to know that our library has now established a special book section for the boys in your biology and botany club. The books that we have obtained are the best available on the subject, and I believe that the members of the club will derive great benefit from their use. Please place a notice on your bulletin board about our library so that the boys may begin borrowing books immediately.

3. In accordance with the contract which you recently signed with our company, you accepted our direct-mail service with the understanding that we could expect a check from you each month. It is now three months since we received your last check. Under the circumstances, you can certainly appreciate the fact that we cannot continue to give service until you have paid the accrued balance of your account. I will appreciate it very much if you would place a check in the mail at once.

4. I had hopes that I would hear from you regarding the details of the advertising program I drew up on Wednesday. You seemed so delighted with the ideas I mentioned that I expected some word from you in a day or two. Did the Board of Directors decide against our dividend plan that would double your advertising dollar? As I told you, there are hundreds of advantages to be gained from advertising in our trade paper; and they should be made to understand that they cannot afford to discard the added advantages of this medium.

5. Our concern is eager to establish a permanent site in your section; therefore, we expect to send a representative to see you next week. We will need at least three hundred acres for our plant and the homes of our employees. We prefer to have this property near the river. The final decision, however, will depend on what our agent tells us after he speaks with you. Any help you may be able to give him will be very much appreciated.

6. Our firm was founded fifty years ago for the benefit of the families in our fine city. Our belief has always been that very few men are fortunate enough to face the financial difficulties that often follow a long illness, and we therefore offer an effective insurance plan to offset a loss of income. If you are fearful for the welfare of your family in times of illness, then call at our office and let our staff give you information about a plan you can well afford.

7. We are going to begin our big luggage sale on Monday. Every single piece of baggage will be offered at bargain prices, and we suggest that you take advantage of the huge savings that we are making available. Bring your wife along so that she may see the gorgeous alligator bags that we also stock. You will both agree that we are giving the best that can be bought for low prices.

DATE LINE

The date line consists of (1) the name of the month, written in full; (2) the day, written in figures followed by a comma; and (3) the complete year. (In military or foreign correspondence, the day may be written before the month; for example, 10 July 19--.)

Position the date on line 15 from the top of the page or three lines below the last line of the letterhead, whichever is lower. The date line usually begins at the center of the page, but it may begin at the left margin or end at the right margin. The horizontal arrangement depends upon the style of letter, the design of the letterhead, and office preference.

INSIDE ADDRESS

The inside address of a business letter, like the envelope address, must contain: (1) the name of the person or company to whom you are writing, or both; (2) the street address; and (3) the city, state, and ZIP code. It may include the person's office title and his department, a room or apartment number, or an attention line.

Begin the inside address on the fifth line below the date, and single space the lines unless the whole letter is double spaced. The block style (all lines flush with the left margin) is universally used for the address in the letter and on the envelope. The letter and envelope should conform in all details. The address may be written in two lines if it is short—the name on one line and the city and state with the ZIP code on the next. If the address is very long, it may be written on four or five lines.

NAME OF PERSON AND TITLE

When writing the name of a person or company in an inside address or elsewhere, follow the spelling and capitalization that appears in the original correspondence. Do not abbreviate or use initials unless the person to whom you are writing uses abbreviations or initials. This also applies to the use of the ampersand (&) in a company name.

Always use a title before the name of a person unless an abbreviation of an academic degree is to appear after the name. If the person has no special

8 Have you had a chance to check the rough draft of the pamphlet which I sent to you on the fourth of March? This pamphlet, which gives the history of photography, has been ready for the publishers for almost a month; and we wish to go ahead with the printing shortly. Will you therefore read it thoroughly and let me have whatever comments you wish to make about its worth. I shall appreciate your help. *83*

9 This is in reply to your inquiry about Miss Irene Wilis. Miss Wilis was hired by our institute five years ago and since that time has proved highly efficient and reliable in her duties. Her ability as a statistical typist made her services invaluable and she displayed genuine initiative in handling the minute details involved in her job. I think you will find her well qualified for the position in your firm. *83*

10 In January you joined our Junior Book Club, and judging by your comments, you are enjoying your membership. This is to let you know that we have just received a manuscript of jungle stories by B. J. Jorkman that will reach you in June or July. If, however, the subject does not interest you, just jot us a note stating your objection. We will send some other book. *74*

11 Thank you for the check which reached my desk today. I am very glad to know that you think highly of our books. We expect to make up your order at once and ship it by truck before the end of the week. I spoke to Mr. Baker about the book for which you have asked, and he thinks that it has not been in stock for some time. However, we will keep looking and will make every effort to locate it as quickly as possible. *84*

12 Following our usual policy, we have mailed you a folder which describes fully the glass bottles that our plant makes. The great skill with which all our able employees do their jobs has never been excelled, and our label on a product is a sure sign of excellent quality. Look through the folder while you have it before you and place your order for holiday glasses immediately. We will be happy to fill even a small order. *85*

13 March is the month when most homeowners make up their minds to do something about the problem of home repairs. If your home is now in need of repairs, remember to communicate with us because we can manage them with maximum efficiency at minimum cost. If you will mail the enclosed information card immediately, we will make arrangements for our men to come to your home to give you a complete estimate. *81*

14 A number of men from your company have recently written to ask us for information concerning our new group insurance plan. I am now writing to inquire if you would consider a plan wherein one of our agents would conduct a meeting in the recreation room in your plant. I know that the entire group of men would benefit from such a general meeting, and it would certainly be to their advantage to hear the answers to the questions raised by the individuals in the group. *95*

FIRST NATIONAL BANK

BROADWAY AND DEEGAN STREET

AUGUSTA, GEORGIA 30900

Narrow Letterhead

Acme Insurance Company

FOR A SECURE FUTURE

Phone 746-0499

965 HARTFORD AVE. • OMAHA, NEBRASKA 68100

Deep Letterhead

Speedwriting® of CANADA LIMITED

▶ 1181 St. Catherine West, Montreal, P.Q.
Telephone: 842-3823

▶ J. Paul Morin, B. Com.
National Coordinator

Speedwriting

abc shorthand
8 languages

Secretarial Typing

Business English

Business Correspondence

Business Spelling
and Word Power

Left-Weighted Stationery

15 I am sorry to inform you that the policy of our company does not allow me to forward the report you ordered. However, in order to be as helpful as possible, I am enclosing a report of our study recently conducted in one of the major counties; I hope that it will prove of some worth to you in your work. If you would consider coming to my office sometime this month, I might possibly be in a position to offer more information to you. [88]

16 Your subscription to our paper has now been properly posted, and your papers should reach you promptly from now on. Most people—especially those who are particularly interested in all phases of sports—will probably be happy to learn that we propose to expand our popular photography pages in the near future. Every important sporting event will be photographed by our reporters, and the captions under each picture will tell the complete story. [90]

17 It has been quite a long time since you inquired about our antique furniture, and I am writing to request that you come in quickly to see our stock. [30] The quality of our antiques has never been equaled in Quincy, and some of our merchandise is so quaint that I am sure you will be quick to see its worth. The prices we quote qualify us to say that we can meet your requirements at the lowest cost available in Quincy. [84]

18 We are returning the radio that you recently forwarded to us for repair. Unfortunately, the parts that require replacement are no longer being manufactured; and we are, therefore, unable to put this radio in working order for you. We are sorry that we cannot provide our regular service to you, and we regret that it is necessary to return the radio in the same condition in which it was received. We hope we can be of better service to you in the near future. [93]

19 Several months ago, we published a series of science books for use in the high schools of our state. These books were designed to stimulate strong interest among students, and the messages sent us assure us that our purpose enjoys enthusiastic success. Since teachers and students have expressed satisfaction with this series, we should like to send some to you for your inspection. May we send them at our expense? [84]

20 Thank you for extending to us the opportunity to test the interesting device for which you recently received a patent. As we stipulated in the last letter that we sent you, we are interested in anything that we think will better the quality of our product; and the tests conducted by our experts indicate that your invention is just exactly what we need. However, the situation in our plant at the present time does not permit the installation of test equipment; but we will get in touch with you at a future date. [104]

Business Letter Stationery

Use letterhead, plain paper for the second page, and envelopes that are matched in weight and color. The standard size of letterhead paper is 8½ x 11 inches. Other fairly common sizes are: Half sheets, 8½ x 5½; Baronial, 5½ x 8½; and Monarch, 7¼ x 10½.

The envelopes used with standard are No. 6¾ or No. 10; with half sheets, No. 6¾; with Baronial, No. 5⅜; and with Monarch, No. 7.

For carbon copies, use manifold, onionskin, or copy letterhead. Manifold is a lightweight paper. Onionskin is a stronger, more expensive paper. Copy letterhead is a lightweight paper with the word COPY printed on it. It may or may not contain the letterhead.

Carbon paper is chosen by weight and finish. The type used is determined by the number of copies to be made and whether you have an electric or manual typewriter:

Copies	Weight	Finish
1-4	Standard	Hard
5-8	Medium	Hard
9-20	Light	Medium

Basic Parts of a Business Letter

A basic letter is composed of a heading, body, and closing. The eight basic parts are:

1. Letterhead or Return Address
2. Date Line
3. Inside Address
4. Salutation
5. Body
6. Complimentary Close
7. Dictator's Name and/or Title
8. Reference Initials

LETTERHEAD

The printed letterhead contains the company name; street address; city, state, and ZIP code; area code and telephone number. Other information such as slogans, the nature of the business, and names of officers may also be indicated. (See page 164 for the heading on personal business letters.)

HOME OFFICE: 1750 ASH PLACE • CHICAGO, ILLINOIS 60600 • Phone 923-0740

ARMA RUBBER COMPANY

FACTORY: 3700 PEACH STREET • ST. LOUIS, MISSOURI 63100 • Phone 224-1835

Average Letterhead

21 Your inquiry about the United Hotel is very much valued, and it is our pleasure to rush the literature you requested. During the past four years, we have built up a reputation for the utmost in quality service; and it is no surprise that we have become the most popular resort in the county. Situated at the top of a huge mountain, surrounded by an unusually beautiful setting, the United provides unlimited opportunities for leisurely hours of luxurious living.

22 Please give us the chance to help you solve whatever problem you have in moving to your new home. Every piece of furniture will be carefully covered to avoid damage; all valuable silverware will be wrapped in velvet to prevent scratching. The drivers of our moving vans are each heavily insured, and your moving job will be over in four or five hours. Let our service save you time and solve your moving problems.

23 The letter you wrote was left on my desk when I had gone away for a week and did not reach me until now. I checked with our foreman and learned the following: The watch which you forwarded to us for repair was sent out by Railway Express on Wednesday. It should reach you within a week. We were sorry to keep you waiting, but we would not allow the watch to leave here until it was in good working order. When the watch arrives, will you please wire us.

24 In reply to your inquiry, I am sorry to say that our factory cannot possibly supply the quantity of yellow party frocks that are necessary to fill your order. As I told you in my conversation yesterday, the holiday season is always a very busy one, and our supply of the style and quality you desire is quickly depleted by orders from all over the country. I hope the twenty dresses that went out to you today will prove satisfactory in every way.

25 According to researchers, Benjamin Franklin originated the concept of daylight saving time in 1784 when he was United States Ambassador to France. Supposedly, he awoke early one morning and, seeing daylight, thought of moving clocks ahead an hour to lengthen the working day. The concept was first used widely in World War I as a means of conserving fuel.

WORD-LEVEL RESPONSE

Set margins for a 70-space line. Try to think and type the word rather than typing letter by letter.

1 we or he my in is be us no go by on if so of at to up an do

2 the and you for are not but all was had our one get can she
3 any has day out her now how did say him his got may two too
4 who new sir let way use few old yet put man car its ago ask
5 off big own pay try boy bad lot men why far saw end run buy

Copy the preceding illustrated letter on plain paper. Check the place-ment table for margin settings and check the illustration for linespacing between the parts of the letter.

Type the letters in Jobs 2 and 3 using your own return address and your name in the closing lines. Use the letter-placement table to determine mar-gins for each letter. Insert capitalization and punctuation where necessary. (P) indicates a new paragraph.

JOB 2 *(115 words in the body)*

unitours/250 grand street south/los angeles/california 90051/gentlemen/ i've just returned from your priceless tour to spain, italy, and morocco and want to thank you for a most wonderful experience. everything was even better than you had described. (P) your tour director, miss draper, should be complimented on her efficiency. all of the details of transportation, bag-gage handling and exits and entries through the various countries were smoothly and unobstrusively handled by her. she also handled all of our questions about where to shop, what to do and see, and the intricacies of foreign money. she was always available whenever we needed her. her extra services really "made" the trip. (P) i will wholeheartedly recommend this trip to my friends./sincerely

JOB 3 *(75 words in the body)*

Norwegian Airways
One Madison Avenue
New York, New York 10024
Gentlemen:
I have examined the brochure you forwarded to me and am extremely interested in the special 21-day European tour described. However, in view of the fact that I have spent considerable time in Amsterdam, I am writing to ask whether it would be possible to choose an alternate city without additional charge.
Will you please have your travel agent call me one day this week to discuss this in-formation with me.
Yours truly,

```
6   your have will this with very from time been when they some
7   send good know just make much copy made same also well here
8   find sent them glad what note come were wish take date work
9   over hope only more must like year line book days able best
10  feel soon next bill case last list part hand call such mail

11  would about which yours price check thank other being after
12  first could reply shall their favor stock cover trust state
13  above again think thing given these three write goods until
14  taken month might since place delay money sorry sales going
15  books small under value offer claim short early doubt wrote

16  please letter matter kindly return amount advise credit before
17  office future prices regard course desire unable prompt report
18  orders little remain expect recent regret school better supply
19  within accept having during direct always reason change placed
20  called notice copies sample enough people either second assure

21  account receipt however company balance service receive believe
22  forward payment further through request special shipped invoice
23  furnish another records ordered whether enclose general subject
24  several freight advance advised against greatly written correct
```

STRAIGHT-COPY TIMINGS

Set margins for a 70-space line and tab key for 5-space indentions. Use double spacing.

Words

1

	Words
The English language is not a static thing; it changes to reflect the usage	17
of the people. Some words drop out of common usage and become archaic.	32
Others are created to give names to the new procedures and the new	46
discoveries of our age. Modern science and technology coin new words	60
constantly.	63
Not only are new words born, but old ones are subject to change. Nearly	76
everyone wrote "catalogue" a short time ago instead of "catalog," which	91
we use today. Not long ago, you always found a hyphen in such words as	106
"non-profit," which is now written "nonprofit."	116
American and English lexicographers are constantly revising, adding,	131
deleting, and compiling the results in new, up-to-date dictionaries. (The	146
latest Italian dictionary was based on Dante's *Inferno* and was published	161
in 1811.)	163

2

	Words
Now that you know how to walk like a winner, you're going to learn how	16
to sit like one. As an executive you'll spend plenty of time sitting. Too	32
much time. So pay attention to this point.	41
Whenever you sit down in a chair, turn so that your back is to the chair	57
and slide one of your feet two or three inches under the seat. Then lower	72
yourself into the seat keeping your head erect and your back straight.	87

```
962 Flamingo Drive
Miami, Florida    32803                    Heading or Return
June 10, 19__


Mr. Lincoln Cradwell                       Inside Address
63 Hyde Street
Tampa, Florida    33602

Dear Mr. Cradwell:                         Salutation

Thank you for helping me prepare my latest
book.  I could not have progressed so
rapidly if you had not been so cooperative.

I thought you would like to know that the
book is now ready for release and that I
have mentioned your name in the preface     Body
as a small token of my deep appreciation
to you.

I have arranged to have a copy of the
book sent to you.

            Sincerely,                     Complimentary Close

            Robert Frailey                 Penwritten Signature

            Robert Frailey                 Writer's Name
```

Almost all of your weight is carried by the thigh muscles of your back leg. 102
Maintain your balance—don't flop into the chair with a bang. 115

Once you are seated, relax. But don't slump down like a sack of potatoes. 131
If the chair is a good one, it will provide support for your back by its 146
contour. Sit back so that the chair fits snugly into the small of your back. 162
Keep your perfect posture position—back straight and head up. 175

When getting up from a chair, simply reverse the sitting procedure: 190
Slide one foot back under the chair before rising and keep your back and 205
head erect as you lift yourself up in one easy motion, with your back leg 220
muscles doing all the work. 226

3 How good is your memory? Your ability to remember is a vital asset. 15
Developing a good memory is an art. Very few people are born with 30
exceptional memories; they have to be developed and trained. Most author- 45
ities question the theory that there are people gifted with "photographic" 60
memories. The human mind accepts only an overall picture and usually 74
omits minor items. A girl working in an office must train her mind to retain 90
a "picture" of all necessary details pertaining to her job. 103

The four most important words in developing a memory are: reason, 118
meaning, interest, and desire. 125

Develop good habits by being an attentive listener, training your memory 141
by repetition, using your memory, and not filling your mind with trivia. 156

"I forgot" are two words your employer should never hear you say. On a 172
given day your employer will have a host of obligations. Alerting him to 187
these commitments and helping him prepare for them are important parts 201
of your job. They needn't worry you if you have a well-organized reminder 216
file. 218

4 You have probably seen the abacus in your local Chinese laundry or 15
restaurant. The abacus is a calculator that was developed by the Chinese 30
around 600 B.C. This calculator consists of a wooden frame strung with a 45
row of two beads and a row of five beads on a single strand of wire. The 60
abacus works in a manner similar to the Egyptian sand calculator, each 75
column representing ten times the amount of the previous column. The 89
number of beads in each column of the abacus is different from the number 104
of pebbles in each groove of the sand calculator. 115

In the abacus, the ten digits are divided into two groups of five; the first 132
half is 1 through 5 and the second half is 6 through 10. When all the beads 148
in the lower rows of the abacus are in the lower position, and all the beads 164
in the upper row of the abacus are in the upper position, the full count in 180
the column is zero. As you count to five, merely move each bead in the 195
lower row to the top position. After all five beads have been moved up for a 211
count of five, they can all be lowered and one of the two top row beads is 226

BUILDING COPYING SKILLS   102

BUSINESS LETTERS

A letter that is attractive in appearance is a goodwill ambassador, and your ability to type an attractive letter is your "hallmark" as an efficient, capable typist or secretary.

Frame every letter, allowing a slightly wider margin on the left than on the right. The margins are determined by the number of words in the body of a letter. A skilled typist or secretary will be able to place letters by judgment. A placement table plus practice will enable you to develop this skill.

Any placement table is just a general guide and has to be adjusted to the many variations, such as size of letterhead paper and special features—attention lines, subject lines, long quotations, and tabulations. The chart that is given here is one that is widely used.

Before studying the letter-placement chart, review pages 11 and 59.

Letter-Placement Chart
(for single-spaced letters on 8½-by-11-inch stationery)

Words in the Body	Length of Line	Date to Inside Address
up to 100	4 inches	5 lines
100-200	5 inches	5 lines
200-300	6 inches	5 lines

A 4-inch line is used for a letter containing 71 words in the body. The margins are set at 22 and 62 for pica and at 27 and 75 for elite. The date is typed 15 lines from the top of the paper and the inside address is typed 5 lines below the date.

Letters containing over 350 words are usually two-page letters for elite as well as for pica type. The line length would vary from 60 to 65 spaces for pica type and from 70 to 80 spaces for elite type.

Personal Business Letters

This letter is typed on 8½ x 11 paper with pica type. A modified block style and mixed punctuation have been used. The heading, date line, complimentary close, and the writer's name begin at the center of the page. There are 71 words in the body of the letter.

placed in the downward position, also representing a count of five. For 241
example, to represent the number seven, you lower one of the upper beads 256
to represent five and raise two of the lower beads to represent two; the total 272
is, therefore, five plus two, or seven. 281

The abacus is capable of calculating numbers up to 99 billion. It is said 297
that skilled abacus operators can manipulate the abacus at speeds com- 311
parable to those achieved by electric desk top calculators. 324

5 Rotterdam has for over a quarter of a century had the reputation of 15
being one of the worst-blitzed cities of Europe. That is why it has evoked 31
world-wide sympathy, and its phoenix-like rise from its ashes was followed 46
with such great interest. Everybody talked of the miracle of Rotterdam. 61

As times reverted to normal, the center of Rotterdam was rebuilt; and 76
the port grew to rank among the world's largest. Admiration for what had 91
been achieved remained, but interest in the city's fight to regain its prom- 107
inence fell off. This was to be expected, and no citizen of Rotterdam 122
expected otherwise. 126

The resurgence from the destruction of war was indeed a miracle but no 142
more so than the original growth of Rotterdam from a small fishing village 157
to a world port. Great difficulties had to be overcome. There were many set- 173
backs; opposition and both political and natural obstacles had to be fought. 189

The tragedy of Rotterdam was twofold. In the early days of the war the 204
heart of the city was destroyed, and at the end of the war the port suffered. 220
It was the port that decided the city's future. Unlike Amsterdam, Rotter- 235
dam has always been a port city, not a city with a port. Most of the citizens 241
depend, directly or indirectly, on the port for their livelihood. Therefore, the 258
decision was not difficult; the reconstruction of the port must come first. 274

Five miles of quays for sea-going ships had been blown up and 40 percent 302
of the port equipment destroyed. Plans had been laid for reconstruction 317
during the Occupation, and in December 1949 the reconstruction was com- 331
plete. Full advantage was taken of the most modern techniques to plan the 346
best layout and distribution of port facilities and to incorporate improve- 361
ments. New equipment was provided and is constantly being added to 375
and improved. 378

6 As a secretary, you will often be required to type manuscripts of business 17
reports, sales handbook materials, office manual inserts, etc. These mate- 31
rials may be dictated or they may be handwritten by your employer in 45
rough draft form. 49

In typing manuscripts, leave top, bottom, and side margins of approx- 64
imately one inch on all pages with these exceptions: leave a two-inch 79
margin on the first page and a one-and-a-half-inch top margin on all other 94
pages if the manuscript is to be bound at the top. 105

CHAIN FEEDING ENVELOPES
BACK-FEED METHOD

1. Place stack of envelopes at the left of the machine face down with flaps toward you.
2. Insert the first envelope so that about ½ inch of the top of the envelope shows.
3. Place the second envelope between the platen and the bottom edge of the first envelope so that it will be fed into the machine at the same time as the first one.
4. Turn the right platen knob bringing the first envelope into writing position and type the address.
5. Twirl the right platen knob to remove the first envelope placing it face down at the right of the machine. At the same time insert the third envelope into the typewriter in the same manner as the second envelope. Remember, the left hand inserts the envelopes and the right hand removes them.

FRONT-FEED METHOD

1. Place stack of envelopes at the left of the machine face up with flaps at the top.
2. Insert the first envelope and address it. Do not remove from the machine.
3. Roll the first envelope toward you until ½ inch of the top of the envelope shows.
4. Insert the second envelope face up between the platen and the top edge of the first envelope.
5. Turn the right platen knob toward you to bring the second envelope into writing position and address it.
6. Remove the completed envelopes that accumulate on the paper table.

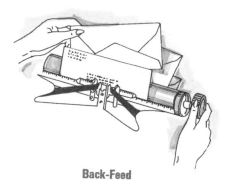

Back-Feed

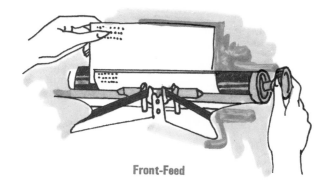

Front-Feed

Unless otherwise instructed, type manuscripts with double spacing on 8½ by 11 paper, indenting the first line of each paragraph five or ten spaces. Quoted material of four or more lines and enumerated items should be single-spaced and indented from left and right margins of the manuscript.

Main headings of manuscripts or reports are typed in solid capitals and centered over the body of the material. Follow the main heading by a triple space.

Side headings are preceded by a triple space and followed by a double space. They are typed with initial capitals, underlined, even with the left margin.

Indent and type paragraph headings with underlining on the first line beginning the paragraph.

If the manuscript is to be bound at the left, type page numbers, beginning with the second page, in the upper right corner of the page even with the right margin and a half inch from the top of the page. If the manuscript is to be bound at the top, however, center the page numbers a half inch from the bottom of the page. Leave a triple space below page numbers in the upper right corner and a double space above those at the bottom.

7   Australia is the world's largest island and its smallest continent. It is approximately the size of the continental United States. It lies between the Pacific and Indian Oceans, with New Guinea and Indonesia to the north and Antarctica to the south. The nearest land to the east is the Pacific coast of South America; to the west, South Africa. Not too long ago, Australia seemed very far away, but the jet age has converted these distances into mere hours.

After many years of comparative isolation, this great country is now attracting hundreds of thousands of travellers. It is a staggering fact that so many people expect to find jolly swagmen sitting under coolibah trees, kangaroos hopping along the streets, aborigines throwing boomerangs in the vast outback, and koala bears up in every tree. The kangaroos are there but under strict scientific control. The koalas are protected in reservations, sanctuaries, and zoos. The aborigines are there as equal members of a society whose standard of living is among the highest in the world. The outback is there, still unpeopled and a wilderness but served with modern highways and a network of air service.

Australia is principally an industrial nation. Farming is still of major importance to the economy, but industry is expanding at a rapid rate. Many more people work in mines, factories, and offices than on the land.

Today the Commonwealth of Australia comprises six states and two territories: New South Wales, Victoria, Queensland, South Australia, Western Australia, the island of Tasmania, Northern Territory, and Capital Territory. Under Australian administration are: Papua/New Guinea, Nor-

Type No. 6¾ envelopes according to the read zone requirements for optical screening using the following information:

Notations	Special Personal Services	Addresses
1. Registered	_____	Mr. Burt Lane 34 Oak Avenue Albany, New York 12203
2. _____	Attention: Mr. George Allen	Baker Brothers, Inc. 42 Water Street Dayton, Ohio 45428
3. Airmail	c/o Artists Associates	Mr. John Hale 71 East Avenue Newark, New Jersey 07102
4. _____	_____	Mr. Fred Grant Box 62 Warren, Arizona 85642
5. Airmail	Hold for arrival	Mr. Harold Burns 7520 North Street Tulsa, Oklahoma 74104

JOB 4

Type No. 10 envelopes according to the read zone requirements for optical screening using the following information:

1. _____	In care of Mr. Fred Lathum	Mr. J. A. Mathewson 1432 Hillside Avenue Dallas, Texas 75216
2. _____	Attention: Mr. James Martin	Acme Art Studio 569 Worth Avenue Dayton, Ohio 45401
3. Special Delivery	_____	Mrs. T. Cole 606 Wellington Drive San Diego, California 92110
4. Airmail	Personal	Miss Wilma Ames 33 Shoreland Drive Seattle, Washington 98145
5. Registered	_____	Randal & Peck 45 Oak Street Rochester, New York 14614

folk Island, Nauru, Cocos Islands, Christmas Island, and nearly half of   360
Antarctica known as Australian Antarctic Territory.   371

One of the outstanding advantages of touring Australia is that cities of   387
great splendor are within reach of many of the beauty spots and tourist   402
areas.   404

8   A fine color sense is not so rare as a fine musical ear, but even the un-   16
trained eye may become educated by careful study. Taste and discrimina-   31
tion as well as creative ability in the use of color may be developed by   46
study, comparison, and selection.   53

Color, working hand-in-hand with line and proportion, can create optical   69
illusions to camouflage figure and feature faults in addition to creating   84
psychological effects both on the wearer and those around her.   97

Color will do things for people, whether they like it or not! Generally   113
speaking, people are divided into two broad classifications: the introverts   129
and the extroverts. The introverts tend to be shy and retiring, while the   144
extroverts are outgoing and responsive to the world around them. Sim-   158
ilarly, these two groups respond differently to color: the introvert tends   174
to feel happier in soothing neutral or "cool" colors; the extroverts, on the 190
other hand, will probably be radiantly happy wearing vivid reds and yellows   206
—the "warm" colors. The introvert will probably feel "uneasy" in bright   221
red; the extrovert will probably feel equally uncomfortable in dull beige.   237

When we speak of "cool" and "warm" colors, the very presence of light   252
can almost be felt. There is warmth on the skin in yellow sunlight, coolness 268
in a breeze that comes from the blue ocean, a clamminess to gray fog and   283
mist. So much of the earth that is warm and dry is orange, yellow, and tan;   298
so much that is wet and transparent is blue and green. So you can readily   313
understand why red, yellow, and orange are considered to be warm colors   328
while blue, green, and violet are of the cool family. Both psychologically   343
and visually, warm colors are advancing and energetic, while cool colors   358
are receding and symbolic of repose.   366

9   One of the signs of a "beaten man" is the aimless way he shuffles along   16
when he walks. Chances are, he drags his feet, making a grating sound with   32
every step. He also probably walks duck-footed; that is, with his toes   47
pointing outward to form a V if viewed from above.   58

All right, you can picture the wrong way to walk. Now let's get down to   74
the right way.   77

When you walk, the length of your stride—the space between your steps—   93
should be approximately one and a half times the length of your shoe. In   108
other words, your shoe is probably 10 to 12 inches long. Your stride should   124
be approximately 15 to 18 inches.   131

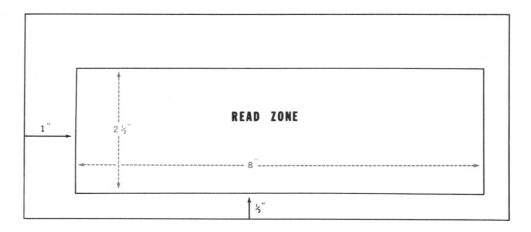

The post office asks that the new two-letter state abbreviations be used with **ZIP** codes so that this line of the address will fit within the read zone. Learn these new abbreviations, which are listed on page 145. (It is still permissible, however, to spell the state name in full, but the letter will not be automatically sorted.)

On-arrival directions are typed four lines below the return address rather than below the main address so that they will not interfere with the reading of the address.

Mailing notations are typed below the stamp position and at least three lines above the envelope address.

CONFIDENTIAL   REGISTERED

```
           I 3.
           Mr. George H. Reynolds
           Martin Manufacturing Company
           15 South Wabash Avenue
           Chicago, IL    60614
```

CONFIDENTIAL   REGISTERED

```
           Mr. George H. Reynolds
           Martin Manufacturing Company
           15 South Wabash Avenue
           Chicago, IL    60614
```

Your arms should hang relaxed at your sides, palms toward the thighs— 146
barely touching them as they swing forward to the front of your body, and 161
then back. Elbows close to the waist. Remember—palms in, elbows close to 177
the waist. Shoulders relaxed. 184

As you walk keep the toes pointed straight ahead and place your feet 199
directly to the side of an imaginary line running down the center. Do not 214
step on this line. Your right foot should be to the right of this line—your 230
left foot to the left. Your feet should point straight ahead—neither duck- 246
footed nor pigeon-toed. And lift them so there's no drag or scrape. 260

Naturally, as you walk you carry yourself in your perfect posture posi- 275
tion—head up, back straight, shoulders relaxed, tailbone tucked forward. 290

If you are carrying an attaché case, hold it with a relaxed grip. Don't 306
swing it wildly at your side as you walk, but rather keep it fairly stable. A 322
very slight motion is essential for balance, but don't overdo it. 336

Also, whenever you enter an office, switch your attaché case to your left 352
hand. This leaves your right hand free to greet people or to hand your 367
business card to the receptionist. 375

10   In the past two hundred years, as civilization became more complicated, 16
the need for more sophisticated calculating machines became evident. 30
Several fairly sophisticated machines were developed before the 19th 44
century that were similar in design and theory to modern-day devices, 58
except that these machines were relatively slow, inefficient, and sometimes 74
didn't work because of unavailability of parts and/or sufficiently intelligent 90
operators. One early calculating machine was invented around 1642 by a 105
French philosopher and mathematician named Blaise Pascal. This machine 120
was an adding machine that consisted of a series of wheels that added up 135
to 10 and then generated a carry into the next column. Multiplication could 151
be performed on this machine by repeated addition. 162

Shortly after Pascal's machine was invented, another machine called the 178
Stepped Reckoner was invented by another philosopher and mathema- 191
tician named Gottfried von Leibnitz. This machine was a gear-operated 206
calculator which allowed for a carry operation between places. Multiplica- 221
tion could be performed directly in this machine. 231

An English mathematician, Charles Babbage, invented a calculating 245
machine in the middle of the 1800's which could solve rather complex prob- 260
lems. However, Babbage could never get his machine to work because the 275
technology of his time was not prepared to produce the accurate parts he 290
required. His invention, therefore, never got past the design stage although 306
the machine was capable of handling up to 1,000 numbers of up to 50 320
numerals each in length! An interesting aside here is the fact that many 335
modern-day computers have number capacities that are much smaller than 350
the capacity of Babbage's machine, which he called the Analytical Engine. 366

Type No. 6¾ envelopes using your name and address for the return address and addressing them to the following:

1. Trade Manufacturing Company, 13 West 15 Street, Albany, New York 12204

2. Mrs. May Leary, 23 North Street, Seattle, Washington 98112

3. Mr. Charles Brown, 259 Oregon Avenue, Austin, Texas 78716

4. Mr. George Press, 21 River Street, Avon, Connecticut 06001

5. Miss Lillian King, 10 Woodlawn Avenue, Atlanta, Georgia 30303

JOB 2

Type No. 10 envelopes (with return address printed) addressing them to the following:

1. Mr. George A. Coleman, Bentley High School, Danbury, Connecticut 06810

2. Mr. Leo Glenn, 1180 Lester Place, Ames, Iowa 50010

3. Miss Eleanor Crandall, 17 Elm Street, Philadelphia, Pennsylvania 19114

4. Central High School, Stafford, Connecticut 06075

5. Mr. James R. Baker, 62 Spring Street, Portland, Oregon 97262

The U.S. Post Office Department now uses Optical Character Readers to hasten the sorting and distribution of first-class mail. The ZIP code and the name of the city and state are read electronically and the letters are sorted into appropriate bins.

The Optical Character Readers can read numbers, capitals, and small letters if they are typed. When a letter is slotted into the OCR, an "eye" reads from the bottom of the envelope or card upward. Another "eye" reads from the left edge inward. If something is wrong with the envelope or something interferes, the envelope is rejected and must be sorted by hand.

Since there are limits to the capabilities of the OCR, envelopes and cards must be addressed in such a way that the OCR will be able to read them. The placement suggested on page 158 will position the address in the read zone that is shown in the following illustration.

		Words
11	Also in the 19th century, another English mathematician, George Boole,	16
	was doing the groundwork for the algebra of logic. The algebra was to	31
	become an important tool in the design of today's digital computers. This	46
	algebra of logic became known as Boolean algebra.	56

In 1890, an American scientist working for the Census Bureau, Dr. Herman Hollerith, invented the forerunner of today's calculating machines that use punched cards. Actually, Dr. Hollerith used punched tape. The punched holes represented the data the machine was to process, each hole representing a different piece of information. The data contained on the punched tape were read by a scanner which was able to perform arithmetic and sorting operations on the data. This method was successfully used in the United States Census of 1890. Later Dr. Hollerith developed the punched card code now used in IBM cards and aptly called the Hollerith code. As a matter of fact, all computer manufacturers, not just IBM, use the Hollerith code for punched cards.

After Hollerith's innovation in 1890, the development of data processing and calculating machines proceeded at a rapid pace. The greatest strides were made by IBM in their development of unit record equipment. Remember that this equipment was relatively slow and depended on wired control panels for instructions.

The first successful large-scale general-purpose digital computer capable of performing automatic computations was developed by the International Business Machine Corporation (IBM) and Dr. Howard Aiken during the years from 1939 to 1944. The machine was originally known as the Automatic Sequence Controlled Calculator (ASCC), and became known as the Harvard Mark I when it was presented to Harvard University in August of 1944. This machine was the culmination of the work Charles Babbage had done; the advanced technology of the 1940's permitted fabrication of the parts not available to Babbage a century earlier. Actually, Dr. Aiken came across Babbage's papers and drawings. Unfortunately, this discovery came after Dr. Aiken had duplicated much of Babbage's work.

12 There are countless dictionaries on the market today—college dictionaries, high school dictionaries, pocket dictionaries, office dictionaries. It's important to pick one that is up to date and thumb-indexed for quick reference. Although it's important to choose the proper dictionary, it's equally important to know how to use it. Here are some hints that may help you develop the dictionary habit.

Examine the table of contents and look through the book. You may be amazed to find such a wide range of information. There are biographical listings, tables of weights and measures, rules for spelling and pronunciation, foreign words and phrases, and signs and symbols. Become aware of the fund of information that is available right at your fingertips.

ADDRESSING ENVELOPES

There are two standard sizes of envelopes. The small envelope is called No. 6¾ and it measures 6½ by 3⅝ inches. The large envelope is called No. 10 and it measures 9½ by 4⅛ inches.

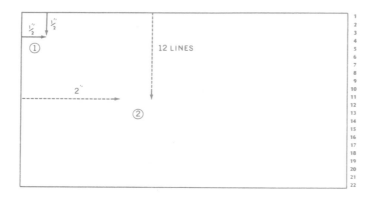

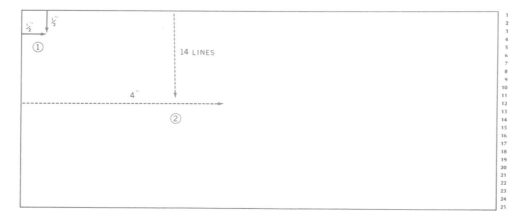

1. RETURN ADDRESS (if not printed) begins on line 3, ½ inch from the edge, and is blocked. No personal title is needed except for Mrs.

2. NAME and ADDRESS begin on line 12, 2½ inches from the left edge of a small envelope; or on line 14, 4 inches from the left edge of a large envelope. Type the address in block style with single spacing. Type the city, state name or abbreviation, and ZIP code on the last line of the address, allowing one to three spaces between the state and ZIP code. Always use an appropriate personal title on an envelope address to an individual.

State house numbers in figures except for the house number one. Spell out street names that are numbers from one through ten. The use of ST, D, RD, or TH after street-name numbers is local preference. The post office prefers them but businessmen tend not to use them, particularly when a word separates the house number and the street number.

Any word defined in the dictionary is called a vocabulary entry. It's | 173

usually printed in type different from that of the definition. | 186

The first and last entries on the page are printed at the top of the page, | 202

indicating that the words between those two alphabetical arrangements | 216

are listed on that page. | 221

Divisions are usually indicated by centered periods or hyphens. | 235

Whenever more than one spelling is listed, the first is generally preferred. | 252

Pronunciation is usually indicated in parentheses following the entry. | 268

To know how to use the phonetic symbols, refer to the pronunciation key | 283

at the bottom of the page. | 289

The grammatical designation is given for each word in this form: n. for | 305

noun, v. for verb, etc. | 310

A brief history is given of each word. This is known as etymology. | 325

Plurals are usually given only if they are irregular. Synonyms appear at | 341

the end of the entry. Antonyms are given after the synonyms. | 354

In addition, you will find labels, usages, and definitions. The prefixes and | 371

suffixes are listed as entries. | 378

13

There was a time when the capitalist was a person of great wealth, but | 16

that is no longer true. The country is full of capitalists today, of people | 32

who have a nest egg. | 37

Millionaires have become proportionately fewer, and people in the middle- | 53

income brackets have prospered as never before. At one time hundreds of | 68

investors with millions of dollars were able to supply all the funds that | 83

American industry needed for expansion. Today industry also looks to the | 98

millions of people with hundreds of dollars. In 1965 the New York Stock | 113

Exchange estimated that more than half of the people owning shares in | 127

American business had incomes of less than $10,000 a year. | 140

Everyone who can afford it should own a share of American business. To | 156

decide whether you can afford to invest, ask yourself these questions: Can | 172

I cover living expenses comfortably? Do I have adequate insurance? Do I | 187

have enough ready cash to meet emergencies? If you can answer yes to | 201

these questions, you should think about investing. | 212

Bondholders, unlike stockholders, are not part owners of a company. | 227

They are creditors of the company. People who buy a company's bonds | 241

lend their money to that company, and the company agrees to pay them | 255

back at a set date and at a set rate of interest. | 266

Bonds are regarded as the safest kind of security because they have prior | 282

claim. If the company fails, the bondholders must be paid before stock- | 296

holders can receive anything. The prices of bonds do not fluctuate as much | 312

as stock prices. | 316

In addition to corporate bonds, there are state, city, and U.S. Government | 332

bonds. The state and city bonds are called municipal bonds, and they | 356

NAMES OF MONTHS IN SEVEN LANGUAGES

English*	Latin*	German*	French	Spanish	Italian	Portuguese
January	Januarius	Januar	janvier	enero	gennaio	janeiro
February	Februarius	Februar	février	febrero	febbraio	fevereiro
March	Martius	März	mars	marzo	marzo	março
April	Aprilis	April	avril	abril	aprile	abril
May	Maius	Mai	mai	mayo	maggio	maio
June	Junius	Juni	juin	junio	giugno	junho
July	Julius	Juli	juillet	julio	luglio	julho
August	Augustus	August	août	agosto	agosto	agôsto
September	September	September	septembre	se(p)tiembre	settembre	setembro
October	October	Oktober	octobre	octubre	ottobre	outubro
November	November	November	novembre	noviembre	novembre	novembro
December	December	Dezember	decembre	diciembre	dicembre	dezembro

Source: Style Manual of the United States Government Printing Office.

*Note that the months are capitalized in these three languages and not in the others.

attract many investors because the Federal Government does not tax the 371
income from these bonds as it does the income from corporate and most 385
U.S. Government bonds. 390

Bonds are usually issued in $1,000 units, but they are usually quoted as 406
though the price were a percentage of the face value. 417

The stock of a company represents the ownership of that company. If you 433
own a share of stock, you own a piece of that company. How much you own 448
depends upon how many shares of stock have been issued by that company. 463

People buy stock to make money. The money they make is known as 477
dividends. The size of the dividends depends upon how much the company 492
earns in a given year. The company's board of directors decides what divi- 507
dends will be paid and when. You and the other stockholders elect these 522
directors and they are your representatives. They are the real heads of the 538
company; other officers are responsible to them. 548

Companies may issue common stock only or common and preferred. 562
Generally, preferred stock carries a set dividend rate, which must be paid 577
before the common stockholder gets anything. However, if a company 591
really booms, the common stockholder can anticipate larger dividends 605
while the preferred stockholder still gets his first set rate. 618

14 Stenographers are often mistakenly called secretaries. There is a great 16
difference between the duties assigned to a stenographer and the responsi- 31
bilities that a secretary carries. The stenographer's job and the secretary's 47
job are alike in only one major respect and that is the ability to take dicta- 63
tion and to transcribe it into a mailable letter. As a stenographer, you are 79
expected to do just the work which is assigned to you. As a secretary, you 95
will participate in the office operation on a far broader scale. You will 110
truly be an assistant to an executive. 118

Many of the things which a secretary must know must actually be learned 134
in school, and others must be learned through experience. 146

What skills does a secretary need? Not only must she be skillful in short- 162
hand and typewriting, but she must also know filing, records, basic office 177
machines, and telephone technique. She must be able to compose routine 192
business letters that are clear, tactful, and complete. She must know the 207
primary sources of information. She must thoroughly understand the pro- 222
cedures in handling incoming and outgoing mail. She must be trained to 236
carry out instructions in an efficient manner. 247

Personal traits are extremely important to your success in secretarial 263
work. In a survey made by the American Management Association, it was 278
learned that about half of the stenographic, secretarial, accounting, and 292
clerical workers who lost their jobs were dismissed because they did not 308
have the right personal traits or because their personal traits or their per- 322
sonalities were definitely undesirable. 331

SMITH STORE

Income Statement

For January, 19__

SALES:		$13,925.00
COST OF SALES:		
Merchandise inventory, January 1, 19__	$20,300.00	
Purchases	14,700.00	
Total	35,000.00	
Deduct merchandise inventory, January 31, 19__	26,550.00	
Net cost of sales		8,450.00
GROSS PROFIT:		5,475.00
OPERATING EXPENSES:		
Delivery expenses	162.00	
Office salaries and wages	300.00	
Store salaries and wages	400.00	
Miscellaneous office expenses	335.00	
Telephone and telegraph	35.00	
Light, heat, and water	55.00	
Total operating expenses		1,287.00
OPERATING PROFIT:		4,188.00
OTHER INCOME:		
Interest income		50.00
TOTAL:		4,238.00
OTHER EXPENSE:		
Interest expense		70.00
NET PROFIT:		$ 4,168.00

If a table is too wide to type in 8½ inches, turn the paper sideways. This allows a 110-space pica or 132-space elite line. There are 51 vertical lines available. Type the following table crosswise on a standard 8½ by 11 sheet.

What are these personality traits? Here are a few which are essential: good appearance, mental alertness, patience, perseverance, personal integrity, and intellectual honesty.

The first step in building a good business personality is developing the right attitude toward your fellow students. You will then be able to carry over this attitude to your fellow employees and to your employer.

As a member of any business organization, your first duty to that organization is loyalty. Loyalty means working for your company and not against it. A person who is really loyal wants the company to succeed and works at all times toward that goal.

Can you keep a secret? Because of the close relationship which exists between the executive and his secretary, you will often learn confidential information about both the business and the personal affairs of your employer. Every business strives for a competitive advantage over other businesses, and often millions of dollars depend on keeping business affairs secret. Other things which should be kept secret are salaries, personnel changes, sales data, and so on. The secretary must be closemouthed about everything that goes on in her office.

As a secretary you must learn to adopt an impersonal attitude toward criticism of your work. There should be no resentment to suggestions or criticisms on carrying out an assignment or on improving work that has not been completed in a satisfactory manner. Sensitiveness has no place in a business office.

Knowing what is important and what is not important should rank high on the list of good qualities. A secretary should have a sense of values. Her attitude toward gossip, toward the shortcomings of others, toward her work, all are important or unimportant in terms of her own sense of values.

15   All of us use numbers every day in the performance of our normal daily activities. Over the years we developed such a great facility with numbers that we are able to add, subtract, multiply, and divide automatically without giving any great thought to the actual processes involved.

Probably the first application of the numbers concept was when man began counting on his fingers. He was, therefore, probably limited to totals of either five and below, or ten and below. This is probably why our number system is based on the number ten and why we have ten numerals, 0 through 9, representing numbers in our system. If primitive man had happened to have six fingers on each hand, then perhaps we would have 12 numerals instead of 10.

As man became more sophisticated, his requirements for numbers and counting became more complex. For example, with the advent of the tradesman came not only a counting system which included numbers greater than nine, but also a requirement arose for recording these counts

SMITH STORE

Balance Sheet

January 31, 19___

A S S E T S

CURRENT ASSETS:
  Cash in bank $17,033.00
  Accounts receivable   21,425.00
  Notes receivable   6,000.00
  Merchandise inventory   26,550.00
    Total current assets $ 71,088.00

INVESTMENTS:
  Investment in corporation bonds   6,000.00

FIXED ASSETS:
  Land (subject to mortgage)   7,000.00
  Buildings (subject to mortgage) 16,000.00
  Furniture and fixtures   3,260.00
  Delivery equipment   1,700.00
    Total fixed assets   27,960.00
                                      $104,968.00

L I A B I L I T I E S   A N D   C A P I T A L

CURRENT LIABILITIES:
  Accounts payable $13,300.00
  Notes payable   6,100.00
    Total current liabilities $ 19,400.00

LONG-TERM LIABILITIES
  Mortgages payable   12,000.00

CAPITAL:
  Robert Smith, Capital, Balance, January 1, 19___   70,000.00
  Add net profit, January 19___   4,168.00
  Total   74,168.00
  Deduct drawing, January 19___   600.00
  Robert Smith, Capital, Balance, January 31, 19___   73,568.00
                                      $104,968.00

for some future use. Each of the nine numerals, therefore, was assigned 225
numeral symbols and a system of adding and subtracting these numerals 239
was devised. This was first done by the early Egyptians around 3400 B.C. 254
when they devised their system of hieroglyphics. The system was obviously 269
devised from the number of fingers being held up for that particular count. 284

With their numerals thus specified, the Egyptians then developed a sand 300
calculator which consisted of columns of grooves etched out in the sand. 315
The hieroglyphic was represented in the sand calculator by placing an 329
appropriate number of pebbles in the right-hand column. The right-hand 344
column could therefore represent any number from 0 through 9 depending 358
on the number of pebbles contained in the groove. The Egyptians also 372
noticed that if the groove contained nine pebbles, there was no more room 387
in the groove for the next pebble. They therefore emptied the groove and 402
placed one pebble in the next column, and this column then represented 417
the number of tens. Further, after 99 pebbles have been counted, not only 432
is there no more room in the first groove, but there is also no room in the 447
second groove. Adding one more pebble caused the first groove to be 461
emptied and caused the second groove to receive another pebble. This 475
caused the second groove to be emptied and caused a pebble to be added to 490
the third, or hundreds, groove. The Egyptians carried this principle further 506
and observed that each groove was representative of numbers 10 times 520
that of the previous groove so that the grooves represented the 1, 10, 100, 535
1000, 10000, 100000, etc., columns. 543

Probably the next number system devised was by the Romans. The Ro- 558
mans, like the Egyptians, assigned unique symbols (called Roman nu- 571
merals) to each of the ten numerals. In addition, symbols were assigned to 587
what the Romans thought were important milestones in the number system 602
(50, 100, 500, 1000). In this system, the number of units, or ones, were repre- 618
sented in the rightmost column, then the number of tens, then the number 633
of fifties, etc. You can see that the number of separate numerals required to 649
write a number can become very large, especially when each numeral in 663
the number to be represented is large. To avoid extremely large numbers, 678
the Romans devised a scheme in which a smaller number to the left of a 692
larger number meant that the smaller number is to be subtracted from the 707
larger number. 710

Even this scheme of shortening the number is limited, by convention, as 726
only one numeral can appear to the left of a larger numeral. 739

The number system we use today is of a Hindu-Arabic origin and our 754
numerals are, therefore, called Arabic numerals. The Hindus are recognized 770
for a most important contribution to mathematical thought: the concept 785
of zero. 787

FINANCIAL STATEMENTS

Financial statements and reports may be prepared in the same way that any other tabulation is prepared. Another method that can be used is the right-to-left method for the body of the statement. This is similar to the backspace method. Instead of beginning at the middle of the page, begin at the right margin:

1. Clear the tab keys and set a one-inch left margin.

2. Move the carriage pointer to one inch from the right edge of the paper and backspace once for each letter, space, or figure in the longest item in the right column. Set a tabulator stop at this point.

3. Backspace for the number of spaces in the intercolumn and the number of spaces in the longest item in the next column. Set a tabulator stop. The machine is now ready for typing this problem.

The main heading is often typed in solid caps with the letters spread. The side heading is typed in solid caps followed by a colon. The account title usually has only the first word capitalized.

Indent the account title two spaces, and indent the total line five spaces from the margin.

For the intercolumn between money columns, allow five elite spaces or three pica spaces.

Keep in mind that all dollar signs in a column must be aligned and that the dollar sign must precede the space occupied by the longest number, which may be at the bottom of the column.

To type a double ruling, use the underscore, backspace, operate ratchet release and move the carriage forward slightly, and type another underscore. Lock the ratchet release and return platen to line of writing.

A total number is preceded and followed by a blank line space.

Type the following jobs as they appear in the illustrations.

16   Imagine the giants of American industry trying to keep their business   15
records on stone tablets. Unthinkable!   23

These businesses cannot survive without highly efficient means for keep-   39
ing records. Under modern business conditions, adequate information to   54
make business decisions cannot be delayed. To survive, the modern firm   69
must quickly adjust to constantly changing conditions—changes in its   83
market, changes in its resources and supplies, changes in its manufacturing   98
and labor situation, changes in its competition. To make decisions based   113
on these many variables, the manager needs vast quantities of information.   129
And he needs this information fast. Tomorrow may be too late.   142

The requirement for timely and adequate information is not new. Since   158
the turn of the Twentieth Century, the need for timely information has   173
increased with the rising production potential created by new and more   188
sophisticated machines. Rising production is not the only reason for which   204
there is an increased need for timely information. The increased domestic   220
market for American production, the geographic dispersion of plants and   235
factories, and the evolution of American industry into the principal sup-   250
plier of the world's needs have also been important factors. Of great   265
importance is the fact that manual methods were becoming inadequate.   279

To meet the demand for more efficient information processing—for ex-   294
ample: sales statistics; inventory controls; production controls—informa-   309
tion processing machines were developed. Machines that used a new   323
concept—the punched card—recorded the information to be processed in a   338
compact and machine-readable form. These new information processing   352
machines could tabulate and reproduce mechanically at much greater   366
speeds than were attainable by manual methods. And these information   380
processing machines could be instructed, by wiring control panels, to make   395
some simple logical decisions.   401

These information processing machines (developed by IBM and com-   415
monly referred to as unit record machines) could perform calculations on   430
punched cards at speeds of up to 150 cards per minute—or 2½ cards per   444
second—and they adequately served the needs of business for many years.   459

By 1950 the information requirements of business had strained the   474
capabilities of these machines. The unit record machines could not process   490
information fast enough to keep up with the increased information require-   505
ments, and their simple logical decision-making ability was not able to   520
cope with the more sophisticated demands of business. A new means of   534
processing information was required—a machine that would operate at   548
higher speeds and that could be instructed to make complicated logical   562
decisions.   564

The electronic computer filled those requirements. Designed in the late   580
1940's, the first electronic computer processed information in thousandths   595
of a second—more than two thousand times as fast as unit record machines.   611

Words

Main Heading: ARDMORE CHINA*   10

11

Secondary Heading: Dinner Service for 12   24

25

26

			Sale Price		39
					40
Column Headings:	Pattern	Decoration	Gold Band	Gold Edge	46

81

Pattern, Blossom; Decoration, Green center; Gold Band, $75.00;

Gold Edge, $68.50   91

Pattern, Bouquet; Decoration, All-over sprays; Gold Band, $59.75;

Gold Edge, $53.50   101

Pattern, Florabel; Decoration, Floral center; Gold Band, $73.00;

Gold Edge, $65.00   111

Pattern, Regis; Decoration, Pink center**; Gold Band, $75.00;

Gold Edge, $68.50   121

Pattern, Springtime; Decoration, Floral center; Gold Band, $85.00;

Gold Edge, $80.00   131

Pattern, Windemere; Decoration, Splatter; Gold Band, $48.00;

Gold Edge, $43.50   140

141

142

145

 *Available for immediate delivery   150

**Available also with Green center   157

Teelman & Sons
Annual Sale
Top-Grade Cutlery

Item	Regular Price	Before Discount Sale Price*
Sewing Scissors	$2.75	$1.83
Straight Trimmer	4.50	3.00
Kitchen Shears	3.75	2.50
Cuticle Scissors	2.00	1.33
Nail Scissors	2.00	1.45
Barber Shears	3.50	2.50
Thinning Shears	3.50	2.35

* In effect only until July 1

These early electronic computers were designed for scientific use. In addition to processing information, the first electronic computers could also be instructed, by external wiring, to make complicated logical decisions. So, although the electronic computer was originally thought of as a tool of mathematics and physics, it quickly became an important tool for business information processing.

17   American business rapidly found new and exciting uses for the electronic computer. Additional requirements for speed and simplicity of instruction became greater as each new use for the electronic computer was developed. The electronic computer was engineered so that it could be given instructions without having to be rewired. Internally stored instructions called programs replaced wiring. The internally stored program made the electronic computer available for different kinds of jobs of information processing without the time-consuming effort of rewiring. In addition, the electronic computer manufacturers increased the speed by steps; from thousandths of a second (milliseconds) to millionths of a second (microseconds) to today's speed of billionths of a second (nanoseconds). Speed of operation and the decision-making ability were now available to American business, and business has put these capabilities to good use.

Today we see evidence of the computer all around us. We receive invoices and bills which have been prepared by electronic computers. When we travel by air, our airline reservations are confirmed by computers. Even travel by auto involves us with the electronic computer. Traffic signals are computer controlled, toll cards on highways are prepared by and will be processed by electronic computers, and automobile registrations are prepared and recorded by computers. These are only some simple examples of the uses of the computer. Business has literally thousands of applications for the electronic computer.

Business information processing requirements such as inventory control, production planning, payroll preparation, just to mention a few, are handled by the electronic computer. Each of these information requirements is different—yet the computer handles them all without much time being spent in giving the computer new instructions. The secret is the internally stored instructions, called a program, which we mentioned earlier. The electronic computer program is a detailed series of instructions that have been prepared by a man or woman called a programmer. The programmer has created the program by breaking a business routine into a series of minute step-by-step procedures. Why does the programmer break a business routine into minute steps? Because all business information processing consists of repeating these minute step-by-step procedures.

For example, let's look at a few of the minute steps required for payroll preparation. First, we must multiply the hours worked by the rate of pay,

Words

AVERAGE CHARGES TO COLLEGE STUDENTS

1968 and 1978

Type of Charge	1968		1978*	
	Public	Private	Public	Private
Tuition and Required Fees	$292	$1,327	$367	$1,855
Board Rates	470	521	470	521
Dormitory Rooms	314	411	409	546

Source: U.S. Office of Education
*Projected

22
23
31
32
33
46
47
101
102
116
126
136
137
138
139
146
148

Main Heading: MONTHLY SALES

Secondary Headings: Total for Branch Offices

Eastern Division

First Three Quarters

Column Headings: Month   This Year   Last Year

In January, This Year, sales were $44,005.67; Last Year, $42,996.63

In February, This Year, sales were $35,119.58; Last Year, $36,608.82

In March, This Year, sales were $38,078.94[a]; Last Year, $38,954.65

In April, This Year, sales were $45,678.20; Last Year, $42,890.06

In May, This Year, sales were $41,876.45; Last Year, $40,246.89

In June, This Year, sales were $33,509[b]; Last Year, $39,228.07

In July, This Year, sales were $43,888.56; Last Year, $28,115.39

In August, This Year, sales were $43,390.75; Last Year, $40,160.43

In September, This Year, sales were $47,995.98; Last Year, $43,726.07

[a]Does not include Boston, Massachusetts

[b]Does not include Rutland, Vermont

[c]Does not include Hartford, Connecticut

8
9
24
35
36
37
62
63
94
95
102
110
118
125
132
140
148
155
163
164
174
183
193

giving us the gross pay for an employee. Then we must calculate the pay- | 546
roll tax deductions from the gross pay to determine the employee's net pay. | 560
Of course, these are only two of the steps we would have to detail in order | 575
to complete a payroll. What do you think the steps would be to calculate the | 590
net pay for the next employee? How about the next thousand employees? | 605
The same steps are repeated for each employee. The wonderful thing about | 620
the electronic computer is that it can repeat the same steps (the program) | 635
endlessly and perform these steps in the same exact way the thousandth or | 650
millionth time as it did the first time. What's more, the electronic computer | 666
does this and never gets tired or bored! | 674

18 Brainstorming is group creative thinking. The popular picture of a typical | 16
business session has half a dozen executives sitting around a room. One of | 31
them throws out a wild idea and the other five jump on him. They show | 46
him all the reasons the idea won't work. Result—few ideas are suggested | 61
for fear of looking ridiculous. That's exactly what brainstorming isn't. | 76

The advantage to the group creative thinking—brainstorming—is that | 91
there are more imaginations involved, each one activating the others. One | 106
man's idea prompts the next man's idea. The third man gets a related idea. | 122
The fourth man twists it and reapplies it. Priority is given to combinations | 138
of ideas—syntheses. In effect, one man's ideas ride piggyback on another | 153
man's ideas. The whole imaginative side to creative thinking is speeded up. | 169

Research has indicated that four men involved in brainstorming the | 184
solution to a problem will create more different possible solutions than | 199
the total number of possible solutions created by the same four men acting | 214
independently. In other words, the four men working together may create, | 229
let us say, 35 solutions to a problem. Working alone, each might create 7 | 245
different ideas—a total of only 28 ideas. The reason is obvious—piggy- | 260
backing. One man's idea creates the impetus for the next man's idea, that | 275
idea for someone else's, and so forth. | 283

How does brainstorming work? Brainstorming works best in a group | 297
that has enough members to keep the ball rolling, but not so many that | 312
each member can't repeatedly get into the act. Four to six people is usually | 328
a good number. | 331

Before starting, the group-leader should set a time limit for the brain- | 347
storming—at least five minutes and no more than fifteen minutes at a time | 362
unless the group is "hot." Someone should be assigned to write all ideas | 377
as they are suggested. | 382

Now the brainstorming session is on. The group is small enough so that | 398
no parliamentary procedures need be followed. It's completely informal. | 413

Someone has an idea and suggests it. Someone else has another and | 428
speaks right up and so on. No criticism of ideas is permitted—yet. All ideas | 444
are listed. Finally, the time is up—the list is quite long. Now what? | 459

Year	Winner		Year	Winner	
					7
					8
					9
1934	Horton Smith		1952	Sam Snead	38
1935	Gene Sarazen*		1953	Ben Hogan	39
1936	Horton Smith		1954	Sam Snead*	49
1937	Byron Nelson		1955	Cary Middlecoff	58
1938	Henry Picard		1956	Jack Burke	68
1939	Ralph Guldahl		1957	Doreg Ford	79
1940	Jimmy Demaret		1958	Arnold Palmer	89
1941	Craig Wood		1959	Art Wall	99
1942	Byron Nelson*		1960	Arnold Palmer	110
1946	Herman Keiser		1961	Gary Player	118
1947	Jimmy Demaret		1962	Arnold Palmer*	128
1948	Claude Harmon		1963	Jack Nicklaus	138
1949	Sam Snead		1964	Arnold Palmer	149
1950	Jimmy Demaret		1965	Jack Nicklaus	160
1951	Ben Hogan		1966	Jack Nicklaus*	170
					180
					190
					191

*Won in playoff

Braced Headings

A braced heading is one that identifies more than one column.

1. Capitalize the first letter of each word unless it is a preposition, article, or conjunction. If such a word begins the heading, however, it should be capitalized.

2. The braced heading is to be centered over the entire space that it braces.

3. Underscore the braced heading, extending the underscore only to the edges of the headings that it braces, even if the columns extend beyond their headings.

4. Allow one blank line between the braced heading and the column headings.

5. In practice, leave space for the braced heading, but do not type it until the column headings have been typed. After typing the column headings, roll the cylinder back and type the braced heading.

Salaries		
Department	Day	Evening
Accounting	$13,478	$4,220

Center the following jobs on a full sheet. Use single spacing.

Now it's time to evaluate. The ideas are read off one by one, analyzed   475
and criticized one by one. Bad ideas are discarded. Good ideas stay on the   491
list. From the list of good solutions to the problem, the best solution is   507
chosen. The others are reserved as "possibilities"—to be used if the best   523
solution doesn't work out. And that's the end of the brainstorming session.   539

What's the advantage of brainstorming, you may ask, if bad ideas are   554
rejected in the end anyway? Why not reject them right away? But that's   569
the very point. If a participant knows that ideas will be subject to imme-   584
diate criticism, he will start censoring his own ideas before he states them,   600
making sure he expresses only "good" ideas. Result: Fewer ideas—good   615
ones or bad ones. Further result: Less opportunity for piggybacking of   630
ideas, yielding a net of even fewer total ideas—good or bad.   643

Many firms use brainstorming, or some close variation, as a basic   657
creativity process. By understanding the process, you will be prepared to   672
participate effectively. As you should recognize by now, brainstorming is   687
simply the application to a group of your individual key to creativity—   702
suspending judgment.   706

19   The first secret of a good memory is concentration. If you concentrate on   16
remembering, you can remember. What does concentration involve? Three   31
procedures: (1) You have to want to remember. (2) You have to exercise   47
your memory. (3) You have to screen out distractions. Here's how you go   62
about developing these three keys to concentration.   73

How many times has a friend of yours asked you to remind him to do   88
something? And how often have you answered: "I'll remind you if you   102
remind me to remind you"? That's more than just a quick quip. You're   117
telling your friend that you don't intend to remember because you have no   132
stake in what he wants to remember.   140

Obviously, you're going to try to remember only those things that are   155
important to you. Your problem is to decide what is important.   168

As an executive you have to remember the basic facts about your com-   183
pany—for instance, whether you produce widgets or what-nots, whether   197
the competition produces cheaper widgets or what-nots than you do, and   212
so forth. You're a storehouse of information. But most important, an   227
executive has to remember people—their names and faces.   239

In an effort to turn his big customers into bigger customers, Andrew   254
Carnegie named his steel plants after them. The Edgar Thompson Steel   268
Works, for example, was named for the President of Pennsylvania Railroad.   283
A pretty transparent gimmick, you think? Maybe so. But the railroad from   298
that day on bought all of its rails from the Edgar Thompson plant.   312

20   Name power is business power, especially in these days of business   15
bigness. Let's face it, you don't have to know a man's name in order to   30
handle his business efficiently. You can serve a Mr. X as well as you can   45

Center the following table on a full sheet. Make the horizontal and vertical rulings with a pencil or pen. Use double spacing.

				Words
Arabic Numerals	Roman Numerals	Cardinal Numbers	Ordinal Numbers	18
				38
				39
				40
				41
1	I	one	first	47
2	II	two	second	53
3	III	three	third	60
4	IV	four	fourth	66
5	V	five	fifth	72
10	X	ten	tenth	78
50	L	fifty	fiftieth	85

Footnotes

Footnotes are separated from the body of the copy by a 1½-inch underline, which is preceded by a single space and followed by a double space.

Center the following tables on a full sheet. Make the vertical ruling with pen or pencil. Use single spacing.

JOB 1

			Words
MIDWINTER FURNITURE SALE			13
Open-Stock Dining Room[1]			15
			31
			32
			33
Piece	Regular Price	Sale Price	41
			63
Shield-back Side Chair[2]	$ 29.50	$ 24.50	75
Breakfront	186.00	173.00	82
Credenza[3]	193.00	178.00	90
			91
			92
			93
[1]Mahogany-finished hardwood			100
[2]Available in other finishes			108
[3]Mahogany front			113

serve a Mr. Witherspoon. But how does Mr. Witherspoon feel about it? 59
Call him "Mr. Witherspoon" and he's a big man. But call him "Mr. X" or 73
"Customer #34-02," and he'd just as soon take his business elsewhere. Mr. 88
Witherspoon, after all, is only human. He wants to be remembered as a 103
human being. So do you. So does everybody else. How do you remember 117
Mr. Witherspoon? Take the next step. 125

Memory power, like muscle power, is built up by use. You have to prac- 140
tice remembering in order to become a rememberer, just as you'd have to 155
practice lifting weights in order to become a weight lifter. You start easy, 171
then you take on harder and harder challenges. Soon you find yourself 186
remembering more than you ever thought possible. 196

At Scotland Yard, detectives are trained in memory. The teacher starts 212
off the new student by having him look at a display of small objects— 226
maybe half a dozen at first. Then the teacher covers the display and asks 241
the student to repeat what he saw. Once the student can recall everything 256
in the display, he's challenged with a harder test. Those Scotland Yard 271
detectives can, at a glance, take in the doors, windows, locks, latches, and 287
details of a room. 291

The only difference between them and you is that their memories are 306
well-exercised—they've practiced this technique of concentrating on details. 322
After you've practiced, you'll be as adept as they. Use photographs in 337
magazines, and practice looking at details until you can remember every- 351
body in a simple picture. Then challenge yourself with more complicated 366
pictures until you can walk out of a real life situation and remember 380
everybody you saw there. 385

Before you can stash anything away in your memory, you first have to 400
get your mind on it. Memory, by definition, is nothing more than the mind's 416
way of retraveling a course it has traveled before. It stands to reason that 432
you have to drive carefully the first time. That's not so easy as it seems. 448
Your mind is eager to wander. And there are all kinds of distractions to 463
lure it off the track. 468

Boredom is the biggest of the built-in obstacles you have to hurdle. You 484
can fake interest without even realizing it. When you meet Mr. Witherspoon, 500
for example, you stare straight at him, you smile, you look alert. But you 515
record nothing. Solution: Tell yourself Mr. Witherspoon may someday 529
become your biggest customer and that you're going to meet him again 543
tomorrow. The trick is to arouse your interest in him and give yourself a 558
stake in remembering. 563

You can use basically the same technique to beat boredom with anything 579
else you want to remember. To arouse your interest in a meeting or lecture, 595
for instance, take notes—not word-for-word records, but translations and 610
summaries in your own terms. Jot down questions that come to your 624
mind, too. In doing this, you'll force yourself to put your mind to work on 640

Center the following table on a full sheet. Make the horizontal rulings with the underscore key. Note that the dollar sign is typed only once in the first line of each column and not repeated unless there is an average or total. The dollar signs are aligned one under the other. (The rulings are not counted in the word count.)

	MONTHLY SALES		Words
			8
	Total for Branch Offices		9
			24
			25
			26
			27
Month	This Year	Last Year	43
			44
			45
			46
January	$44,005.67	$42,996.63	54
February	35,119.58	36,608.82	62
March	38,078.94	38,954.65	69
April	45,678.20	42,890.06	76
May	41,876.45	40,246.89	83
June	33,509.00	39,228.07	90
July	43,888.56	28,115.39	97
August	43,390.75	40,160.43	104
September	47,995.98	43,726.07	116
			117
			118
AVERAGE	$41,504.79	$39,214.11	126

what's being said. You can also use this method with a book that bores you: 656
Translate, summarize, and question. Don't take excessive notes, though, 671
or your notetaking will become a distraction in itself. 682

Outside distractions sometimes are easier to combat, sometimes harder. 698
Often your mind wanders because your attention is caught up by something 713
else. A bit of stray conversation from the next office sounds interesting—the 729
view out the window catches your eye—the room feels too hot or too cold. 744
Screen out these distractions before you get down to business. Close your 759
office door before you start your work. Draw the blinds. Get the radiators 775
or air conditioning working properly. Remember, though, that in an office 790
you can't rid yourself of all distractions unless you work in solitary confine- 806
ment. You'll just have to discipline yourself to concentrate on the single 822
situation at hand. Place a mental shield around this focal point. 836

All right! Now you know how to concentrate. You learned, first, that you 852
have to want to remember. Next, you learned how to exercise your memory. 867
Then you learned how to screen out distractions. Half the job in remember- 882
ing is done. 885

21 You have five senses—sight, hearing, smell, taste, and touch. These five 16
senses feed your mind. Your mind takes impressions from your eyes, your 31
ears, your nose, your tastebuds, your fingertips, skin, and muscles. Every 47
mental note is first an impression on your senses. The greater the number 62
of impressions—of any name or any thing—the greater the impact on your 77
memory. 79

If you can gather five kinds of impressions, you'll store all five. Granted, 96
this usually is impossible. How can you taste a name? You can't. You can, 112
however, store three impressions of a name instead of just one. 125

To remember the name of a person as you meet him, listen to it carefully 141
first. You'll get and store the sound of it. Second, visualize the name. In 157
your mind, see how it looks. You'll get and store the sight of it. Third, write 173
the name if you can. You'll get the "feel" of it. Also, repeat it aloud so that 189
you get another "feel" of it. 195

Make sure, though, that you get the name right the first time. If you 211
don't catch a name when it's mumbled at you, ask to have it repeated. If 226
necessary, ask for the spelling. That will help you visualize it, too. 240

Your memory for names isn't going to do you much good, however, unless 255
you can connect the names with the right faces. How do you do that? By 270
adding to your visual impressions of each name. 280

When you meet a man and his name at the same time, get a clear impres- 295
sion of both face and name. Concentrate on the face. Then visualize the 310
name, as if it were printed in capital letters across the man's collar. Try to 326
burn this image into your memory. You'll remember the face more easily— 341
and the name, too. Why? Because you will have added to your visual 355
impression. 358

Center the following table on a half sheet. Double space the body. Determine the spaces between columns and use open leaders. Note that the percent sign, unlike the dollar sign, is repeated.

TREND IN SHARE OWNERSHIP

Year	Number (millions)	Percent of U.S. Population	Words
			14
			15
			16
			27
			66
1952	6.5	4%	76
1956	8.6	5%	86
1959	12.5	7%	93
1962	17.0	9%	108
1965	20.1	10%	118
1968	24.0	12%	129
1969	26.4	13%	140

Boxed Tables

A boxed table is one with both vertical and horizontal ruled lines. The lines divide the columns and headings but do not close in the sides. Arrange and type the table as usual, leaving spaces for the lines (one extra line space for each ruling), and then draw the lines with pen or pencil.

Horizontal lines extend a quarter of an inch beyond the two sides. To draw horizontal lines, place the pencil point or pen through the cardholder (or on the type bar guide above the ribbon) and depress the carriage-release lever while drawing the carriage across the line. (If vertical rulings are not needed, the horizontal rulings may be made with the underscore.)

Vertical lines are centered within the blank-space columns. To draw vertical lines, operate the ratchet release and place the pencil point or pen through the cardholder (or on the type bar guide above the ribbon). Roll the platen up until you have a line of the desired length. Remove the pen or pencil and reset the ratchet release and return the platen to the typing line.

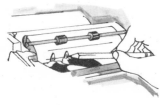

Horizontal

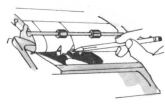

Vertical

The next step works on the same principle. The difference is that you 373
associate the man with something or someone else. You paint a picture 378
around him. There are two ways to do this. One of them helps you remem- 402
ber the man's face and the important facts about him. The other helps you 417
remember the name. 421

To remember the face and the facts, visualize the man in the setting 436
that's most meaningful to you. If you know that he works at the XYZ 450
Company, for instance, picture him there—at his desk or in the plant or 465
wherever he should be. If the XYZ Company produces, for instance, mouse 480
traps, picture the man examining a mouse trap. Throw in as many 493
significant details as you want, but make it a clear sharp picture. Then 508
focus on your picture—burn it into your memory. See him clearly in the 523
pose you've painted so that whenever you meet him again, you'll see that 538
picture instantly. 542

With some names, you try a different approach. First you picture the 557
man. Then you paint a mental picture of the visual image that the name 572
itself conjures up. 576

Take Mr. Baker. Imagine him pulling a pie from the oven. Get a clear 591
mental picture of it. The next time you see Mr. Baker, your mind will 605
flash back to that impression. Know a Mr. Carpenter? A Mr. Hunter? A 619
Mr. Fisher? Use the same kind of picture. 627

Elongate Mr. Long; stretch him until he's ten feet tall. Know a Mr. 642
Small? Shrink him down to one-quarter inch. 651

But how about Mr. Edgington? Visualize a one-ton weight—with a lace 666
edging around it. Stand Mr. Edgington on top of it. 677

Silly? Of course. That's the point. The sillier the picture you paint, the 694
more you're likely to remember it. Almost every name lends itself to some 709
kind of silly picture. Remember, though, that you have to take a few 723
seconds to concentrate on each picture after you paint it. You have to let 738
it burn into your memory by concentrating and associating. 750

Once you've stashed away a memory, you still have no guarantee that 765
it will stay where you put it. Memory is the mind's tendency to retravel 780
a course it has traveled before. It's like a habit. You have to fix a memory 796
as you fix a habit, by repetition. You remember in order to reinforce your 811
first impression. How do you do that? 819

When you're first introduced to a man, you have a golden opportunity 834
to practice his name. You simply use it as often as you can in talking to 849
him. For instance, instead of saying, "How do you do?" you say, "How do 864
you do, Mr. Witherspoon?" Address him by name frequently during the 878
conversation. And close it with "Good-bye, Mr. Witherspoon." (Bonus: 893
You'll flatter him by doing this.) 900

Paint your mental picture of Mr. Witherspoon immediately, while you're 916
you're talking to him and using his name. Visualize him in the setting in 931

Center the following table horizontally and vertically on a full sheet. Double-space the body. Determine spaces between columns and use close leaders.

1968 WINTER OLYMPICS MEDAL TABLE

	Gold	Silver	Bronze	Total	Words
					19
					20
					21
					51
Norway	6	6	2	14	61
USSR	5	5	3	13	71
Austria	3	4	4	11	81
France	4	3	2	9	91
Netherlands	3	3	3	9	101
Sweden	3	2	3	8	111
West Germany	2	2	3	7	120
United States	1	5	1	7	130
Switzerland	0	2	4	6	140
Finland	1	2	2	5	150
East Germany	1	2	2	5	160
Italy	4	0	0	4	169
Czechoslovakia	1	2	1	4	179
Canada	1	1	1	3	189
Rumania	0	0	1	1	199

which you met, or at his office, or with the mutual associate who intro- 945
duced you. Visualize your image of his name printed in capital letters right 961
across his collar. Visualize the picture you painted of his name. 975

Later on, if someone mentions Mr. Witherspoon to you or if you have 991
other reason to think of him, visualize him in those pictures you painted. 1006
This takes only an instant—a split second. But it goes a long way in rein- 1021
forcing your memory so that the next time you meet Mr. Witherspoon, 1035
you'll know him by name and call him by name. And, who knows? Some 1049
day Mr. Witherspoon may be worth a million dollars to you. 1061

22   The longest memory is shorter than the shortest pencil. One sure-fire 15
way of remembering is to write it down! Although you have to remember 30
many names and faces and facts and figures, there are some things you 44
simply don't have to commit to memory. Your day's schedule, for instance, 59
is better kept on an appointment calendar than in your mind. No sense 73
in putting yourself to the trouble of remembering it. 84

There are dozens of memory joggers that will do your remembering 98
for you. Here's a list to consider as a starter. Decide which ones are best 114
for you. Then remember to use them. 122

A desk calendar lets you note, briefly, everything you have to do during 138
the course of a day—calls, letters, meetings, and so on. It also lets you 153
note major projects well in advance of the deadline. You make a note on 168
the day you want to get started. And you can include tasks that merely 183
have to be done "sometime." Then keep entering them on the calendar 197
until they're done. Some calendars serve also as records of what you've 212
done in the past. With others you have to tear off the page each day to 227
get to the next one. 232

Here are some tips to make your desk calendar a more effective tool: 247
"X" out holidays and vacation days so you won't inadvertently schedule 262
business for those days. Underscore any time notations for conferences, 277
appointments, and so on. Enter your "must-be-dones" in red, your personal 292
notations in pencil. Cross off each notation as you finish the job. Reenter 308
anything that's left over when the day runs out. 318

A tickler file is a set of tabbed guides for each month of the year and a 334
set of tabbed guides numbered 1-31. The daily guides are placed behind 349
the current month guide. You write notes to yourself on index cards and 363
file them behind the appropriate date guides. Each day you pull out the 378
reminder cards and move the guide card for that day behind the next 392
month guide. 395

To make a tickler file more efficient, list instructions for recurring jobs 411
on one card. You can move it from month to month if your instructions 425
include your deadline schedule. 432

When a column has been totaled, underscore the column concerned.
The underscore is followed with one blank line.

133	805	20	436	6
6513	3744	260	73	12
585	24	1201	789	18
3961	8857	83	5002	25
167	56	545	760	37
				38
10859	13486	2109	7060	46

JOB 4

The dollar sign is not repeated except in the total. Align the dollar sign
in the total with the one at the top.

William L. Parker	Columbus, Ohio	$1,302	10
Marion Gordon	St. Louis, Missouri	627	20
Richard Gibbons	Atlanta, Georgia	3,158	29
Warren Loyde	Trenton, New Jersey	1,293	39
John R. Davis	Fort Worth, Texas	767	48
Dorothy Kennedy	New York, N. Y.	2,013	58
Shirley Adams	Forest Hills, N. Y.	830	69
			70
TOTAL		$9,990	75

JOB 5

MASON HARDWARE COMPANY   14

    15

Report of Sales   24

    25

    26

New   29

Item	Quantity	Stock No.	Price	
				65
Door Chimes; 1; 603; $8.15				73
Rubber Hose; 18 feet; 6254; $3.80				82
Shovel; 1; 118; $5.35				88
Tool Chest; 4; 85; $24.90				96
Steel Cabinet; 3; 437; $45.00				104
Manual Drill; 6; 79; $9.00				111
Brackets; 8; 2061; $16.35				119

Leaders

    Dots or dashes (leaders) are used in a table to make the reading lines easier to follow. The leaders may be typed with no spaces between characters (close) or with a space between characters (open). In either style, the dots or dashes are aligned one under the other with each ending at the same point. Allow two or three spaces open at the beginning and end of each line.

A month-at-a-glance calendar gives you a general picture of your month's work. Of course, there's no room for detailed instructions. A monthly calendar is just a useful supplement to a more detailed reminder system.

Pocket reminders tell you what to do when you're out of the office. They're like small desk calendars. Usually you have a page for each day, and each page is marked off into hours or half-hours so you can list your appointments in order.

If you need more detailed reminders, carry 3 x 5 index cards with you. You can include time, place, and everything else you need to know. You also can jot down memos on the results of the meetings.

A contacts file is useful if you deal regularly with people you don't know. File your people alphabetically by their names or the names of their companies. On each man's card, list everything you have to remember about him as well as anything that will help you remember him. Include his company, title, address, phone and extension numbers, secretary's name, the hours you're most likely to find him in, his association with your company, a brief description of anything else that will help you recognize him. You can even note his wife's name and his personal interests.

If you deal with people mainly on a company-to-company basis, list the name of the company first. Then list your contacts at the company and go on from there.

The Memindex guide is a combination calendar, memo book, and record book. You get a daily guide, a weekly guide, and a yearly summary. Appointments can be listed prominently in order of time, separate from unscheduled tasks. Important jobs can be highlighted on the daily calendar pages. Spare-time jobs can go on the weekly sheets.

There's room for memos on sales and purchases. And you get separate cash account sheets. Memindex includes an address book, too. It's an all-in-one system that helps you plan ahead as well as remember.

23   Before you give a talk you have butterflies, naturally. How to overcome your nervousness? By remembering that it is natural. You're concerned about doing well. As soon as you start talking, the jitters will go away. You'll concentrate on what you have to say and forget yourself. Remember, your enthusiasm will win out over your self-consciousness if you've "earned the right to talk."

There are a couple of other things you can do to help forget yourself. For one, be on time. This will help you relax. For another, be sure you're groomed and dressed appropriately. Appropriate clothing doesn't call attention to itself and away from your speech.

Walk confidently to the front of the platform. Put your notes or outline inconspicuously on the stand. Never read a speech—better dead than read! You're supposed to talk to your audience, not read "at" them. Have your

Words:
448
463
488
503
518
533
538
554
569
581
598
613
628
642
657
672
687
701
716
730
735
750
764
778
793
804
819
833
846

16
31
46
61
76
80
96
112
126
136
152
167
182

JOB 1   TWO-LETTER ABBREVIATIONS FOR STATE NAMES

				Words
				25
				26
				27
Alabama	AL	Montana	MT	34
Alaska	AK	Nebraska	NB	42
Arizona	AZ	Nevada	NV	49
Arkansas	AR	New Hampshire	NH	57
California	CA	New Jersey	NJ	66
Colorado	CO	New Mexico	NM	74
Connecticut	CT	New York	NY	83
Delaware	DE	North Carolina	NC	92
District of Columbia	DC	North Dakota	ND	103
Florida	FL	Ohio	OH	109
Georgia	GA	Oklahoma	OK	117
Hawaii	HI	Oregon	OR	124
Idaho	ID	Pennsylvania	PA	132
Illinois	IL	Puerto Rico	PR	140
Indiana	IN	Rhode Island	RI	148
Iowa	IA	South Carolina	SC	157
Kansas	KS	South Dakota	SD	165
Kentucky	KY	Tennessee	TN	173
Louisiana	LA	Texas	TX	180
Maine	ME	Utah	UT	187
Maryland	MD	Vermont	VT	194
Massachusetts	MA	Virginia	VA	203
Michigan	MI	Washington	WA	211
Minnesota	MN	West Virginia	WV	220
Mississippi	MS	Wisconsin	WI	229
Missouri	MO	Wyoming	WY	238

JOB 2   NUMERALS

Arabic	Roman	Small Roman	Words
			5
			6
			7
			13
			36
			37
1	I	i	40
2	II	ii	44
3	III	iii	48
4	IV	iv	52
5	V	v	55
6	VI	vi	58
7	VII	vii	62
8	VIII	viii	67
9	IX	ix	70
10	X	x	74
11	XI	xi	78
20	XX	xx	81
30	XXX	xxx	86
40	XL	xl	89
50	L	l	93
60	LX	lx	97
100	C	c	100
500	D	d	104
1000	M	m	108

thoughts clearly organized in your mind. Make notes of facts and figures.
And, if you like, outline your key points. Don't try to memorize, though.
A memorized speech never sounds like talk.

Acknowledge your introduction with a smile, a nod to the man who
introduced you, and a "thank you." Nod to your audience.

Start your speech slowly. Relax the group with your attention getter: a
question, a show of hands, a funny story, and so on. Later, when the
audience is with you, you can speed up a little.

Keep your eyes on your audience. Talk to them—not to a clock at the
back of the room or to your notes or to the microphone. Look at their
faces to gauge their reactions. If they look puzzled, slow down and reem-
phasize your point. If they look pleased, you're right on the beam.

A simple trick is to pick out an individual in the audience who is obviously
"with you"—someone who laughs at your jokes and nods in agreement—
someone obviously tuned in on your wavelength. Concentrate on talking
to that one person. His enthusiasm will reinforce yours, and yours will
enthuse the entire audience. Of course, don't constantly stare at that one
person; but, whenever you need moral support, turn your gaze to him and
talk just to him for a few moments.

To keep your audience's interest alive, keep your speech alive. Be excited
about it. You'll communicate your enthusiasm. Don't be worried about
expression and gesture. If you're relaxed and enthusiastic, your expressions
and gestures automatically will be right. Don't be afraid to let your feelings
show.

When you hold up your visual aids, pick them up just when you're ready
to use them. Hold them high enough so your audience can see, low enough
so you don't cover your face. And don't talk to your visual aids—talk to
your audience! Naturally, have them prepared in advance so that you don't
fumble till you find the right one.

No matter how well you're doing up there, don't overstay your welcome.
How long should you talk? There's an old adage among public speakers
that says: If you don't strike oil in twenty minutes, stop boring! We suggest
you use this as your motto, too, when you've become an accomplished
speaker. At the moment you're probably a beginner, so a talk of one minute
probably seems an eternity. That's a problem with most speakers. When
they're beginners, you can't get them to stand up. When they're experienced,
all too often you can't get them to sit down!

When you've said your last word, smile and nod to the audience. Pause,
then walk away confidently. All in all, Abraham Lincoln's advice on delivery
can't be topped: "Be sincere, be simple, be seated."

When we talked about speeches, we said that preparation was more
important than delivery. It's the same with reports, only more so.

			Words
Main Heading:	INCOMING SHIPS		9
			10
Secondary Heading:	Wednesday, August 12		23
			24
			25
Column Headings:	Ship	From	37
			38
	Olympia	Athens	42
	Ocean Rover	Antwerp	47
	Royal Sails	Southampton	52
	Queen Anne	Bermuda	57

JOB 3

Sales Record
Week Ending January 15

Branch	Amount
Albany	$ 15,008.78
Hartford	12,640.23
Elmont	3,503.89
White Plains	8,003.39

Tables Containing Three or More Columns

When a table is composed of three or more columns, follow the same procedure for tabulating as you used for two columns.

To facilitate copying longer tables, use a line guide (an envelope or ruler) that you can slide down the page as you begin each line.

Type the following jobs on a full sheet, double-spacing the body. Determine the spacing between columns.

When you prepare a report, don't worry too much about anecdotes and 776
dramatic effects. You'll be talking to a selected audience—people who are 792
concerned with what you have to say. They'll be interested in facts, sup- 807
porting evidence, and conclusions. Your purpose is to make yourself clear 822
and to present your material quickly and completely and interestingly. If 838
they're asleep, they can't hear you. So in making your points, apply the 853
Action Formula. 857

The format is the same as the speech format. "Tell 'em what you're 872
going to tell 'em, then tell 'em, then tell 'em what you've told 'em." You 888
announce your topic, state your points in logical order, then summarize. 903

You may want to write out your report then read it to your audience. 918
This is all right if you use conversational language. For a report to read 933
well, it has to sound like talk. Wherever possible, however, try to give a 948
report from notes rather than read it. If your report is technical, and you 964
must read it, read your report through a few times so you can lift your 979
head and keep that valuable eye contact with your audience. Remember, 993
you're reading to people. Don't race ahead in a mumbled monotone. Speak 1008
up, with expression in your voice. Although you don't have to pamper your 1023
audience as you do when you make a speech, you should do all you can 1037
to make their listening painless. There is no harm in pointed illustrations 1053
and anecdotes. Keep your report interesting. 1063

24   Fashion is a phenomenon that has been puzzling sociologists and psy- 15
chologists for years. Exactly how and where new cycles of fashion begin 30
are still enigmas, even for the professionals. One thing is known for sure, 46
though. Fashion has been going in cycles ever since Eve first stated her 61
preference for fig leaves rather than grape leaves. 72

Our own century alone has brought about radical changes in both 86
women's and men's fashions. A glance into the family album is all that's 98
needed to get a clear picture of the devious ways of the fantastic and 112
exciting subject we call "fashion." 120

At the turn of the century, the bustle had given way to the amazingly 135
toppled-over silhouette of the Gibson girl and her hourglass figure. As this 151
figure became boring to its wearers, skirts became so hobbled that women 166
could scarcely walk. World War I brought about the shorter skirt and 180
looser dress. Further up went the skirts in the jazz era of the twenties, 195
only to come down again in the thirties as women again discovered their 210
waistlines and bosoms. 215

In the early thirties, fashion began to show a softer, more graceful, 230
willowy silhouette conforming more to the feminine form. But this did 245
not last for long! As the storm clouds again gathered over Europe, the 259
fashion silhouette took on more of a masculine look until, during World 274
War II, the style reached its peak when women were more often seen in 288
slacks and uniforms than in frilly clothes. 297

C. Using the backspace method, center each heading above its column.

BACKSPACE METHOD

A. Move the carriage to the beginning of the column.

B. Tap the space bar once for each two letters, spaces, or figures in the longest line in the column. Do not space for an odd letter. This will move your carriage to the midpoint of the column.

C. Backspace once for each two letters in the heading that is to appear above the column.

3. If a column heading contains several words, the heading should be divided into two or more lines, each centered above the column.

4. Underscore the last line of the column heading to separate it from the body of the table.

		Number of	Number of Doctors in
HOSPITAL	FOUNDED	PATIENTS	ATTENDANCE

5. Allow one blank line before typing the table.

Using one of the methods outlined, tabulate the following jobs on half sheets. Single space the body of each tabulation and determine the number of spaces you will use for intercolumns. Note that the column of figures in Job 3 is aligned on the right and the dollar sign is used with the first amount only.

JOB 1

			Words
Main Heading:	WALDON HIGH SCHOOL		11
			12
Secondary Heading:	Departmental Chairmen		26
			27
			28
Column Headings:	Chairman	Subject	48
			49
	Mrs. T. Ludlow	English	55
	Mr. P. Browne	Biology	60
	Mr. L. Clarke	Music	65
	Miss H. Dunn	History	70
	Mr. S. Suskind	Psychology	76

In 1946, a mammoth fashion revolution was engendered by Christian Dior with his New Look, dropping the hemline from 18 inches to 11½ inches off the floor and returning to softer shoulders, large hats, and voluminous skirts. About 1951, the influence of the Directoire period started to make its mark; the high-belted Empire look started to infiltrate the pages of fashion magazines. Approximately seven years later, the no-belt "sack" dress, or Chemise silhouette, was born—much to the unhappiness of most men.

Partially because of this male disapproval, the Chemise did not survive its full cycle and, in 1962, its style was greatly modified into the flattering A-line made so famous by Jacqueline (Kennedy) Onassis. With seasonal fashion changes, the A-line still persisted as THE basic silhouette of the late sixties. Along with the booted Courreges look, and so forth, most high-fashion designers still stick, in their basic clothes, to the A-line style because it satisfies every facet of the fashion formula successfully.

You must therefore learn to recognize a basic silhouette as opposed to a seasonal fashion change. A silhouette is the outline or contour of a figure or costume. The new silhouette at the beginning of any season relates to the general contour in fashion at the time, especially with respect to the waistline, the hemline, and the shoulder width.

A basic silhouette lasts from seven to eight years; a seasonal change is merely a variation on the basic theme or trend. It may be a season of ruffles or leather or fur trim, but none of these seasonal changes affects the basic silhouette.

When does a basic silhouette become dated? When it becomes tiresome to the eye. And, as you have already learned, this boredom with seeing or wearing the same general silhouette generally occurs about every seven or eight years.

The designer who makes a big hit with a new line does so because he has created a new silhouette that is in keeping with the times. It is the psychological time for change, and the designer has met the challenge.

25   Probably no question of etiquette will give a man more trouble than the confusing one of tipping. Some men overtip out of ignorance, believing it is the best way to get extra service. Some undertip, resenting the entire tipping operation. Others tip just the right amount at the right time, but in the wrong way. There's a lot more to tipping than being a walking adding machine with the necessary coins in pockets.

First of all, tipping begins with your "attitude." Make up your mind that you can't beat the system. Tip, you must. Next, since you must, do it graciously, privately, but personally. Whenever possible, tip face to face and say, "Thank you." And smile as if you meant it—even if it kills you! With your attitude determined by fate, you only need to meet the demands of the going rates.

1. Type the main heading in all capital letters.

2. Center it above the table.

3. Allow two blank lines below the main heading (one blank line when it is followed by a subtitle).

4. A main heading that extends beyond the width of the table should be divided into two lines. In such cases, make the first line a little longer than the second.

SECONDARY HEADING

1. Capitalize the first letter of each principal word.

2. Center the secondary heading above the table.

3. Allow two blank lines below it.

COLUMN HEADINGS

1. Capitalize the first letter of each principal word.

2. Center column headings above the column. First locate the center point of the column. Finding this center point may be done by using either the arithmetic or the backspace method. Study the steps involved in each method.

ARITHMETIC METHOD

A. Divide the length of a column by two. Drop any fraction.

$$33 \mid 12 \div 2 = 6 \mid \quad (33) \qquad\qquad 12 \quad 10 \div 2 = 5 \mid 33 \quad (57)$$

B. Add the above result to the beginning point of each column to get the center point of the column.

$$33 + 6 = 39 \qquad\qquad 57 + 5 = 62$$
$$33 \mid 12 \div 2 = 6 \mid \quad (33) \qquad 12 \qquad 10 \div 2 = 5 \mid 33 \quad (57)$$

As a starter, let's consider those people that are never tipped: | 177

Club members give Christmas presents, but they do not follow the daily | 192
habit of tipping waiters, locker room attendants, stewards, etc., at their | 207
clubs. Nor do you, as a guest at a private club, tip the employees. That's up | 223
to your host. | 226

Stewardesses or stewards, pilots, limousine drivers, or porters who | 241
wear the airline uniform are never tipped. Porters who work for the | 255
airport, rather than a particular airline, are tipped. Their rate of tip may | 271
be an announced rate per piece of baggage (as with train Red-Caps) and, | 286
if so, you should add a tip of 5 to 10 cents per piece of luggage. If not a | 302
stated rate, the porter who takes your baggage from either the limousine | 317
or the taxi should be tipped 25 cents a bag, but not less than a total of | 332
50 cents no matter how light you are traveling. | 342

While you can't always judge the position of the man who greets you by | 357
his looks, take a quick glance at his clothes. If he's dressed similarly to you, | 373
chances are he's either the owner, manager, or head waiter—the latter also is | 389
usually nontippable. If in doubt, the best you can do is offer the tip and | 404
re-pocket it with as little embarrassment as possible if turned away. If you | 420
are handed over to a section-head waiter by the owner, manager, or head | 434
waiter, you may be sure that the section-head waiter is tip-hungry. | 448

If you're not sure whether tips will be accepted or rejected, offer the tip | 464
as if you were asking a favor. Then, again, you can pocket it with little | 479
embarrassment if you're lucky enough to have it rejected. | 491

One tip-off you'll find is the presence of a little silver tray or saucer | 507
equipped with glued-on or decoy quarters. | 516

Another tip-off is to be found in the change you receive. If you receive | 532
little or no change in return for your bill, you can assume one of two things | 548
—you are expected to tip with a full bill or you're not expected to tip at all. | 565
If you question the doling out of an entire dollar, ask for change. | 579

The current rate for waiters is 15 percent of the check unless you are at a | 595
first-class restaurant or have received exceptional service. Then the rate | 610
swells more toward 20 percent. If the service is terrible, or the waiter or | 626
waitress surly, then let your conscience be your guide and shade your | 640
tip downward. | 643

At a table, 25 cents per person is the minimum. In a diner or tea room, | 661
15 or 20 cents a person may be adequate, but in a swank spot the minimum | 676
would be about 50 cents per person. | 684

Now here's where your mental calculator comes into use. When 15 | 698
percent of a check goes above $2.00, you may begin to shave the tip off a bit. | 714
Thus, you would tip $2.00 for a $12.50 check. In addition, you might also | 729
get by with $2.00 on a $15.00 check but with this is on the low side. You | 743
could leave $2.50 on a check of about $18.00, and whether the service has | 758
been up to par or not would decide whether you left $2.50 or $3.00 on a | 773

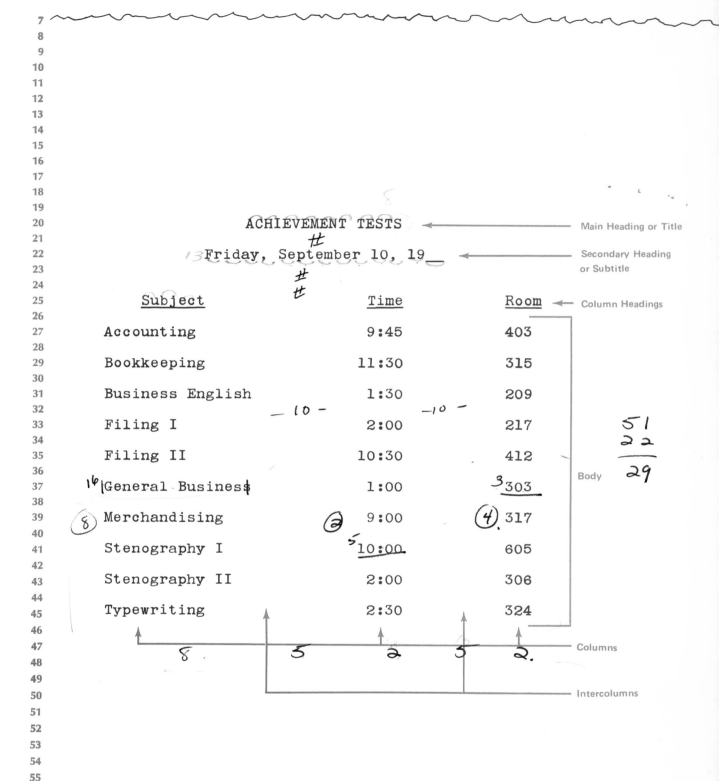

ACHIEVEMENT TESTS ⟵ Main Heading or Title

Friday, September 10, 19__ ⟵ Secondary Heading or Subtitle

Subject	Time	Room	⟵ Column Headings
Accounting	9:45	403	
Bookkeeping	11:30	315	
Business English	1:30	209	
Filing I	2:00	217	
Filing II	10:30	412	
General Business	1:00	303	
Merchandising	9:00	317	
Stenography I	10:00	605	
Stenography II	2:00	306	
Typewriting	2:30	324	

Body

Columns

Intercolumns

$20.00 check. The usual practice is to leave even change, ignoring nickels and dimes in either direction.

Eating at a counter usually pulls the 15 percent down to 10 percent, except that a dime is your smallest tip even if your checks covers only 10 cents for a cup of coffee.

As a rule, cafeterias eliminate the need for tips, but it is still a custom to leave the cleaning-up fellow at least 10 cents per person for the dirty work.

In a fancy restaurant, if the waiter serves you drinks, but there is a wine steward, the waiter still receives 15 percent of the check and the wine steward receives 10 percent of the wine check, but not less than $1.00. If the wine steward handles his own check, you have no problem. Since folding money is easier to pass, most men even the tip off to the nearest bill.

Once you've left the waiter's tip, you are faced with the tipping of section captains and head waiters and all others who wear starched shirts. It is not necessary to tip these people unless you have caused them extra trouble or they've given you extra service. If the top man does nothing but turn you over to the second man, who does nothing but hand you a menu and write down your order, forget the tip. However, if you are trying to establish yourself in a restaurant which you would like to visit often, or if you've had any kind of fuss about your order, or if you've ordered a dish that requires special "floor show treatment" by the captain—then hand over the folding money. A folded dollar bill is adequate in most places; two singles in a very expensive restaurant. If you are, or would like to become, a "regular" at a restaurant, then you may be wise to give five dollars to the head waiter every third or fourth trip.

Busboys are not tipped. It is assumed that the waiters "share the wealth" with them.

In a night club, tip as you would in an expensive restaurant. Entertainers are not tipped unless you have asked for a special number to be played for your date. If so, the number will cost you a buck.

Hat check girls should be tipped 25 cents per person. Ditto if you order cigarettes from a cigarette girl. Again ditto for the men's room attendant even though he only hands you a towel and makes a vague sweep at you with a whisk broom. A quarter is also standard for a doorman who tucks you into a cab; more if he goes whistling into a rainy night to bring one to the curb for you. Incidentally, it is not considered sporting to flag down your own cab if there is a doorman to do it for you.

It isn't cricket to tip an usher unless he has taken a note backstage for you. In this case, the gratuity is usually 50 cents. The usual 15 percent is called for if you are in a theater which serves alcoholic beverages. No tip is expected by the man who sells choclate goodies or orange drinks at exorbitant prices.

788
795
810
824
830
847
863
878
894
910
925
940
957
973
988
1003
1018
1033
1049
1065
1080
1095
1110
1126
1132
1148
1151
1168
1183
1195
1211
1226
1240
1255
1270
1286
1297
1313
1329
1375
1389
1393

CORNWALL DAILY PRESS

Editorial Staff

Foreign News	Charles Spoor	32
National News	Ivy Bolder	39
Books	Norman Lewis	42
Movies and Theater	Allen Porter	50
Science	R. T. Ryme, Jr.	56
Medicine	Morton Linn	61
Television	John Noble	66
Space Age News	Henry Arnold	73
Social News	Alice Goodley	79

13
14
23
24
25

JOB 3   (10 spaces between columns)

Scheduled Courses all cap.

Room Directory

Archaeology of Mexico 1105
Art Styles Through the Ages 1118
Graphic Design Workshop 1219
Literature of the Sixties 1012
Sculpture in Metal 1217
Voice and Diction 1006

More About Headings

The headings that are typed above a tabulation may be divided into three general groups:

1. Main heading—the title of the table.

2. Secondary heading—the subheading.

3. Column heading—the title of each column.

A quarter is considered adequate for the doorman who takes your bags out of the cab, whether he dumps them on the sidewalk and calls a bellhop, or carries them to the desk. To the bellhop who takes your luggage to your room, tip 25 cents a bag, but not less than a total of 50 cents even if you are carrying only a briefcase. Twenty-five cents is also minimum to a bellhop every time he does something for you. Waiters for room service are tipped 15 to 20 percent—but never less than 25 cents.

In commercial hotels, chambermaids are usually not tipped by transients. In resort hotels or anywhere you have stayed for several days running, it is a good idea to stick to the old rule of tipping $1.00 a night for the maids—left on the bureau in an envelope, on which you write "Housekeeper." If on a business trip of more than one night's stay, it's good public relations to give the head housekeeper a few dollars to divide among the day, night, and relief maids.

Bell captains, elevator operators, and telephone operators are seldom tipped by hotel guests but, if you live in a hotel, folding money at Christmas time is expected and sometimes a tip throughout the year at the rate of about 50 cents to $1.00 a month. Desk clerks and assistant managers are not tipped. Nor are clerks who get transportation or theater tickets for you. Bellboys, however, who deliver the tickets to you are tipped.

In most towns you can safely get by with a 15 percent tip on a taxi fare. In larger cities—such as New York, Chicago, San Francisco, Los Angeles, Dallas, and the like—25 cents on a dollar ride is expected; 40 to 50 cents on a $2.00 meter. If a large-city cab driver does more to bestir himself than simply hold out his hand, consider yourself a miracle-worker. Tip him 50 cents. Should you "forget your property" and have it returned to you by a cab driver, let your tip reflect the value of the lost article.

A Pullman porter should be tipped 25 to 50 cents at the end of a daytime trip. If he has done anything more than lift your bag off the platform for you, make it a dollar. The porter serving your berth or roomette should be tipped a dollar a night per person; two dollars a night if you are occupying more posh quarters. Dining car attendants should be tipped the same as waiters in a good restaurant. If you require anything special from the head waiter—such as a table for two when he is trying to hold his tables for four—he also should be tipped the usual dollar or two. Club car waiters are tipped the same as in a good bar; waiters who bring things to your room are tipped as if they came from room service in a good hotel.

As mentioned previously, Red-Caps (porters at the station) usually have an announced rate for a piece of baggage—whether they carry it or simply toss it on a cart. As a rule, you should add 5 to 10 cents per piece, depending on the service rendered. A Red-Cap who actually gets you to your seat with baggage intact or sees you into a taxi, thereby taking himself out of circulation, deserves at least 50 cents over the stated fee.

1408
1423
1438
1454
1469
1484
1494
1508
1523
1539
1553
1568
1583
1591
1606
1722
1737
1752
1767
1751
1783
1798
1814
1829
1844
1859
1872
1888
1904
1919
1935
1950
1966
1978
1994
2009
2022
2038
2053
2069
2084
2100
2112

Birthstones all caps

January	Garnet
February	Amethyst
March	Bloodstone
April	Diamond
May	Emerald
June	Pearl
July	Ruby
August	Sardonyx
September	Sapphire
October	Opal
November	Topaz
December	Turquoise

Subtitles or Secondary Headings

A subtitle gives additional information. It is centered a double space below the main title and is followed by a triple space. A subtitle is typed with initial caps for the principal words and may be arranged on more than one line.

Tabulate the following jobs on half sheets.

JOB 1   (10 spaces between columns)

		Words
CLUB OFFICERS		8
		9
Effective January 24		21
		22
		23
Harold Fisher	President	29
William T. Brooks	Vice President	37
Mary Henderson	Treasurer	43
Elizabeth Collin	Secretary	49

For a haircut, 25 cents is the minimum tip, and it's easy to work up to 50 cents in a good shop—especially in one where you are hoping against hope to teach the barber how to cut your hair properly. If you have run into a "hair stylist," your tip increases according to his fees. As a general rule, however, 50 cents or 10 to 15 percent of your bill is about right when you've had a shave, the lamp, and "the works" in addition to a haircut; 25 cents is about average for the shoe shine boy, and 10 or 15 cents for the porter who whisk-brooms you.

Perhaps you aren't invited away for the weekend every weekend—but, you never can tell when an invitation may be in the offing. You may be just the sort of eligible bachelor the boss's wife will latch onto as a prized possession. If so, there are a few rules to follow about tipping household help whenever you have spent a night or more in a private home as a guest.

A Friday-to-Monday weekend can cost a nominal sum or a fortune depending on the size of the household.

The rules are simple, but strict. Tips should go to everyone who has given you personal service. This includes the maid who has tended to your room, seen to your unpacking, or pressed any needed articles. This also applies to the chauffeur who drove you from the station or washed your car. Should you, by any chance, encounter a butler on your entrance, be prepared with a folded dollar bill in your palm at your exit.

Tips should never be given in front of your host or hostess. The usual procedure is to leave money in an envelope in your room for the maid; tip the butler in the hall as you are leaving; and the chauffeur at your car or at the train station—all at the very last moment.

The same scale and rules apply in a smaller and more simple household. If there is a maid-of-all-work who has cooked, served, made up your bed, and pressed your trousers, two dollars is the minimum and five dollars the maximum tip for any one person. Here you may be in a dilemma as to how to track down Jenny, who has been your handmaid for a weekend. Obviously, you can't crash into her domain. Your best bet is to resort to the envelope tactic with her name written on the front and propped in an obvious place in your bedroom.

Using one of the methods just outlined, tabulate the following jobs on full sheets.

JOB 1 (12 spaces between columns)

Words

15 WORDS THAT HAVE GROWN TOGETHER *1*   19
                                                       20
                                           3   21

antechamber   blindfold *4*   27
armchair   bookcase *5*   31
backdoor   bookkeeper *6*   36
bathtub   businesslike *7*   41
bedroom   lawmaker *8*   46
bedside   meanwhile *9*   50
bedtime   newsdealer *10*   55
beefsteak   playwright *11*   60
blackmail   postmark *12*   65
bygone   scrapbook *13*   70
classmate   turnover *14*   74
commonplace   viewpoint *15*   80
copyright   worksheet *16*   85
farsighted   workout *17*   90
handbook   yearbook *18*   94

JOB 2 (10 spaces between columns, double-spaced)

12 CHRISTMAS PARTY COMMITTEE *1*   15
                                                16
                                      3   17

Harold Fisher   -10-   Sales *4*   22

William T. Brooks   Purchasing *6* 29

Mary Henderson   Payroll *8*   34

L. Charles Tremont   Bookkeeping *10* 42

Elizabeth Collin   Secretary *12* 48

Mary Chambers   Secretary *14* 54

Alice G. Vickers   Typist *16*   59

Gertrude Blanchard   Receptionist *18* 67

Louis Bellford   Messenger *20* 73

B. P. Leiland   Mail Room *22* 79

Section 6
JOB TYPING

4. If you are using the elite type, your page is 102 strokes wide. Therefore, subtract the number of strokes in the tabulation (34) from 100 (102 is rounded off to 100) to determine the number of unused spaces remaining for the right and left margins. With pica, subtract 34 from 85.

$$100 - 34 = 66 \text{ spaces available for margins, } or$$
$$85 - 34 = 51 \text{ spaces available for margins.}$$

5. These unused spaces are to be divided equally between the left and right margins—therefore, divide by two.

$$66 \div 2 = 33 \text{ spaces for each margin, } or$$
$$51 \div 2 = 25 \text{ spaces for each margin.}$$

6. Write this figure on the diagram in the spaces representing the left and right margins.

7. Check your calculations by totaling all the numbers indicated on your diagram. The total should equal the full width of your paper. In this example, which is based on elite type, the total should equal 100.

$$33 + 12 + 12 + 10 + 33 = 100$$

8. We must now determine the position for the margin and tabulator stops. First, start with the left margin—we know this to be 33 and can enter it on the diagram. Then the position for the second column is determined by adding to the left margin the width of the first column and the intercolumn. (The right margin need not be set.)

Now that the diagram is complete and the figures checked, you can set your margin and tabulator stops at the correct positions.

9. If you are using pica type, follow the same procedure using 85 instead of 100.

CENTERING

Horizontal Centering

All typewritten work should present an attractive appearance. To achieve this, some lines (for example, a title of a manuscript) must be centered.

How many letters or spaces can be typed across the line of an 8½-inch page with elite type? _102_ with pica type? _85_

Dividing these numbers by two indicates the center point of the paper—50 (51 is rounded off to 50) for elite and 42 for pica. When material is to be centered horizontally, always begin at the center point on the page. Here are the steps to be followed:

1. Make sure that the paper guide is at *0* (see page 10).
2. Move margin stops to ends of scale.
3. Clear tab stop settings.
4. Set a tab stop at the center of the page.
5. Tabulate to the center point and backspace *once* for every *two* letters, spaces, figures, or punctuation marks in the line.
6. Begin typing at the point where the backspacing ends.
7. Type the line.

To center the words FINAL NOTICE, mentally spell the word as follows: *fi na lspace no ti ce*, backspacing once for each pair of letters and spaces. Begin typing at the point where the backspacing ends.

Center each line of the following jobs horizontally, using the linespacing indicated in the copy:

		Words
JOB 1	Muncie	4
	Philadelphia	12
	Washington	18
	Austin	22
	Muskegon	28
	Peoria	32
JOB 2	GASLIGHT	5
	RESTAURANT	12
	Specializing	20
	in	22
	LUNCHEON	27
	DINNER	31
	Reservations	39
	Accepted	44

the 12 letters in the word *accommodated* and another
12 times for the spaces to be left between the first and
second column (57 for elite and 49 for pica).

7. Set the tabulator stop for the second column. Your
machine is now properly set for typing the table.

8. Vertical placement is determined by the same method
used for centering. The heading is followed by a *triple*
space. There are 11 lines needed. (See page 130 for vertical centering.)

9. The title is centered horizontally and typed in solid caps.

ARITHMETIC METHOD

We will now outline the steps for planning a tabulation using the arithmetic method. So that you may compare procedures, we will use the same
problem previously solved by the backspace method.

1. On a piece of paper, draw a simple diagram of the
problem to be set up, using a bracket to represent
each column and a circle within which to write the
tabulator stop.

2. Count the number of letters in the longest item of each
column and place this number in the bracket that represents the column. (In this example: accommodated—
12, noticeable—10.) Also indicate on the diagram the
number of spaces to be left between the first and second
columns—the intercolumn. In this example, we will
again use 12 spaces.

3. Total the number of strokes and spaces for the width of
the entire tabulation.

$$12 + 12 + 10 = 34$$

JOB 3

ATLANTIC MOTOR SALES 10

Holiday Specials

CHEVROLETS

29

RAMBLERS

PONTIACS

Open Every Evening

JOB 4

The Westside Players Present
Jane Hall and Ray Peel
in

Here We Go Again all caps.

by
Judith Bartons
Tickets on Sale at Boxoffice

JOB 5

Garden Apartments
Free Garage
Air Conditioning
Swimming Pool
Immediate Occupancy

Vertical Centering

```
⌐ Line 1
  Line 2
  Line 3
  Line 4
  Line 5
⌐ Line 6
```

Most typewriters provide six lines to a vertical inch. To leave one inch blank, advance the paper seven lines—six lines for the blank inch and the seventh line to start typing.

Standard typing paper is 11 inches long. There are 66 possible lines of vertical spaces on a page (11 x 6 = 66). There are 33 lines of vertical spaces on a half page (5½ x 6 = 33).

Arranging Two-Column Tables

As already stated, the aim in tabulation is to arrange columns so that they are neatly and attractively spaced. To do this, you can employ either of two methods for planning the positioning of columns in table form—the backspace method or the arithmetic method.

BACKSPACE METHOD

The backspace method is simply an extension of the centering technique you have been using.

Let us assume that we wish to set up our tabulated material as in this example:

		Lines
WORDS OFTEN MISSPELLED		1
		2
		3
accommodated	interfere	4
affect	knowledge	5
bureaus	maneuver	6
disappoint	noticeable	7
develop	occurred	8
embarrass	parallel	9
familiar	referred	10
hygiene	separated	11

1. Move margin stops to ends of scale and clear tab stop settings.

2. Determine the longest word in each column.

```
accommodated                        noticeable
```

3. Starting at the center of the page, backspace once for each two letters in these words. Do not backspace for an extra letter at the end and do not allow for the spaces between columns.

```
ac co mm od at ed no ti ce ab le (11 backspaces)
```

4. We must now provide for the spaces between the two columns—the intercolumn. (In this example, we will arbitrarily allow 12 spaces.) To do this, backspace once for each two spaces to be left between columns (6 backspaces). The carriage is now positioned at the starting point for the first column.

5. Set the left margin at the point located in Step 4 (33 for elite and 25 for pica).

6. We must now determine the position for the second column. Strike the space bar once for each letter in the longest word of the first column and once for each space between the columns. Thus, we will space 12 times for

To center copy vertically, follow these steps:

1. Count the lines needed for the copy. (Remember to allow one blank line between double-spaced lines.)

	Lines
JUNIOR BIOLOGY CLUB	1
	1
Announces	1
	1
Annual Field Trip	1
	1
All Members Invited	1
	7

2. Subtract needed lines from available lines on the paper. To type the illustration on a half sheet of paper, subtract the 7 (needed lines) from 33 (lines available on a half sheet).

3. Divide this number by two to determine the top and bottom margins. If there is an uneven number, place the extra line in the bottom margin (33—7=26). Divide 26 by 2 to determine the top and bottom margins. The illustration would begin on line 14 (13 lines for a top margin).

Center the following jobs vertically and horizontally on half sheets of paper using linespacing as indicated:

		Words
JOB 1	LOOKING FOR A TEMPORARY POSITION?	20
	Many Openings for	31
	STENOGRAPHERS	40
	EXECUTIVE SECRETARIES	53
	OFFICE CLERKS	61
	MORGAN OFFICE SERVICE	74
JOB 2	FOR PEOPLE ON THE GO	13
	New Dimensions in Travel	28
	LOW BUDGET PRICES	38
	to	40
	MEXICO	42
	PERU	47
	MARTON LAKE TOUR SERVICE	62

	Words
LOWELL PUBLISHING COMPANY	30
	31
Presents	36
	37
A STIMULATING COLLECTION	52
OF BOOKS	58
FOR CHILDREN AND YOUNG ADULTS	76
	77
A D V E N T U R E	88
	89
F I C T I O N	97
	98
T R A V E L	105
	106
S P O R T S · S C I E N C E	123
	124
At all bookstores throughout the nation	149

	Words
S T Y L E W I S E · F A S H I O N S	22
	23
PRESENTS	28
	29
T H E · N E W · L O O K	43
	44
I N	47
	48
W I N T E R · F A S H I O N S	66
	67
Midtown Shopping Center	81
139 East 72 Street	93
	94
Saturday, September 19	109
	110
Admission by invitation only	127

TABULATION

Tabulation is a simple process of typing columns for ready reference. As a typist you will frequently be called upon to type such material. A knowledge of the techniques involved will enable you to do this work attractively and neatly.

The tabulating mechanism is one of the greatest time-saving devices on your typewriter.

Relocate these parts on your typewriter: (1) Tabulation clear key; (2) tabulator set key; and (3) tabulator key or bar. Review the operation of these parts on page 29.

Always type tables or columns line after line across the page as though you were typing sentences.

JOB 3

SPRING DANCE

All Students Invited

PARK PLAZA HOTEL

8
20
31

JOB 4

SUMMARY
OF
HORIZONTAL CENTERING
Move carriage to center of paper
Backspace once for each two letters or spaces
Do not backspace for extra stroke
Start typing at point reached in backspacing

4
5
18
19
38
66
86
93

JOB 5

Clearance Sale

X   X   X
X

Low Prices
X   X

One Day Only

Center the following jobs on a full sheet of paper using double spacing:

JOB 1

MORTON CRANE
Interior Decorator
cordially invites you to attend
the opening of his new shop
at
15-36 East 907 Terrace
Friday, April 28
from 2 to 4 p.m.

8
19
38
55
56
70
80
91

JOB 2

OFFICE SPACE AVAILABLE
Entire 4th Floor
HEAT — ELEVATOR — WATCHMAN
INCLUDED IN RENT
LEASE FOR 5, 10 or 20 YEARS
Rand Associates
469 Bradley Avenue
Or see your own broker

14
24
39
49
67
76
88
101

Spread Titles

To spread words for extra impact, leave one space between letters of a word and three spaces between words. To center a spread line, use the same method you learned for horizontal centering *except* that you backspace *once* for *each* letter or space between words rather than backspacing once for every two letters or spaces. Example: T H E   E N D. Backspace once for *t, h, e,* space, *e, n, d.*

Type the following jobs on half sheets, centering vertically and horizontally, and spreading words as indicated. Use single and double spacing as indicated.

		Words

JOB 1

C I T Y — 5

B i r m i n g h a m — 17

A n n i s t o n — 26

P i m a — 31

Q u i n c y — 38

JOB 2

R E C O R D   P E R F O R M A N C E — 22

M i s t e r   R o b e r t s — 39

M y   F a i r   L a d y — 53

T o g e t h e r   A g a i n — 70

JOB 3

M I L L E R   P L A S T I C   C O M P A N Y — 27 / 28

i s   p l e a s e d   t o   a n n o u n c e   t h a t — 41 / 42

R i c h a r d   B a r t o n — 53

a n d — 54 / 56 / 57

E d w a r d   A .   B l a c k s t o n e — 70 / 71

a r e   n o w   a s s o c i a t e d   w i t h   u s   i n   o u r — 91 / 92

E A S T E R N   R E G I O N A L   O F F I C E — 107

N E W A R K ,   N E W   J E R S E Y — 118